Praise for
The Joy of Talking Politics with Strangers

As someone who feels passionately about the possibilities inherent in talking with voters at their doors, I was thrilled, inspired and moved by Chur's book. Had I taken everything useful I've learned about canvassing over many years and put it into words, I still wouldn't come close to the wisdom, large-heartedness, and humanity contained in this slim volume. Chur has written something that will show you not only how to change voters' minds, but quite possibly how to change yourself, and gain greatly in the process. A must-read.

—Jessica Craven,
author, "Chop Wood, Carry Water" daily action email

One of the most important lessons I learned as an organizer was that often the most radical action we can take is having a one-on-one, face-to-face conversation. *The Joy of Talking Politics with Strangers* is an ode to the transformational nature of meaningful conversations that take place on porches nationwide.

—Yasmin Radjy,
executive director, Swing Left

The Joy of Talking Politics with Strangers contains a wealth of strategies for connecting with voters, especially those too often left out of the conversation – Latinos, young people and working class people. It demonstrates how to make respectful, mutual connections from the heart which have the potential to win elections and transform our country.

—Carla Rivas-D'Amico,
manager, National Latino Engagement
Democratic Congressional Campaign Committee

ELIZABETH CHUR

THE
JOY
OF
TALKING
POLITICS
WITH
STRANGERS

HOW TO SAVE DEMOCRACY,
ONE CONVERSATION AT A TIME

Talk with Voters Publishing

Copyright © 2024 by Elizabeth Chur
Cover design by Damonza
Interior design by Damonza
Map design by Suzanne Service
Author photo by Tom Shaw

All rights reserved. No portion of this book may be reproduced without written permission from the publisher or author, except as permitted by U.S. copyright law.

Talk with Voters Publishing
P.O. Box 460631
San Francisco, CA 94146

First edition: August 2024

The Joy of Talking Politics with Strangers is a work of nonfiction. Some names and identifying details have been changed.

ISBN 979-8-9909017-0-4 (Paperback)
ISBN 979-8-9909017-1-1 (Ebook)

*To all the volunteers
working to protect
our beloved, imperiled democracy;
and to all the voters
whose lives have touched mine,
and who have taught me so much.*

Contents

Introduction 1
    How to Make the Most of Every Conversation. 5
    The Central Valley: A Sense of Place. 9
    Cultivating Seeds of Hope 11

Chapter 1: Out of Bad Things, Good Things Can Come 13
    Hard Times and Compassion. 15
    An Unlikely Activist. 17
    Starting Small. 21
    The Rewards of Phone Banking 22
    Knock, Knock: Canvassing for Change 24
    Platinum Linings. 27
    Build on Your Strengths. 31
    Unexpected Gifts. 35
    Summary. 38

Chapter 2: Why Canvass and Phone Bank?. 39
    Opportunity for Dialogue 41
    How Voter Engagement Can Help *You* 43
    Bringing 'Beginner's Mind' to Voter Engagement. 45
    Introducing 'Skylar the Skeptic'. 46
    Practice Makes Progress 47
    Experiment with the Recipe Book 49
    Summary. 51

Chapter 3: Safety First 53
    Safety When Phone Banking 55
    Taking Measured Risks. 55
    Respect Your Limits. 57
    Pay Attention to Small Clues 59
    Trust Your Judgment 61
    Summary. 61

Chapter 4: Always Say Yes to the Water 63
Learning to Receive 64
Food for the Journey 66
Breaking Bread (or Tearing Tortillas) Together 67
Summary 69

Chapter 5: 80% Them, 20% Me 71
Listen More than You Talk........................ 74
Gather Intel About Their Priorities................... 75
Strategies for Engaging Voters 77
Ask Them About Their Passions 84
Seek Their Expertise............................. 85
'Teaching to a Need'............................. 89
When Is It Time for '20% Me'? 91
Let Your Nonjudgmental Curiosity Lead the Way 95
Summary 96

Chapter 6: Empathize, Empathize, Empathize 97
Take the Time to Listen 99
An Empathetic Witness – Not a Therapist 100
The Language of Empathy 102
Two Conversations.............................. 103
Can You Observe the Voter like an
    Anthropologist Would? 106
The Importance of Reflective Listening 107
Strategies for Navigating Challenging Conversations 110
Summary 114

Chapter 7: Talk with the One in Front of You 115
Talk with the Neighbors.......................... 118
Take Advantage of Chance Opportunities to Connect..... 119
Prioritize People over Checklists.................... 121
Workers Are Voters, Too.......................... 122
Vote Tripling and Expanding Your Reach 124

    Everyone Is a Potential Ally 126
    Talk to the Doorbell. 127
    Don't Be Afraid to Ask for Help. 131
    Accept Invitations for Respectful Dialogue. 132
    Talk with the One Who Answers the Phone, Too. 136
    Summary 138

Chapter 8: Seize the Day (and the Night!). 139
    Concierge Follow-Up. 141
    Make Voters Feel Special 142
    Become a Taxi Driver for the Day 143
    Accompany Voters on That 'Last Mile'. 145
    Effective is Better than Efficient 146
    Take Your Time 147
    Seize the Night, Too. 150
    Think like a Social Worker 151
    Build on a Good Connection. 153
    Summary 155

Chapter 9: Help Them Visualize Voting. 157
    Take a Picture. 157
    Create a Map 160
    'Every Vote Adds Up' 161
    Summary 163

Chapter 10: Embrace Your Inner Detective. 165
    Keep Going Until You Hear 'No' – or 'Yes'! 166
    Learn Something from Everyone You Meet 169
    Invite People to Help You. 170
    Wait for Your Moment. 172
    Summary 172

**Chapter 11: Making 'I Don't Vote' the Start,
Not the End, of a Conversation**
(written with Jacqueline Tulsky, MD) **175**

High-Potential Voters: (At Least) 34% of the Electorate 176
Three Types of Voters 179
Helping Voters Find Their Inner Motivation to Vote 181
Motivational Interviewing: A Tool for Making
    Positive Changes 183
The Spirit of Motivational Interviewing 184
A Different Way to Communicate 187
How to Start a Conversation – and Keep It Going 189
Sample Dialogue: OAR in Action. 191
Change Talk vs. Sustain Talk 195
'Name the Hidden Hope, the Buried Yearning' 196
Dig Deeper 198
Sample Dialogue: Eliciting Change Talk. 201
'You Just Asked Questions and Listened' 205
Summary 208

Chapter 12: Navigating the First Minute of a Conversation . . 209

Approaches for Navigating Grumpiness 213
What if the Voter is a MAGA Republican? 214
Summary 216

**Chapter 13: For Grassroots Leaders:
How to (Re)Engage Volunteers** *(written with Victoria Levi, MD,
and Dara Friedman-Wheeler, PhD)* **217**

Helping Volunteers Overcome Ambivalence. 220
Sample Dialogue: Meeting Volunteers Where They Are . . . 223
The Power of Listening and Gratitude 228
Summary 229

Chapter 14: Spanish for Activists
(written with Mayela Amayrani Galindo Vásquez) 231
   Hacer un Clic (Make a Connection) 234
   Overview.. 236
   Presentaciones (Introductions) 237
   Expresiones de Conversación (Conversational Expressions) ... 240
   Identificación del Votante (Voter Identification) 242
   Identificación de Temas Prioritarios
      (Identifying Priority Issues) 242
   Votación: Hacer un Plan (Voting: Making a Plan) 244
   Triplicar el Voto y 'Cerrar el Trato'
      (Vote Tripling and 'Closing the Deal') 246
   Las Despedidas (Goodbyes)......................... 247
   Found in Translation: Other Language Tips 247
   Summary... 250

Chapter 15: Gear: Tools of the Trade 251
   My Essential Items for Canvassing 252
   Bonus Items for Canvassing 256
   My Essential Items for Phone Banking................. 259
   Bonus Tools for Phone Banking 259
   Summary... 264

**Chapter 16: Preventing Burnout: Self-Care for
the Long Haul.**.. 265
   Summary... 273

Conclusion 275
   Coming Full Circle 276
   Three Journeys 278

Acknowledgments.................................... 281

Glossary 289

Appendix A: Activities to Build Your Listening Skills 293

Appendix B: Engaging with High-Potential Voters:
   Phrase List 295

Appendix C: (Re)Engaging with Volunteers:
   Phrase List 299

Appendix D: Spanish for Activists: Phrase List 301

Appendix E: 'Election Spanish' for Absolute Beginners:
   Phrase List 309

Endnotes 313

About the Author 317

Introduction

It's a balmy spring morning in March, and I'm knocking doors in California's Central Valley. Today is Super Tuesday, when the biggest number of states hold primary elections. I'm getting out the Democratic vote for one of the hottest Congressional races in the country. In California's "jungle primary" system, the top two vote-getters advance to the general election in November. I'm here to help ensure my candidate isn't squeezed out by two Republicans.

Driving to my assigned neighborhood, I pass acre upon acre of fruit orchards. Oranges hang heavy from their boughs and stud the ground like bright croquet balls. This Congressional district is nearly three-quarters Latino, and many of the voters I talk with work in the fields. Registered Democrats outnumber Republicans. But it all comes down to voter turnout, and Republicans have represented this district for almost all of the last four decades.

I approach a light-blue house and ring the doorbell. I'm here to talk with a voter I'll call Adelina. She's in her 20s, according to my voter contact app. Her older brother, Ricardo, answers the door. He says, "She's a night owl, so she won't be up until 5 this evening. Actually, though, I've been thinking about voting for the first time."

I say, "That's fantastic! Tell more about that." He gestures to a couple of folding chairs on the porch and we take a seat. I ask him, "I'm curious to know what's important to you. If you were president of the United States, what two or three things would you change?" He says, "I think the U.S. needs to have less testosterone in its foreign relations, and should get people together and broker peace."

Wow, that's not a response I was expecting from someone who's never voted, but it sounds promising. I ask him what he does for work, and he says he's worked construction, agriculture, anything he can do with his hands. Ricardo points to his toned biceps curving out from his black sleeveless shirt. "I stay fit carrying 80 pound bags up and down ladders, and never have to go to the gym," he says. "You don't see many people around here using workout equipment, because they get all their exercise at work."

The conversation goes in many directions as he jumps from one thought to the next. He tells me he got all Ds and Fs in high school. "Numbers and words were hard for me, but I could learn how to fix things or use a piece of machinery in a couple of hours," Ricardo says. I say, "There are lots of different kinds of intelligence. It sounds like you're off the charts when it comes to fixing and making things." He mentions that he drank a lot in his younger days, but is getting his life together. He says he knows he doesn't have a filter and says whatever pops into his head – but he's working on changing that, because it hurts people's feelings or makes them angry.

I ask if he identifies as a Democrat or a Republican. He doesn't know the difference between the two parties and asks me to explain. I tell him that based on what he shared with me about wanting more peaceful relationships between countries and how he earns a living using his hands, he sounds more in tune with Democrats, who stand with working people rather than the bosses.

I tell him I'm there in support of the Democratic candidate for Congress and give him a flyer. I ask what, if anything, he knows about Congress. Nothing, he tells me. So I briefly explain the roles of the three branches of government – the president leads the federal government, Congress makes laws, the courts interpret the laws. "Oh, it's a system of threes – that way it's balanced!" he says with excitement. "Exactly!" I tell him. "That's the whole idea, so no one part has too much power."

I tell him that today is Election Day, and that he can vote at the Veterans Memorial. I pull up a picture of it on my phone, which I took the day before when I got into town, and ask if he recognizes it. "Oh yeah," he says confidently. "In high school, me and my buddies used to drink 24-packs in the back of that building." I say, "Awesome! You can go back to your old stomping grounds to vote, anytime before 8 tonight."

I hesitate. California allows voters to register to vote on Election Day. However, given what he told me about having trouble with words and numbers, I worry he might have a hard time filling out the bureaucratic registration form. Since he's never voted before, he might feel intimidated or just leave – if he even makes it to the polls. I say, "Hey, since we're talking now, why don't I just register you to vote online?" Ricardo says sure, so I pull up the website on my phone and walk him through the form. We enter all his information and submit it.

There's just one catch. Since it's Election Day, it's too late for the registration to be in the official records at the polling site. The website says to fill out another registration form at the polls. I ask him, "Will you be home for another 20 minutes?" He says yes, so I ask him to wait for me. I go to my car, where I have a portable printer in my trunk. I download and wirelessly print the voter registration affidavit from my phone. I fold the form, put it in an envelope, and bring it back to him. "Just show this to the poll workers when you go vote, and they should let you fill out your ballot," I tell him. "But just in case you have questions or run into any problems, can I give you my phone number? You can call or text me." We exchange numbers, and I test out calling him to make sure I entered his number correctly.

I ask when he can vote. Ricardo says he can go that afternoon, after he renews his driver's license at the DMV. In my head, I think it's a long shot – maybe a 10% chance he'll vote, given that he's never done it before and seems easily distracted. But I say, "That sounds like a great plan. And if you do vote, I'd love to see a selfie with your 'I Voted' sticker!"

We say goodbye. I head to the public library to use the bathroom, then eat my bag lunch in the backseat of my car. It's turning into a hot afternoon and I'm tired, a little grumpy, and wondering if I spent too much time talking with Ricardo when there are so many other doors to knock. Well, at least I got him registered, which might not have happened otherwise.

As I'm finishing lunch, I look at my phone and see I have a message. It's from Ricardo, and it's just one word: "Finished." He also sends me a selfie with – yes – his "I Voted" sticker. I'm so excited I almost drop the rest of my sandwich. I text him back and say, "Oh my goodness! You totally made my day! Congratulations! How did it go?" He writes back that everything went smoothly. The poll workers looked at the voter registration affidavit I printed for him and handed it back before giving him his ballot.

That night, a little after 7 p.m., I circle back to Ricardo's house. I'm hoping to catch his sister Adelina, the voter I originally was there to talk with. She's awake this time, and is a very sweet young woman who tells me she's "really liberal." But she seems anxious about voting, and nervously wrings her hands. "I'm not comfortable voting, because I haven't done any research," she tells me. I tell her how easy it is, and gently inquire about her priorities. Still, I can tell she is feeling more and more uncomfortable.

Just then, Ricardo comes back from work. I say, "Hey, Ricardo, good to see you again! Congratulations on being a voter! I'm just talking with your sister about voting – maybe you can tell her about your experience today?" He says it went fine, and during his short wait in line to vote, he even Googled a YouTube video to learn more about the difference between Democrats and Republicans. I feel embarrassed about underestimating his initiative earlier in the day. I joke about what a productive day he's had – going to work, renewing his driver's license, *and* voting for the first time.

Even hearing about Ricardo's positive experience, Adelina still doesn't want to go to the polls. As the protective big brother, he asks with concern, "Oh, do you feel nervous? Do you want me to go there with you?" She says no and awkwardly tells me, "I'm sorry, I just don't want to vote this time."

I'm disappointed, but I understand. The polls close in 45 minutes. She has the right to make her own decisions, and I can see that pressuring her further will only increase her discomfort. Even though I would have been thrilled if both of them voted, one out of two is an accomplishment. Now that there are two registered voters in the house, maybe Ricardo's example will rub off on Adelina. I thank them both for their time, wish them a good night, and head out into the darkness to knock a few more doors before the polls close.

How to Make the Most of Every Conversation

Behind every vote there is a story. Stories of courage, overcoming obstacles, transformation. For every election, there are millions of stories like Ricardo's. All these stories woven together make up the grand narrative of our country: Who do we want to lead us? What are our collective values? What kind of future will we choose?

While some voters never miss an election, there are many more for whom a knock on the door, a call on the phone, or the power of multiple conversations before Election Day will make the difference between voting and not voting.

That's where we come in. Ordinary people like you and me, without any special qualifications besides a desire to make our country better. I started phone banking in 2017, ventured into canvassing the following year, and unexpectedly fell in love with voter engagement. My conversations with my fellow Americans have been surprising, enlightening, humbling, and unbelievably enriching. I have talked with more than 1,000 voters so far, and learned so much that I teamed up with several other activists to teach online workshops that have trained 2,500 volunteers nationally.

This book is a compilation of everything I've gleaned from my conversations with voters. In the chapters to come, I'll explain some of the approaches that can help you get the most out of every interchange with a voter – including the techniques I used with Ricardo. Not every conversation is as involved. I might spend less than a minute thanking a voter if they've already turned in their ballot, and ask them to encourage like-minded family members and friends to vote. I might spend a couple of minutes telling another voter where their polling place and ballot drop box are, or five minutes asking someone about their priorities and sharing information about the candidates.

I'm always on the lookout for ways to keep building my toolbox of skills, and I'm excited to share what I've learned with you. Whether you're a first-time canvasser or phone banker, a seasoned campaign volunteer, or just someone who wants to make difference in the next election, I hope you'll find some useful tips and strategies for your own voter engagement work.

Because your level of experience may vary, I encourage you to "choose your own adventure" when reading this book. Feel free

INTRODUCTION

to skip around and start with the parts that seem most relevant to you. Since not everyone will read the chapters in order, I have repeated some information throughout so you'll still be in the loop.

As I'll describe in Chapter 1, I'm a rather reluctant activist. Until 2016, I didn't do much beyond read the paper, vote in elections, and phone bank once every four years. My evolution from spectator to participant in our democratic system arose swiftly and urgently after November 2016 – and now my life has gone in a completely new direction.

In Chapter 2, I'll explain why canvassing and phone banking are so important, and some general practices that can help you get started and stay motivated. Because some of you may have hesitations about jumping in, Chapter 3 addresses the issue of safety, and how you can address possible fears and minimize any risk associated with this work.

In Chapters 4 through 10, I will share some of the most valuable lessons I've learned from my time in the field and on the phone. Those include earning respect, making connections that are relational rather than transactional, and listening with nonjudgmental curiosity. I also encourage you to take advantage of chance encounters, whether it's with a voter's household member, a shop employee, or the person who picks up your call and says it's a wrong number. I suggest some creative approaches to help voters get to the polling place or put their ballot in the mail.

Chapters 11 and 12 give you tools for navigating particularly challenging situations. Those include people who start a conversation by saying, "I don't vote," or are ready to hang up the phone or close the door before you even get started.

So many volunteers stepped up after the 2016 elections, and we need all those people and more to jump back in for this election cycle. If you are a grassroots leader, or are trying to encourage your friends and family to get involved, Chapter 13 offers helpful approaches for encouraging people to start or resume their volunteer work.

Latino voters are a key (and growing) part of the electorate, and some of them may feel more comfortable communicating in Spanish. Chapter 14 includes helpful phrases and approaches for engaging with Spanish-speaking voters in a respectful, meaningful way.

Whether you are canvassing or phone banking, Chapter 15 includes my recommendations for helpful tools and gear to support your work and make your efforts as effective and efficient as possible. And finally, shoring up our democracy is rewarding yet challenging work; it's truly a lifelong effort. To help maintain a spirit of joy for the long haul and prevent burnout, in Chapter 16 I offer some ideas for taking care of ourselves while we tend to our democratic system.

To help explain some of the jargon used with canvassing and phone banking, I've also included a Glossary at the end of this book. The Appendices have handy phrases when talking with voters, prospective volunteers, and Spanish-speaking voters.

A brief note about the stories in this book. I recognize what a profound gift it is to hear about other people's lives, and to learn about some of their joys and struggles. To protect the privacy of the people I talked with, I have changed most names and identifying details. I have recounted our conversations as accurately as I can remember them, in accordance with notes I made to myself at the end of each day. In a few cases, I include excerpts from videos or audio recordings that voters gave me permission to make.

INTRODUCTION

THE CENTRAL VALLEY: A SENSE OF PLACE

I'd also like to share a bit of geographic context for this book. I've spent most of my time canvassing and phone banking in California's Central Valley, since that's where my closest swing districts are located. In particular, I've focused my efforts in California's 22nd Congressional District (CA-22). Since the 2018 election cycle, it has consistently been rated as a toss-up, where either the Republican or Democrat could win the Congressional race.

The district is one of the poorest in California, and Latinos make up a majority of the population. More than half the population reports speaking Spanish at home.[1] Registered Democrats outnumber registered Republicans, but it all comes down to turnout: Republicans have represented this area for most of the last four decades. Bakersfield is the largest city in CA-22, and about half is included within the current district. There are also many small towns spread out across this sprawling district, which covers more than 4,300 square miles and takes a couple of hours to drive across.

The district's main industries are agriculture – including grapes, almonds, citrus, vegetables, dairy and cotton – and oil production. There are also several prisons in the district. The agricultural town of Delano was home to the 1965 Delano grape strike, led by Larry Itliong, César Chávez and Dolores Huerta, which laid the foundation for the creation of the United Farm Workers of America.

The district has some of the worst air quality in the country, which contributes to high rates of asthma and exacerbates heart disease, lung disease and diabetes.[2] The COVID-19 pandemic hit this community hard. Many people were essential workers who could not afford to shelter in place, and it is common for them to live in multigenerational homes.[3]

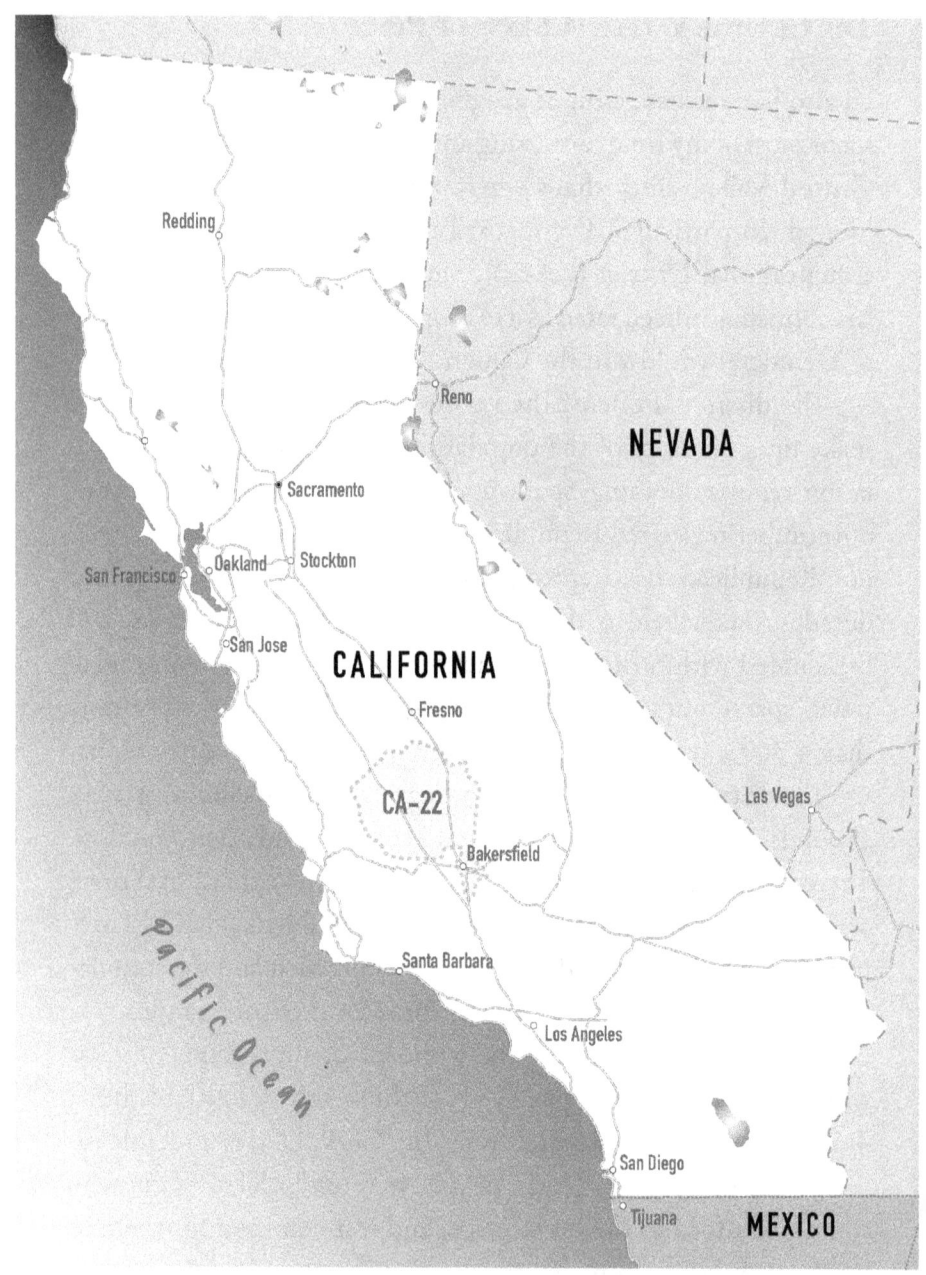

California's 22nd Congressional District (CA-22)

Since 1972, Kings County, one of three counties which make up the district, was subject to the "preclearance requirement" of Section 5 of the 1965 Voting Rights Act.[4] This required jurisdictions with a history of discriminatory voting practices to get advance approval from the federal government before changing their election laws, to ensure any changes would not harm minority voters. The Supreme Court struck down this provision in the 2013 *Shelby County v. Holder* decision.[5]

The residents of CA-22 are hardworking, proud of their important role in feeding the rest of the country, and often overlooked by those in power. While many of my stories take place in the Central Valley, I hope some of the general principles will be useful in other districts and regions across the country.

Cultivating Seeds of Hope

In some ways, talking with voters is a leap of faith. Just like some voters wonder if their one vote will make a difference, I sometimes question whether my conversations with voters have any impact.

When I get discouraged, I think of a memento from my 40th birthday party. My friends Bren and Doug prepared dozens of tiny jade plants in three-inch pots to give away as party favors. I kept a couple for myself, transplanting them into bigger pots as they outgrew their original homes. Now more than a dozen years later, those dwarflike starts have grown into abundant plants that live on top of my microwave. Their long green strands of leaves spill over the edge like the tresses of a punk rock Rapunzel. Sometimes when I visit friends, I see how their jade plants from that long-ago night have flourished. All this time, they've been quietly growing into abundance, in places far removed from their beginnings.

Talking with voters is similar. Most of the time, I'll never know if someone ends up voting, or if they decided to support my candidate. But like most important endeavors, making a change is a journey composed of many tiny steps. Maybe a voter thought about how the elections might affect their day-to-day lives for the first time, or got a little closer to filling out their ballot. And if enough of us step up to initiate these conversations before Election Day, hopefully our collective engagement helps people move a bit closer to voting each time.

From talking with more than a thousand voters, I have witnessed firsthand how forging empathetic connections, helping people navigate obstacles to voting, and talking about what's most important to them is vital to rebuilding our democracy. It's like offering them a tiny jade plant. Not all will flourish. Yet if voters give these tender shoots a little sunlight, water and care, these moments of connection can grow into a vibrant fullness that neither of us can imagine in the moment.

I, too, receive gifts from voters. Each conversation teaches me something. I may get a glimpse into another person's struggles and joys, discover a new way to navigate a challenging topic, or have an opportunity to transform theory into practice. This book is like my jade plant collection, which I've gathered over time, cultivated with love, and assembled for your consideration. I offer it to you, in the hopes that a few buds may be worthy of joining your own garden. May they help our democracy to flourish.

Chapter 1
Out of Bad Things, Good Things Can Come

I grew up in a decidedly apolitical family. I came of age in Oakland, California, during the tumultuous 1970s and 1980s – the era of the Black Panthers, the assassinations of San Francisco Mayor George Moscone and Supervisor Harvey Milk, the Jonestown massacre, and the beginning of the AIDS crisis. While some of my peers went to demonstrations in utero and later in strollers, my family didn't even have bumper stickers on their cars. I lived in another world, filled with weekly piano lessons, ballet classes, and the blue-and-green plaid skirt uniform of my Catholic elementary school.

Politically, my parents were polar opposites. My dad was a Republican – fiscally conservative, but socially more laissez-faire. He loved to fish and hunt and was a card-carrying member of the National Rifle Association. In the years after Nixon resigned from the presidency, he'd watch the news, shake his head, and mutter, "They're all a bunch of crooks." When the occasional political canvasser or nonprofit fundraiser would come to the door, he would play devil's advocate, verbally sparring with them and yanking their chain. I'd listen in from the dining room and squirm, feeling sorry for these poor souls who had come on this fool's errand. He hated paying taxes and often referred to "the government" with a disdainful tone – a bit ironic, since he worked for 40 years as an engineer for the State of California.

My dad came from one of the only Korean families on Maui, where his father was a foreman on a Maui Pineapple Company plantation. They raised much of their own food on a small plot of company land, growing vegetables and raising chickens. My dad put himself through college by working summers in the pineapple fields, leaving the house each morning with a sack lunch and one or two old ketchup bottles filled with water. In the first weeks he was so exhausted after a day of hard labor in the unforgiving sun that his crew threw him into the back of the truck "like a sack of potatoes" so he could get home at the end of his shift. Midway through college he transferred to the University of Wisconsin, Madison, arriving with his Hawaiian wardrobe of flimsy shoes and a thin coat to face his first Midwestern winter. He joined the U.S. Air Force ROTC to help pay for tuition, serving a few years after graduation at the Air Force base near Omaha, Nebraska.

Throughout his life he maintained the green thumb he developed as a child. He faithfully watered pink fuchsias in planter boxes hanging above our front deck, and devised ever more elaborate ways to protect his tomato plants from ravenous deer. One year he raised snails to make escargot, fattening them up on a diet of cornmeal and lettuce and hosing them off individually when he got home from work. He and a buddy even bought a small plot of land in the Central Valley town of Manteca, trying to cultivate a pistachio farm. They were spectacularly unsuccessful and sold the farm after a few years, but one of my earliest memories was sitting on his lap in the tractor, pretending to drive the machine.

My dad could be gruff, but he showed his love in practical, understated ways. He built me a tree house, and designed a go-cart out of plywood, a two-by-four and tricycle wheels. My best friend next door and I raced that go-cart down the hill, squealing with terror and laughter. When I expressed an interest in the night sky, he took an astronomy class at the Lawrence Hall of Science and built me a telescope. We stayed up way past my bedtime to stargaze and record our observations in a star log that he created. One winter day, my only pair of school shoes got soaked with rain. He stayed up late, drying them in front of the kerosene space heater we used to save on the electricity bill, turning them from side to side for hours so I could wear them the next morning.

Hard Times and Compassion

Although my mom was also born and raised in Hawaii, she had different experiences which likely contributed to her identity as a lifelong Democrat. She grew up in Honolulu, and was eight years old when Pearl Harbor was attacked. She had been on her way to Sunday school but had to turn around. On the drive home, somebody told the children to get down on the floor of the car and not look up. She later found out that some buildings in her neighborhood caught fire because of the bombing.

Hawaii was still a territory, and it was immediately placed under martial law for almost three years. The army censored the press, long-distance telephone calls, and the mail. More than one-third of Hawaii's population were Japanese American, including my mom and her family. The federal government couldn't incarcerate such a large portion of the population, especially on a small island. Only community leaders were imprisoned, unlike Japanese Americans on the mainland – including some of her extended family members.

Nonetheless, all Japanese schools were closed immediately and people were ordered to stop speaking Japanese, which is why my mom barely learned any of that language. She also had to stop using her Japanese middle name and switch to her "American" first name. She once told me that growing up, her parents told her she had to be twice as good and work twice as hard as the *haoles* (white people), because she needed to show them that she was hardworking and trustworthy.

In addition to the challenges of wartime, it was a difficult time for her family. My grandmother died of cancer when my mom was 10. My grandfather quit school after about sixth grade to support himself, and eventually became an auto mechanic. When my grandmother was dying, he temporarily stopped working to take care of her, and sent his four children across the street to his in-laws' house to eat. He eventually remarried a widow with three children of her own.

When my stepgrandmother lost her eyesight due to inadequate health care, my teenaged mother – as the oldest girl – became responsible for cooking and cleaning for a family of nine. "I had to grow up fast," she often told me. She frequently bought food on credit, since money was tight. When the neighborhood grocery store was no longer willing to extend credit, she walked to stores further and further away to get enough food for her family.

To put herself through college, my mom worked the graveyard shift at the Libby pineapple cannery, earning 91 cents an hour. She remembered running across a dark, deserted field late at night to get from the bus stop to the cannery. In the factory, the acid from the pineapples ate through her rubber gloves, and the noise from the machines was enough to drive her crazy. It was excellent motivation for earning her college degree, and she became an elementary school teacher. My mom wanted to see the world, and landed teaching jobs in Levittown, Pennsylvania, the military base in Bremerhaven, Germany, and finally in Oakland, where she met and married my dad and lived for more than 50 years.

My mom was the only Catholic in her family, joining the church to attend a Catholic school. After she retired, she coordinated a monthly dinner for homeless residents in Berkeley through our church for 20 years. While she said she never went hungry as a child, her teenage experience of struggling to feed a large family on a shoestring cultivated a sense of compassion for people going through hard times.

My parents had very different political beliefs, though they had a tacit agreement to agree to disagree. "Our votes just cancel each other out!" my mom often joked. Even though they read *San Francisco Chronicle* each day and listened to AM talk radio while driving and doing chores, we seldom talked about politics. And although they both voted in every election, I can't remember a single time when they ever called an elected official, wrote a letter to the editor, or made a campaign donation. Even though they both had strong opinions about current events, I can't imagine them ever phone banking or canvassing.

An Unlikely Activist

Given my parents' upbringing and their focus on working hard, saving money, and securing themselves a place in the middle class, it's not surprising to me that they didn't become activists. I followed their lead, studying hard in school and always working to prepare myself for college. In third grade I also started piano lessons with a fantastic but incredibly stern teacher who taught with passion and precision. The parent of another student once remarked, "I'd rather be caught blatantly cheating on my income taxes than send Mary unprepared to a lesson!"

I loved books and writing, and dreamed of becoming a journalist – perhaps a foreign correspondent or a music critic. I also developed a politically progressive outlook, maybe from growing up in the liberal Bay Area and hearing my mom's opinions about the news and the many books she read. However, my days and evenings were filled with school, homework, editing the school newspaper, practicing piano two hours each day, and spending time with my friends.

Even though I went to a famously liberal college in a swing state – Oberlin College in Ohio – I didn't become politically involved in college. I didn't even reregister to vote in Ohio, since I felt more connected with my home state of California and didn't understand the concept of a swing state. In any case, my timing was off: I turned 18 after the 1988 election, disappointed that I wasn't eligible to help defeat George H.W. Bush. By the time Bill Clinton was elected I had graduated from college. A few friends talked about canvassing voters or taking all-night bus rides to marches in Washington, D.C. Those activities were so far out of my comfort zone that it was like hearing someone describe their honors thesis on quantum mechanics – fascinating to listen to, but nothing I could ever do myself.

I savored my time at Oberlin. The students were quirky, brilliantly creative, and pursued multiple interests – not just academics. I majored in English and music, went to scores of incredible concerts and performances, had many nurturing professors, and went dancing in the campus disco five nights a week. My friends and I stayed up late, talking in the dorm hallways after our roommates went to bed. We discussed the world's problems and how we would solve them, with the grandiose idealism of youth.

One weakness, however, was not learning skills for engaging productively with people who held different opinions. My peers heatedly split hairs between progressive and radical perspectives, and the handful of conservatives on campus (including future conservative political commentator Michelle Malkin) were regarded alternately with amusement or outrage. For the most part, political discussions felt distasteful. As someone who enjoys collaboration, making connections with different kinds of people, and discovering common interests, the tone of most political discourse turned me off. Other people seemed to know so much more than I did, and were more interested in promoting their own viewpoints than understanding my evolving opinions. I also disliked the whole vibe of politics: the winner-takes-all nature of elections, the big egos of the candidates, the focus on glad-handing, prestige and power – not to mention the tales of corruption and the personal foibles and misdeeds of various candidates.

Still enamored with journalism, I wrote and edited for the school newspaper, and landed reporting internships at the *Milwaukee Journal* (before it merged with the *Sentinel)*, the *Seattle Times* and the *Chicago Tribune*. Part of the ethics of journalism was maintaining an impartial stance: we did not sign petitions, participate in protests if we weren't covering them, display yard signs, or put bumper stickers on our cars. (I once heard that some journalists didn't even vote, thinking that might compromise their impartiality, but that seemed like an extreme interpretation.) So that was another reason I stayed away from personal involvement in politics.

After graduation, I had the great fortune to obtain a Thomas J. Watson Fellowship, which allows new college graduates the opportunity to spend a year anywhere in the world outside the U.S. pursuing a self-designed project. It was shortly after the fall of the Berlin Wall, and I chose to research the development of free press in Eastern Europe. I interviewed about 150 journalists about what it was like under authoritarian regimes, and how their practices and business models had changed in those first few years of democracy and the free market. It was one of the most formative experiences of my life. Those conversations taught me a lot about the fragility of democracy, and how important a free press is to maintaining a democratic government.

By meeting many foreign correspondents that year, I realized that path was more grind than glory. I had already started to burn out from the stress of daily deadlines, so I investigated other career paths when I returned to the U.S. I worked in social service and arts education nonprofits for over a decade, then studied documentary radio at the Salt Institute for Documentary Studies in Portland, Maine. When I returned to the Bay Area, I became a freelance radio producer, and paid the bills by working as a freelance medical writer.

As my parents developed more health issues, I continued the medical writing but chose to step away from the time-consuming, low-paid radio work. As an only child, I felt responsible for my mom and dad in their time of need. With my dad's stroke and my mom's struggles with cancer and then heart failure, many of my non-working hours were filled with family care. I spent my limited free time hiking, traveling, going to the theater, and visiting my wonderful dance studio several times a week to boogie down to Latin, hip-hop and pop tunes.

My dad died in 2011, and my mom in 2016. In the months after my mom's death, I was grieving and utterly exhausted. I was, however, concerned about the surprising popularity of Donald Trump, and his clinching of the Republican presidential nomination. In the final weeks of the campaign, I did a little bit of phone banking. I even spent a few hours canvassing in Arizona with my friend Rochelle, on our way to hike the Grand Canyon. Yet it all felt like too little, too late. And indeed, it was – as we found out in the early hours of November 9, 2016.

Starting Small

Before that fateful day, I thought I was a pretty good citizen. I read the paper, voted in every election, and did a little phone banking for presidential elections. But mostly, I figured other people would be doing the heavy lifting of knocking on doors and making phone calls to voters. I'm not sure who I thought those other people were. Elves? Idealistic college students? But I figured they'd be much better equipped to do this kind of work, and "they" would magically take care of it.

Obviously, it didn't quite work out that way. After the 2016 election, I wandered around in a nightmarish daze for weeks. It was hard to celebrate the start of 2017; instead, I was filled with dread about what the new year would bring. I wanted to do *something*, but I had no idea what I, as one lone person, could accomplish that would have any impact on the vast challenges we were facing. When the start of the Trump administration proved even worse than I'd feared, I counted down the months until our next presidential election. I anxiously hoped our country could survive four years of increasing chaos and damage to our civic institutions. I knew I'd never again be complacent about our democracy.

When I'd done a few hours of last-minute phone banking before the 2016 election, I hit a brick wall when I was completely unable to communicate with Spanish-speaking voters. Living in California, I'd always had vague aspirations of learning Spanish, but never found the time to do it. So when Trump kept saying, "I'm going to build a wall!" I thought, "I'm going to learn Spanish so I can talk with more voters and get you out of office!" I started taking Spanish classes in mid-2017, with the goal of learning enough by 2020 to have basic conversations with voters. I wanted to at least be able to introduce myself, say why I was calling, and engage in simple back-and-forth about the candidates and the logistics of voting.

I also committed to spending at least two hours a month taking concrete action. Worrying, reading the news or going to talks didn't count toward that goal. When choosing between something that might make me more knowledgeable and something that might actually result in a few more Democratic votes in the next elections, I chose the latter. I started by writing postcards to voters, and stood in the rain to vote in elections for my local Democratic committee leaders. I got on some local progressive activist email lists and saw a lot of opportunities to volunteer. Though I was too scared to canvass, given the increasing polarization of the country, I thought phone banking would be a good way to dip my toe back into talking directly with voters.

THE REWARDS OF PHONE BANKING

I started in fall 2017 by calling Alabama voters on behalf of Doug Jones, the Democratic Senate candidate in the special election to fill a U.S. Senate seat after Jeff Sessions was appointed Attorney General. The two candidates couldn't have been more different. Jones had successfully prosecuted two members of the Ku Klux Klan who, decades before, had killed four young girls in the 16th Street Baptist Church bombing. His Republican opponent, Alabama Supreme Court chief justice Roy Moore, faced multiple accusations of sexually assaulting minors.

The phone bank was held in the spacious apartment of one of the organizers. Volunteers spread out on comfy brown sofas or sat at white folding tables, squinting at their laptops and tablets as they made calls. Silver desk bells and bowls filled with candy were scattered around the room. When I started dialing, I mostly got voicemails, disconnected lines or wrong numbers. Even so, I was so nervous about encountering a nasty voter or not knowing the right thing to say that I had to take a 10-minute break every hour to go outside, stretch, and do some deep breathing.

I had thought I needed to be an expert in politics, history and economics to make these calls. However, when voters did pick up, most of the time I was just explaining the basic differences between the two candidates, and answering logistical questions about where and when they could vote.

There was a buzzy excitement in the room. Every time someone finished a good conversation with a voter, they rang one of the silver desk bells to celebrate and encourage other volunteers. That cacophony was the sound of democracy in action – a symphony of civic engagement, where I got to contribute a few bell rings of my own to that chaotic, beautiful chorus. I realized I was part of a cast of thousands of voters and volunteers, joined by a collective spirit of courage, generosity and hope as we struggled to make our country just a little bit better. And Doug Jones did prevail that December, eking out a win with a margin of less than 22,000 votes.

That victory was so sweet, and far from assured. I was elated to know I might have helped bring in a few of those votes! I also was filled with an unfamiliar emotion in those days: hope. For the first time since the 2016 election, instead of feeling smothered by a leaden blanket of dread and helplessness, I felt a tiny gleam of excitement. Rather than just reading about the latest terrible tweet or outrageous executive order, I could actually have a say – no matter how minuscule – in what happened next.

I continued to phone bank as the 2018 midterms got underway. While many of my friends and acquaintances agonized about the news, most weren't actively involved in electoral work. Unsurprisingly, going to phone banks was a great way to meet people who were far more engaged than I was. Some had been phone banking and canvassing longer than I'd been alive. I eavesdropped on many of them as I made calls and picked up little tips.

It was also a fantastic way to get immediate support for difficult phone calls when a voter was particularly cantankerous, or told me to take them off the call list. One of the other women at my table got hung up on, and she turned to her friend and said, "And... scene!" (As in, "Curtains.") We all burst out laughing.

It was also exciting to tell fellow volunteers about the uplifting calls that make a whole shift worthwhile. One of my most rewarding early calls was with a woman who went from not voting because she didn't think it would make a difference, to mentioning that before Obamacare she'd had difficulty getting health insurance because of a preexisting condition, to committing to vote for the Democratic candidate I was supporting, and even accepting a yard sign! The adrenaline rush of participating in another person's evolving thought process (and behavioral choices) was a thrill like none other I had ever experienced.

Knock, Knock: Canvassing for Change

Phone banks were also useful for gathering intelligence about other volunteer opportunities. I chatted up seasoned volunteers after those phone banks to ask them about their experiences with door-to-door canvassing. One of them, Martha, encouraged me to try it at least once, since in her opinion it was more fun than phone banking. "Fun?" That wasn't a word I'd ever considered using in the same sentence as "canvassing," but it intrigued me enough to sign up to canvass in Turlock, a small town in the Central Valley, home to our nearest Congressional swing district.

I couldn't convince anyone else to go with me, but the universe gave me several signs that I was headed in the right direction. Although I barely slept the night before, out of nerves and excitement, when I cracked an egg for breakfast it turned out to have a double yolk – twice the nourishment for my big day ahead. As I drove the nearly two hours to Turlock, I heard Lulu Garcia-Navarro on NPR's Weekend Edition, reporting on the critical role of Latino voters in the midterms. Since Latinos made up more than 40% of Turlock's population, I was definitely headed to the right place! And instead of just listening to the news from home, how wonderful that I heard that story on my way to actually *doing* something that could shape the outcome of the district's election – and the balance of power in the House of Representatives.

When I arrived at the launch site, I was the only person without a buddy. The organizers said I could head out alone, but I was way too nervous to canvass solo. Gordon, a kind and generous retired physician, saw my alarmed look and volunteered to knock doors with me. He had only been canvassing a few months longer than me, but just knowing that someone else was at the door with me was hugely reassuring.

We fumbled with the voter contact app, but finally figured it out together. After we struggled (and failed) to connect with one chain-smoking, cynical voter, we joked about outrageous things we could have said to get his attention. When I got to use my rudimentary Spanish with a voter for the very first time, I was elated! There are few things more exciting than setting a goal, like learning Spanish to communicate with voters, and actually achieving it – with endless opportunities to keep practicing and improving.

Gordon shared my excitement, and kept telling me how impressed he was. When I explained how I'd started studying Spanish the previous year for this very purpose, he said, "Wow, you're like the Koch brothers – you're playing the long game!" (Billionaires Charles and David Koch are megadonors to conservative and libertarian candidates and causes.) I burst out laughing and said, "I never thought being compared to the Koch brothers would be something positive, but I guess I'll take that as a compliment!"

I ended up driving Gordon home, and we chatted nonstop – not just about politics and canvassing, but about our work, families and hobbies. We stayed in touch, and I became friends with both Gordon and his wife Sally – two of the many wonderful, unexpected friendships I have developed from doing this volunteer work.

After that auspicious start, I was hooked! In the coming weeks I returned to the Central Valley half a dozen more times, venturing even further south to a district that was rated as a toss-up. I was so smitten with political activism that I spent Thanksgiving weekend in 2018 driving around Bakersfield, helping to cure ballots. That involved tracking down voters who had supported our candidate but had a signature mismatch between their ballot envelope and their signature on record, or had forgotten to sign their ballot at all. I helped voters "cure" their ballots by giving them a one-page form to sign which certified that they resided in their county, had indeed voted, and were the person whose name appeared on their ballot's envelope.

That Congressional race was the last in the country to be called. Nearly a month after the election, we flipped that district from red to blue – by a mere 862 votes. It was an unbelievable thrill to realize that I helped secure a few of those 862 votes through my canvassing and ballot curing. I was ecstatic to be one drop of the "Blue Wave" that swept through the country – the outpouring of Democratic voters who made their deep unhappiness with Trump known at the ballot box. Together we flipped seven governorships from Republican to Democrat. We also gained 40 seats in the House of Representatives, handing the gavel back to my hometown Congresswoman, Speaker Nancy Pelosi.

Platinum Linings

I was on a roll. I joined a local activist group, Swing Left San Francisco – one of hundreds if not thousands of political grassroots organizations which sprung up after the 2016 elections. I also canvassed in Virginia in 2019 for their state legislative elections, and went back to the Central Valley in early March 2020, knocking doors before the California primary election.

In early 2020, I had also been working with two fellow Swing Left San Francisco activists, Myra Levy and Debbie Benrubi. We were developing a "Canvassing for Introverts" workshop to encourage people on the fence about canvassing to give it a try.

Then COVID hit. In those early days of the pandemic, filled with fear and uncertainty, some unexpected "platinum linings" emerged – positive outcomes that defied the odds and opened possibilities far beyond anything I could have imagined. During the early weeks of the pandemic shutdown, Debbie, Myra and I repurposed our material for Zoom and renamed it "Phone Bank Training for Introverts (& Friends)."

We tried to demystify phone banking by explaining how it works, why it's so important and effective, and some useful approaches for having good conversations with voters. We also tried to bring a lighthearted approach. As an icebreaker, we encouraged people to brainstorm in the chat about all the reasons *not* to phone bank. (People might be mean, workshop participants hate getting these calls themselves, and so on.) As introverts, we could speak from experience about how our ability to listen thoughtfully and take our time with voter conversations help us to be effective in this work.

While it was a steep learning curve to figure out how to make an online training interactive, interesting and hopefully a bit fun, there was a huge up side. Instead of training 15 people at a time in friends' living rooms, we suddenly had the potential to reach volunteers at scale. Word got out, and we ended up leading 18 workshops that trained a total of 1,400 volunteers from more than 30 states and the District of Columbia. Some of these participants had little to no previous experience phone banking, but in survey feedback the vast majority said they were somewhat or very likely to phone bank in the next two weeks.

In addition to the Introverts workshop, I have been able to co-develop other online trainings. Right before the shutdown, I spent a couple of weeks doing a language intensive course in Oaxaca, Mexico; after I returned home, I continued working online with Mayela Galindo, one of my Spanish teachers. In spring 2020, she and I developed an online "Spanish for Activists" course, and ended up training nearly 200 Spanish-speaking volunteers nationally on "election Spanish."

I recruited many of our "alumni" to phone bank in key races across the country, including California's Central Valley and to Spanish-speaking voters in Wisconsin. It was deeply satisfying to see people we'd trained at various phone banks, knowing that the approaches and Spanish-language phrases we'd shared with students were being put into practical use with voters who too often are overlooked.

Before COVID, I'd had fantasies of moving to South Texas for a few months to canvass full-time in a swing district there. Obviously, in 2020 that was off the table due to the pandemic. Instead, besides doing a lot of phone banking from home that year, I co-taught about 50 workshops, between our Introverts and Spanish trainings. In retrospect, those workshops helped me make a bigger contribution to voter engagement efforts than anything I could have accomplished just knocking doors on my own.

Building on the success of those workshops in 2020, I wanted to take it a step further. A secret joy of teaching is that is allows me to investigate the areas I want to know more about, like how to learn election Spanish, or how to turn introversion from an obstacle into a superpower. Then I get to share what I learn with others who are also wrestling with those same questions.

Case in point: One of the thorniest issues I'd encountered as a phone banker and canvasser was voters who told me, "Oh, I don't vote" before hanging up or closing the door. I knew there must be a better way to handle this, but I wasn't quite sure how to proceed.

My friend Rochelle is a longtime volunteer with Citizens' Climate Lobby, and one of their volunteers made a video[6] about how to use Motivational Interviewing (MI) to engage with voters. MI was originally developed by two clinical psychologists to help patients struggling with addiction, and has since been widely adopted in many helping professions to address issues related to behavior change – weight loss, exercise and many other hard-to-change habits.

In my day job as a freelance medical writer, I interviewed Jacqueline Tulsky, MD, an addiction medicine and HIV primary care doctor at San Francisco General Hospital. In addition to her deep experience caring for some of our most vulnerable community members and her wise, generous spirit, she also turned out to be an MI trainer. I invited her to collaborate with me to develop a workshop using MI tools specifically to engage with people who are not in the habit of voting. In 2021 we created a new workshop called "You and the 34%: How to Have Meaningful Conversations with High-Potential Voters."

"High-potential voters" is a positive reframing of a group traditionally referred to as "low-propensity voters" – people who rarely or never vote. The "34%" refers to the (shockingly high) percentage of eligible voters who did not vote in 2020. You can read more about how to effectively engage with this large and vitally important group of voters in Chapter 11, "Making 'I Don't Vote' the Start, not the End, of a Conversation." To date, we've trained more than 1,100 volunteers nationally on how to employ these powerful tools.

In keeping with the theme of how this volunteer work can not only strengthen democracy but help us personally, a number of participants in our "You and the 34%" trainings reported how useful these skills are in their personal life. Some have even told us that incorporating these approaches into their everyday lives has improved the way that they interact with their family members, friends and co-workers. It's a huge gift to be part of something so important and so meaningful. Stepping up to make the world a better place really can lead to amazing outcomes that I could never have predicted at the outset.

As much as I love teaching, I also missed canvassing. In fall 2022, once the pandemic had eased, I took a month off work and spent an entire month in the Bakersfield area. To maximize opportunities to use my Spanish, I volunteered mostly in rural parts of the district. I thought I was a pretty good canvasser before this monthlong immersion. But just as my Spanish improved rapidly when I spent a couple of weeks studying the language in Oaxaca, my canvassing skills got so much better with repeated practice and opportunities to improve in the field. Afterward, I put together a slide presentation of my biggest learnings and shared it with a few groups. When I tried to summarize my learnings in an essay, I realized I had more to share. The result is this book, which I hope will provide you with some useful tools for your own voter engagement work.

BUILD ON YOUR STRENGTHS

One of the things I love most about canvassing and phone banking is that it uses everything I've ever learned from various parts of my life. It's also given me opportunities to develop new skills, like learning Spanish. Here are a few of the influences that have shaped my thinking and practice so far:

- *Journalism*: Though I discovered the intense pace of journalism was not for me, I later pursued training in documentary radio, and eventually fell into my current freelance work as a medical writer. All these types of writing and storytelling helped me cultivate invaluable skills that support my voter engagement work. For example, I learned to ask a lot of open-ended questions (ones that can't be answered with "yes" or "no") as well as follow-up questions. I also try to count silently to 10 to give people a chance to think and respond. I'm a hard-core introvert and normally rather shy. However, give me a microphone or clipboard plus an assignment, and I'll boldly approach complete strangers.

    I also document notable conversations with voters. If I'm phone banking, I jot down interesting points in a spiral notebook while we talk. If I'm canvassing, I keep a small notebook in my pocket and write down follow-up tasks for myself, like if someone requests a yard sign or has a policy question I can't answer and need to research and get back to them. My journalism background has been especially useful when canvassing and ballot curing. It's helped me be persistent, get creative, and not feel shy about enlisting the help of household members, neighbors, and even the UPS delivery driver to find an address or reach a voter.

- *Music:* I studied classical piano for 14 years, and later jazz piano for five years. In addition to all the technique and theory, a huge part of my musical training was about *listening*. As a child I was taught how to listen to a musical phrase that someone else played, sing it back, and then transcribe it. My teacher sometimes had me listen to three different recordings of a Beethoven Sonata and evaluate the similarities and differences, describing the nuances and artistic choices each performer made. Playing piano duets, chamber music and in the school orchestra taught me how to play in sync with others. I had to learn my own part well enough so I could hear other musicians' lines, while staying true to my own.

  Today, these experiences help me listen to a voter's words with intention and focus, and hear the nuances within them. That musical background has also helped me tune my own word choice and pace in a conversation, which can help a voter feel more comfortable and earn their trust.

- *Travel:* I've always loved learning about different cultures and visiting different parts of the country and world. There's something invigorating about witnessing how people live in other places, how local influences shape their lives, the ingenious solutions they come up with, and the stories they tell. I appreciate opportunities to go beyond "checklist tourism," where I'm just rushing from one famous site to another to take a few selfies to prove I was there. Instead, I try to slow down and get a deeper understanding of place, whether that's taking a cooking class in Bali or chatting with a local on a Greek ferry about his recommendations for the best islands to visit.

As a visitor to a community, I also know how important it is to come with humility and an open mind. The people who live there are the experts in their lives and their community. While I've been truly touched and inspired by the generosity and kindness of many people I've met in the field, I know it is not an entitlement, but rather a gift. Often that gift comes in the form of story, of people sharing their time and allowing me a glimpse into their lives.

- *Elder care:* I helped my mom and my dad in their later years as they dealt with the challenges of aging, chronic illness and end of life. For almost 20 years, I watched as my smart, hardworking, fiercely independent parents slowly declined. I tried to help them navigate the labyrinths of the medical, legal and financial systems. I learned a lot about patience and tenacity. I tried to find joy in the little victories. When my dad needed to move into a skilled nursing facility for over a month to receive daily intravenous antibiotics, I mailed him a letter, postcard or pack of gum each day to help ease the boredom and isolation. I figured out that my mom got relief from insomnia by listening to books on CD that I borrowed from the library (they put her right to sleep). Out of desperation, I came up with creative solutions to logistical problems, like placing a three-way phone call with my mom, me and 911 on the line when she was reluctant to call for help.

  I was awed by my parents' inner strength and enduring sense of humor as they traversed difficult paths. I got a lot of practice muddling through times of great uncertainty, when the stakes felt high. My dad was on life support for seven days, and my mom was on hospice for seven months, each day potentially their last. Even if I couldn't always make things better for them, I saw the value of heartfelt listening and bearing witness to other people's journeys. It was one of the hardest, yet most rewarding chapters of my life. Whenever I start feeling tired or overwhelmed by my volunteer work with voters, remembering that period of time helps me keep it all in perspective.

- *Nonprofit work:* I spent about a decade at St. Anthony Foundation, a social services organization in San Francisco's Tenderloin neighborhood which serves homeless and low-income people. Besides serving about 2,500 free meals every day, St. Anthony's also provides free clothing, medical care, social work, drug and alcohol rehabilitation, and other vital services. They also have a wonderful service-learning program which engages students, corporate groups, faith communities, and others in learning about the root causes of poverty, and provides opportunities to volunteer. Each day ends with a reflection session to discuss what participants experienced and ways to advocate for more just policies and structures.

    I learned so much from that environment that translates into voter engagement. It was a great training ground for learning how to do excellent work on a shoestring. (My co-workers and I joked that our motto could be, "High quality, low cost – it's the St. Anthony way!") Although I attended Catholic school for 12 years, it wasn't until St. Anthony's that I learned about liberation theology, which emphasizes the liberation of oppressed people and working for justice. I saw those ideals embodied daily through our direct service and advocacy programs. I witnessed how the spirit of welcome and kinship was as important as providing food, medical care or other necessities.

I also felt the hazards of burnout: no matter how hard I worked, there would always be more to do. Self-care was an absolute necessity in such a challenging environment. Perhaps most of all, I experienced the life-giving energy of being in community with people who shared the same values. Their passion, exuberant humor, creativity and incredible generosity of heart showed me how to find joy in the struggle. Even when our progress can feel microscopic and imperfect, wrestling with some of the biggest questions of our time is ultimately worthwhile and rewarding.

This is just some context about the particular perspectives that have shaped my approach. You don't need these exact experiences to make meaningful connections with voters. Instead, I hope this book helps you to draw upon your *own* rich life experiences as you connect with voters in person or over the phone. Whether that includes skills from your career, your experiences as a parent or caregiver, your discipline as an athlete, or some other combination of life learnings, you have many deep wells of wisdom to draw from. You bring all of this to one-on-one conversations with voters.

Unexpected Gifts

From my own experience, if you're feeling overwhelmed and disheartened by the state of the country, consider taking a small action. You never know where it may lead. While my initial goal was to do something to help bolster our democracy, one thing led to another, in surprising ways. I met like-minded volunteers who shared ideas, inspiration and practical tips. I built my skills and gained confidence in my abilities, which allowed me to push the boundaries of what I was willing to do. The urgent need to work for change inspired me to convert good intentions – like learning Spanish – into practical steps like taking classes, doing homework, and applying my new skills to conversations with voters.

Before all this, I had lifelong dreams of being a teacher. In truly unforeseen ways, the confluence of the 2016 election and the COVID pandemic helped create the circumstances that allowed my collaborators and me to teach volunteers on a national level. Writing a book was also on my bucket list, but I'd never found the time or the topic that felt like it *needed* to be written. With the cosmic realignment of the last several years, this book really called to me to be written, and fast. My goal has been to crank out a book as soon as possible, in time for the 2024 election cycle, rather than honing this material into a beautifully crafted work that I might publish 10 years from now. I've never felt the urgency of a deadline more than with this project. I don't need to tell you how important this year's elections will be for the future of our country – and our entire planet.

Finally, perhaps the biggest gift of these last several years of civic engagement has been the community I've formed with people from across the country, and even internationally. My co-trainers for these various workshops have become treasured friends as well as collaborators. Other volunteers continue to inspire me with their dedication, humor, intelligence and generosity. My life has become unbelievably richer for their presence in my life.

Don't get me wrong – the precipitating events behind all of this have been scary and stressful. It's been heartbreaking to witness the damage to our democracy. If I could wave a magic wand, I'd happily trade all I've learned in recent years to change the results of the 2016 election, eliminate the COVID pandemic, and undo all the other hardships of recent years. In a nanosecond.

But that's not an option. No amount of wishful thinking or obsessive worrying can undo the past or change what's happening now. However, you and I *do* have the power to respond to what's going on right now. Given that all this is true, what are we going to do about it? What are our options? How can we pool all our courage, passion and creativity to meet this moment?

Most people have heard about post-traumatic stress disorder (PTSD). Interestingly, there is also a phenomenon called post-traumatic *growth*, described by clinical psychologists Richard Tedeschi, PhD, and Lawrence Calhoun, PhD, as the experience of positive change that occurs as a result of the struggle with highly challenging life crises.

We each need to find our way through the thicket of challenges that recent years have brought to our doorstep. I can testify to the incredible power of taking small actions. In isolation, they may seem insignificant, too small to succeed, laughably puny in the face of what we're up against. Yet each action adds up over time. And we are not alone. This effort is so much bigger than any one of us – but it needs *each* of us in order to succeed. All of us contributing what we can is what will make the difference between despair and hope, between the death of democracy and its rebirth into its next incarnation, between the triumph of cynical greed and the emergence of a more just, kind and inclusive society.

So which direction will prevail? Together we are writing that next chapter. Our decisions, our actions or inactions, will shape what kind of country and world we will call home. It is my hope that this book will be a resource to support you in the vital work you are doing toward the good.

Summary

- Start from where you are. These times present a golden invitation to reach beyond your comfort zone, whether that's phone banking or canvassing for the first time or learning new tools for connecting more effectively with voters.
- Engaging in this work not only helps win elections – it can reduce your anxiety and lead to unexpected gifts.
- You have a lifetime of wisdom and experience to bring to this work. This is a great time to channel those gifts toward shoring up our democracy!

Chapter 2

Why Canvass and Phone Bank?

So, why canvass or phone bank? Simply put, these are the two most effective ways of reaching voters.
According to a Sister District Action Network analysis,[7] voter engagement methods that use live conversation are more effective than other methods, such as texting, postcarding and letter-writing. Research suggests that canvassing is *the* most effective way to increase voter turnout,[8] and phone banking is the next best way. Various studies indicate that direct voter engagement can boost turnout by a few percentage points. That may not seem like a lot, but keep in mind how incredibly close many elections are. As just one example, less than 43,000 total voters spread out among three key states – Arizona, Wisconsin and Georgia – decided the outcome of the 2020 presidential election.[9, 10] For comparison's sake, all those voters could fit into the California Memorial Stadium on the UC Berkeley campus, with more than 20,000 empty seats left over.

Also, not all conversations are created equal: studies also suggest that the *quality* of interactions with voters impacts how effective those conversation will be.[11] This book is devoted to exactly that topic: how to have the best conversations possible with the voters you reach.

There is often a lot of pressure, especially as Election Day approaches, to talk with as many voters as possible. At the end of many phone banks, organizers sometimes invite people to share how many calls they made, as if they were racking up points in a video game. I understand that there are millions of voters to reach, and we want to connect with as many supporters and potential supporters as we can.

However, just like the "slow food" movement focuses on quality over quantity, and sustainability over maximizing profit, I'm an advocate of "slow canvassing and phone banking." I strive for conversations that are *relational* rather than transactional. I try to build rapport and trust, rather than swooping in and out as quickly as possible.

There is a whole field of voter engagement called deep canvassing, which uses longer conversations and respectful engagement to help change hearts and minds. Deep canvassing was pioneered by Steve Deline and Ella Barrett at the Los Angeles LGBT Center after the 2008 passage of Proposition 8, which banned same-sex marriage in California. After that big defeat, they talked with voters to learn more about why they had supported Prop 8. From those conversations, they developed a method of reaching out to voters that includes empathy, in-depth conversations, remaining respectful even when there is disagreement, and inviting people to share their own stories as a means to fostering understanding and compassion with others.

Using these approaches, in 2012 they helped defeat a Minnesota constitutional amendment that would have banned same-sex marriage. Deline and Barrett co-founded the New Conversation Initiative to promote this effective approach, partnering with groups such as People's Action, a national network of progressive organizations, and others.

I don't claim to be practicing deep canvassing, since that is a specific approach pioneered and honed by the New Conversation

Initiative and their partners. However, some of my approaches are aligned in spirit with theirs, and I encourage you to incorporate any and all useful field tools from various models. It is inspiring to know that many groups across the country are actively incorporating more relational, heart-based, empathetic methods for reaching across divides. Doing the hard work of listening helps us connect with others who might seem very different from us on the surface. I'm honored to be part of this community, and hope to contribute something to this conversation.

Opportunity for Dialogue

Part of the magic of canvassing and phone banking is that these mediums allow us to engage in dialogue with voters. One-way communications like TV, radio and social media ads definitely have their place in a campaign. More personalized forms such as postcarding, letter-writing and texting also provide important information and encouragement to vote; they can remind voters of upcoming deadlines for turning in their vote-by-mail ballots, share information about early voting, and prompt them to bring their driver's license or state ID if they live in a state that requires that.

However, there's no substitute for two-way forms of communication. These real-time conversations allow us to confirm we have accurate contact information for a voter, elicit their specific questions and concerns, and make a human connection that may encourage them to vote for our candidate.

For example, in 2022 I phone banked with the Northeast Arizona Native Democrats, a wonderful organization led by tribal organizers and leaders working across sovereign lands. I asked a voter I'll call Nelson if he'd received his vote-by-mail ballot yet, and he said no. He'd actually called his county recorder earlier that day to find out where it was, but never got a call back.

I confirmed all of Nelson's contact information and asked if I could put him in touch with his local organizer, who might be able to help him sort this out. He said yes. He didn't have a pen or paper handy, but said I could text him. I sent him some follow-up information and wrote a detailed note in the file.

Nelson and I chatted for about 15 minutes. He mentioned that he got his mail at a post office box, but only checked it once a month because the post office was only open half-time. So this was a voter who might not get a reminder postcard in time for the election. Yet he *did* pick up the phone and was quite happy to talk. And I got important information from him that I would never glean from a one-way communication like a postcard or letter. Nelson was obviously a committed voter – and maybe just needed a little help navigating the bureaucracy.

Volunteers like you and me are like the backstage crew at a Broadway show. Think of it as "Democracy: The Musical!" We're helping out behind the scenes so everything is ready when the actors get on stage. The voters and local organizers are the stars. But it's a huge team effort. Without a full backstage crew, it's hard to put on a musical. Our friends in swing states and districts need our help to make the best use of the local staff and volunteers' precious time, and to connect with the tens of thousands of voters we want to reach.

And for people who rarely or never vote, having an in-depth conversation is probably the most effective way to help move them a step closer toward the ballot box. In Chapter 11, "Making 'I Don't Vote' the Start, not the End of a Conversation," I devote an entire chapter to this hugely important topic.

Some of you may be devoted postcarders, letter-writers and texters. Your work is incredibly valuable, and a vital part of the overall strategy. At the same time, there are many voters who have moved since the last election, have specific questions about the logistics of voting, or need to talk through their priorities and concerns with someone. In order to earn their votes, we may actually need to *talk* with them. And with so many critical races coming down to a handful of votes, the results may hinge on whether or not enough of us step out of our comfort zone to engage in actual, real-time conversations in person and on the phone with our fellow Americans.

I know some of you would rather have a colonoscopy than talk politics with strangers. I get it! Until fairly recently, I was in a similar boat. Even if the thought of talking with voters makes you queasy, I'm gently inviting you to consider giving phone banking or canvassing a try. By adding this to your portfolio of activism, even if it's just occasionally, you'll expand the scope of your efforts and help connect with some voters we can't reach any other way.

How Voter Engagement Can Help *You*

I've described some of the benefits of canvassing and phone banking for winning elections. Just as important, there can be unexpected and amazing benefits for *you* as well. In my own experience, it feels so good to channel a fraction of the energy I previously spent on worrying into actually *doing* something, no matter how small. I went from feeling like a helpless victim to making a terrible situation just a little bit better.

There are vast and complex forces at work, designed to pit us against one another and to keep us separated into our microbubbles of likeminded thinkers. Those are beyond the scope of this book, but they include the consolidation and privatization of media outlets, social media algorithms that prioritize profit over truth, dark money from veiled sources that goes into influencing elections and public policy, and so much more. As just one human being, I can't do a lot to counter those forces singlehandedly. However, I *can* risk discomfort and choose to talk to people who would likely never enter my orbit in any other way.

How often do I get a chance to have a meaningful conversation with a stranger? When was the last time I got to learn from someone with a completely different life experience, unmediated by someone else's interpretation – not just the curated snippets I read in the *New York Times* or hear on NPR? (Yes, I'm revealing my own media consumption biases here.) Listening to other perspectives can be enriching and transformative. Just like I need two eyes to have depth perception, opening myself to other ways of thinking and living helps broaden my understanding in a way that just reading about it never will. Even if I think I'm right, really keeping an open mind and hearing someone out can help me better understand the world and myself.

Think of it like the difference between reading guidebooks about Turkey compared with actually getting on a plane and *going* there. Sure, you can watch videos of the Hagia Sofia and the Turkish Bazaar. But there's nothing like hearing the mesmerizing buzz of the call to prayer from mosques all around you, having a random group of Turkish teenagers walk half a mile out of their way to guide you to your destination and say they hope we meet again one day, *inshallah*, or watching whirling dervishes spin in ecstatic circles while their voluminous white robes create a palpable breeze that lifts your hair.

Similarly, talking with voters in swing districts or states offers a chance to develop a much richer, more nuanced understanding of other people's lives and communities, far beyond what you will learn just by reading a newspaper story or watching a four-minute television piece. And those encounters may expand your perspective, or even change it.

Bringing 'Beginner's Mind' to Voter Engagement

One of the most useful approaches when talking with voters is bringing a beginner's mind to each conversation. This concept from Zen Buddhism encourages us to bring an open, eager attitude which is free of preconceptions, even when doing something at an advanced level.

Beginner's mind helps me to connect with voters, and also prevents me from losing heart when I have a difficult interaction. I would love to have every voter enthusiastically receive my call or visit, and jump out of their chair to support my candidate. While other parts of this book will hopefully provide a few strategies for increasing the likelihood that you'll have productive and meaningful conversations with voters, there will inevitably be bumps in the road.

It's important for me to remember that I'm not there to evangelize, lecture or badger voters into doing what I think is best. Voters are the experts on their own situations, and they have a whole lifetime of experience that shapes their worldview. In addition to working to win elections, one of my personal goals is to be changed for the better by the process – perhaps even transformed. In order for that to happen, I aspire to bring friendly, nonjudgmental curiosity to every conversation. I try to cultivate an attitude of humility, and to assume that each person has something to teach me, something to share that I might not have considered. I also try to express gratitude to voters for taking the time to talk with me and listen to what I have to say, even if we disagree.

If I encounter voters who refuse to vote or hold opinions diametrically opposed to mine, it's tempting to ask, "How can I change their mind?" And while this book includes some ideas for navigating those challenging situations, I also try to balance this with some different questions to myself. These include, "What can I learn from talking with this person? What stereotypes or beliefs can I challenge within myself? How can I support other people's internal desires to create a better world for themselves, their families, and their communities?"

At the end of a canvassing or phone banking shift, I try to reflect on questions such as, "What did I learn today that I didn't know at the start of my shift? Who could I ask for suggestions on other ways to handle tricky issues? What are one or two things I might want to try next time?"

For me, staying the course means that part of success is coming out of a conversation, volunteer shift, or election cycle changed in some way. Maybe it's gaining some nuanced perspective or reconsidering one of my beliefs after encountering new evidence in the field. Perhaps it's better understanding the human-level effect of how health care policy or economic disparities affects individuals in their day-to-day lives. Or maybe I've learned something about a different part of the state or country that I never would have known otherwise.

At its best, canvassing and phone banking provides opportunities for mutually enriching encounters through the give-and-take of talking with other human beings.

Introducing 'Skylar the Skeptic'

It can be hard to engage with the unpredictable, messy business of interacting with other people. Even if my phone bank or canvass has a script, we can't script how voters respond. And no strategy, no matter how well-planned, is foolproof.

To help illustrate my response to the inevitable challenges in the process of voter engagement, I'd like to introduce you to "Skylar the Skeptic." I like to think of him as my internalized (or occasionally externalized) critic, who is quick to see all the shortcomings of every approach and to come up with examples of how they would never work. If something I try isn't completely perfect, the very first time, he's ready to throw the whole idea out the window.

If I were hard at work digging a ditch, Skylar the Skeptic would stand on the side of the road with his arms crossed, pointing out how I'm not working fast enough and how the ditch isn't straight enough. Never would he dream of picking up a shovel and getting in the trenches to help me out. From time to time in this book, I'll bring in Skylar the Skeptic's questions and criticisms, and share how I would answer them.

Practice Makes Progress

When I teach voter engagement workshops or share stories from the field, I'm flattered that people think I have some useful tips for canvassing and phone banking. However, please don't let this deter you from giving it a try yourself. Skylar the Skeptic might say, "Oh, I could never do what you do! I'm just not good at talking on the phone, or talking with strangers."

The biggest hurdle to phone banking and canvassing is just making the decision to do it the first time. And one of the next biggest hurdles is feeling bad if you're not amazing at it right out of the gate. As Myra Levy, my dear friend and one of my co-teachers for our "Phone Bank Training for Introverts (& Friends)" workshop says, talking with voters involves a set of skills that can be improved with practice. Sure, some people may naturally be more comfortable with aspects of it, whether that's talking with strangers or dealing with the app interface. Nevertheless, most of us can get better with intentional practice. I know I have.

As I mentioned earlier, the first time I ever canvassed in the Central Valley I was paired up with Gordon, a retired physician who had a few more months under his belt than I did. I remember kicking myself for forgetting to ask an enthusiastic voter to make sure three people they knew also voted. He said, "Don't worry – we're honing our craft." Giving myself permission to learn on the job, to make mistakes and grow from them, is critical to my ability to get better.

I trained as a classical pianist as a child and through college, and later took jazz lessons. I'm always inspired by a story that pianist and singer Dena DeRose told at a scat singing workshop I took at the Stanford Jazz Workshop. (I'm an off-key but cheerfully enthusiastic singer.) Back in the day, Dena lived on the seventh floor of a New York apartment building. Eric Alexander and Joe Lovano, two jazz sax players who went on to become famous, shared a practice studio in the basement. Each of them got it for 12 hours a day.

One afternoon, she heard Eric playing arpeggiated chords – for four hours straight. The first hour started off slow, with the metronome. The second hour, he picked up speed and started adding in other notes. "He did all kinds of things to get beyond the superficial level – to find the inner workings of the piece," Dena said. She encouraged us to take a similarly patient, methodical approach to practicing. "It might seem overwhelming, but all of a sudden it becomes part of what you do to learn every song you know. We can do more than we *think* we can do," she said.

Even a jazz great like Eric Alexander had to put in the hours in a basement practice studio to improvise as effortlessly and gorgeously as he does today. Each conversation we have with a voter, no matter how it goes, is our basement practice studio. We can learn from every interaction – what went well, what we can improve, which approaches seem to work with which personality types. By trying out different approaches and observing what happens, we learn how to more effectively navigate the inner workings of a conversation.

Because human interactions are complex, with a lot of moving parts, it's worked well for me to pick one or two things to work on, and try to get a little better for a few shifts. If I see some improvement, then I pick another area to work on. It's another great reason to start phone banking and canvassing early in the election cycle. It gives you more time to hone your craft and build your familiarity with the apps, the candidates' platforms, and most importantly, how to engage effectively with voters.

However, if you are feeling inspired (or anxious enough about the looming election) to jump in the week of Halloween, by all means, go for it! Don't let the perfect be the enemy of the good. Every conversation you have is laying the ground for the ones that follow, and the elections yet to come. Just remember to cut yourself a lot of slack and give yourself permission to start off clumsy. With a little patience and practice, you'll likely be amazed by how much better you get.

EXPERIMENT WITH THE RECIPE BOOK

As I mentioned earlier, many experiences have shaped my particular approach to talking with voters. We all have our own style and flair when engaging with other people. I've tried to distill some general principles that might be helpful for your own conversations with voters. The idea is not that you should try to sound like me, but rather to channel the best of your own life experiences into canvassing and phone banking.

Skylar the Skeptic might say, "Where's the evidence base for what you advise? It sounds like a lot of work, but will it make any difference?" I agree – these approaches may take more time, and I can't guarantee that they will result in more votes. Some of what I describe in this book is just what I've found to help me in the field or on the phone. This is not a scientific treatise. I'd actually be delighted if an academic thought any of these ideas would be worth studying more rigorously to evaluate their efficacy on a wider scale. As I mention earlier in this chapter, there have been some studies about the effectiveness of approaches like deep canvassing, but it's expensive and time-consuming to rigorously investigate every aspect of voter outreach. So I can't guarantee this will lead to more votes.

Instead, think of this more like a recipe book for my favorite home-cooked meals. When I browse through a recipe book, I know I'll never make all the dishes. I'll pass on "Escargot Three Ways," skip the recipes with 30 ingredients, and forego ones that require the outdoor grill I don't own (and the patio I don't have). But if something does look interesting, I may substitute chicken for pork, or throw in some extra fresh herbs and cayenne pepper. I invite you to do the same with this book. Feel free to adapt any of the ideas to your own style, as well as the specific culture and conditions of the community you are currently working within. Whether you've been canvassing and phone banking for decades or are gearing up to try it for the first time, I'd be thrilled if you came away with one or two new ideas that you could put to use in your upcoming conversations with voters.

I'll also note that for all the limitations of what I outline in this book, the status quo is not that fantastic. In my experience, most phone bank or canvassing orientations focus on how to use the voter contact apps, and share some talking points about the candidates and issues. But what do you do if someone actually picks up your call or answers the door? That's when things get more complicated. I hope that some of the approaches in the coming chapters will help you better engage with our fellow citizens, and maybe even make you excited about talking with voters.

Summary

- Canvassing and phone banking are *the* most effective tools we have for winning close elections because we can engage in empathetic, meaningful dialogue with voters.
- No matter your starting level of ability, you *can* improve your skills through practice.
- Give yourself permission to learn from your mistakes, try new approaches, and adapt ideas from this book and other volunteers to suit your own style.

Chapter 3

Safety First

The first step toward trying something new is facing any fears that may hold me back. When my collaborators and I teach our "Phone Bank and Canvassing Training for Introverts (& Friends)" workshops to shy or first-time volunteers, we start by asking participants to list all the reasons *not* to phone bank or canvass in the chat. It's a juicy question which prompts a deluge of responses. One of the biggest obstacles people mention is fear for their safety.

I get it. For almost two years after the 2016 election, I was completely unwilling to consider canvassing because of these fears. I'll talk more about how my thought process has evolved since then, but I'll say up front that after talking with more than 1,000 voters in person and on the phone, I have never been cussed out or physically threatened. Yes, some people have been annoyed at the interruption in their day, but in my experience, I am 100 times more likely to meet a politically disengaged voter than a hostile one. Honestly, the greatest risk I usually take when canvassing is the chance of getting into a car accident on the drive there and back.

At the same time, we all navigate decisions around risk and safety every day, whether we're boarding a plane, making choices related to COVID, or living in an area prone to earthquakes, wildfires or hurricanes. We each get to decide what is right for us at a particular moment, in each situation. It is also helpful to discern the difference between feeling *uncomfortable* – perhaps inevitable with some aspects of voter engagement work, especially at the beginning – and feeling *unsafe*.

As one activist, Michelle, told me, when her friends say they don't feel comfortable phone banking or canvassing, she wants to tell them, "I don't know about you, but I'm feeling *really* uncomfortable with the things Trump is doing right now. That's why I'm willing to call strangers or go canvass." When I am discerning my own line between feeling uncomfortable and unsafe, there are precautions I take to mitigate risk, which I'll touch on below.

I also want to acknowledge the risks of remaining passive. If I stay home or am unwilling to phone bank solely because of what *might* happen, I'm letting the forces of division and fear control my life. One of my superpowers (as well as Achilles' heels) is that I'm ornery. I don't like other people telling me what to do. I don't want to cede my freedom of movement or speech to those who want to take those away from us. In recent years there has been an escalation in violence against Asian Americans. I stay alert and aware of my surroundings, but I continue to carry on with my life.

I have some family members who were incarcerated at Heart Mountain, Wyoming during World War II, just because they were Japanese American. I can only too easily envision a future America where that could happen again, either to me or others, because our collective silence and fear prevented us from acting while there was still time. Many immigrants are already being imprisoned at the border. And I think of all the Civil Rights activists who risked far more than I am ever likely to face. How would history have been different if all of them had stayed home, too afraid of what might happen?

Safety When Phone Banking

In the rest of this chapter, I will focus on canvassing, but I do want to say a word about phone banking. I know some people are so nervous about talking with strangers on the phone that they don't want to give it a try. I have phone banked hundreds of voters, and I have never been threatened. Many people hang up on me, some ask me to take them off the call list, and a few are cranky. However, I have never felt in personal danger from these calls. Many phone banks also use a toll-free call-in number that masks your own phone number, so you won't need to reveal it to voters.

Some phone banks, especially less well-funded ones earlier in the cycle or low-budget campaigns for local or state campaigns, do require you to use your own phone to make calls. In Chapter 15, "Gear: Tools of the Trade," I describe some free or inexpensive ways to create a temporary phone number on your cell phone that allows you to shield your personal phone number.

When talking with voters, you don't need to give your last name; in my experience, most people don't ask where you are calling from. You can also use a nickname or a pseudonym if you prefer. If you really feel uncomfortable during a call or someone becomes threatening, just hang up and make a note for the campaign to remove them from the call list. No one should *ever* endure threats or hateful behavior in this work, and you have a right to feel and be safe.

Taking Measured Risks

Canvassing involves a different kind of risk exposure. As I mentioned earlier, I started with postcarding and phone banking in 2017, then started canvassing in fall 2018. Along with the thrill of connecting with voters in a critical swing district, there were a few potholes. My third time canvassing, I blindly followed directions from the campaign staff, who told me we needed to knock on every door listed in our "turf" – the particular neighborhood we were assigned to visit, with a list of specific voters to contact, along with their addresses.

When I got to one house that had not just one, but two gigantic Trump signs in the windows, I hesitated. Being the rule-following, former Catholic schoolgirl that I am, I forced myself to knock on the door. I prayed that the voter wasn't home. Unfortunately, he answered the door. When I timidly asked if there was any chance he'd consider voting for the Democratic candidate for Congress, I could feel his animosity. He just shook his head with rage, looking like the veins in his forehead might pop open, and closed the door.

I was reeling for the rest of the day and barely slept that night, constantly replaying the look of disgust on his face. That was almost the end of my canvassing career. But I didn't want fear to have the last word. I spoke with a lot of experienced advocates, including Mary, who was volunteering in another district. She has become one of my fairy godmothers of activism. When I explained what had happened, she encouraged me to come out to her district. It was further away but had a majority Latino electorate, and more registered Democrats than Republicans. She said, "Down here, we have so many Democratic doors to knock, we don't have time to talk to Republicans. If you see a house covered with Trump signs, just mark 'Not home' in the app and move on to the next one." That was a revelation! I went down, had an incredible experience, and have made many trips since then – including my monthlong immersion there in 2022.

Respect Your Limits

That encouragement to trust my gut reminds me of advice I received at the start of my reporting internship at the *Chicago Tribune* back in the 1990s, a few weeks after I graduated from college. It was quite the macho atmosphere, with some interns trying to outdo each other to impress editors. There was social pressure to enthusiastically pursue every story assignment, even potentially risky ones. Early on, a veteran reporter named Bill Recktenwald must have seen my look of terror and took me aside.

If anyone had earned bragging rights to glamorize aggressive reporting, it was Bill. He was a Pulitzer Prize-winning investigative reporter who had gone undercover as a prison guard, nursing home aide, bar owner and ambulance driver, among other personae. To my surprise, he basically told me, "If any of these editors tries to send you out to a place where you don't feel safe, or you get there and it seems dangerous, just come back to the office. Some of these editors haven't been out in the field for decades, and they don't know what it's like today." He told me that no story was worth risking my life over.

I was so grateful that someone who had chosen to put himself in risky situations and had received one of the highest honors in journalism urged me to trust my own judgment, and to prioritize my safety over what editors might think. I keep his advice in mind when I'm canvassing. The campaign staff may tell me to knock on every door, but only *I* can assess the safety of each situation – depending on the atmosphere, environmental clues, tone and body language of a voter, and my intuition. Giving myself permission to bail on a dicey situation frees me to knock on the vast majority of doors where my Spidey-sense is not sending me warning signs. It doesn't have to be all or nothing. I get to choose which risks are worth taking, depending on what my six senses are telling me.

I want to acknowledge the role that privilege plays in this calculus. People of color, sexual and gender minorities, and other marginalized groups may face increased risk, depending on the community and context. If this applies to your situation, it can be helpful to do some research about the specific area you will visit, and talk with others who have canvassed there. Tougaloo College, a historically Black college in Mississippi, hosts a database[12] listing "sundown towns." (The term comes from towns which posted signs warning people of color to leave town before sundown.)

Based on the work of sociologist James W. Loewen, this database is a national registry of communities where African Americans and other people of color have been systemically excluded. It assesses past and current "sundown town" status, lists racial and ethnic Census data from 1860 to the present, and includes comments contributed by nearby residents. While some towns may have made progress from their racist past, it can provide some helpful context.

I had an informative experience in 2019 when I was canvassing south of Richmond, Virginia, for the state legislative races. The campaign wanted to send me to Colonial Heights (which I later found out was nicknamed "Colonial Whites"). It was the hometown of Kirk Cox, a conservative Republican who at that time was the incumbent speaker of the House of Delegates. I had looked up the voter registration demographics of that area (it was deeply red), and had heard that Confederate flags were common there. I had zero desire to canvass there. When I told the volunteer organizers that I wasn't comfortable canvassing there, they tried to persuade me. "But you'll only be knocking on the doors of Democratic voters!" they said, doing the hard sell. I told them, "I don't care – give me another turf. I'm not going there."

One of the campaign staffers, Kate, told me how it had been a tough place for her to canvass, and added, "You shouldn't have to go to places like that. I'm white, and it's different for me. Let the white staff and volunteers take those turfs." I appreciated that Kate had my back and validated my concerns – an important piece of volunteer recruitment and retention.

It is humbling yet realistic to accept that I'm not meant to knock on every door. Knowing and respecting my own limits – which includes situations that cross the boundary of uncomfortable into unsafe – is part of what allows me to do this work. We all get to decide where those lines are for ourselves, without judgment from ourselves or others.

Pay Attention to Small Clues

All that being said, there are a few common-sense steps you can take to mitigate your risk. Canvass with a buddy if that works for you. In general, I prefer to canvass solo, because I can move at my own pace and I find it easier to develop rapport with voters; however, that's just personal preference. In lieu of a canvassing partner, I always let someone at the campaign and an emergency contact at home know where I'm going. I text them several times during my shift to let them know I'm fine, and message them once I wrap up for the day and am heading home. You may also want to share your location on your phone, and carry a whistle or pepper spray.

If you are new to canvassing, see if you can talk with the organizers ahead of time and discuss any concerns you might have. You might want to ask for an easier turf to start – one that is mostly Democrats who just need a reminder to vote.

Campaigns generally say to never go inside a voter's house. I take that with a grain of salt; if the voter is an elder or a mother with young children, I may step inside, especially if it's too hot or cold for them to talk with me outside, or if they have trouble standing. This is particularly true for my encounters with Latino voters, where it feels like part of the culture to accept an invitation to enter their home.

On the other hand, if I see any indications that give me pause, I mark the voter "Not home." That includes Trump signs, decals for the National Rifle Association, and stickers that say, "The Second Amendment is my gun permit." I once saw a sign meant to deter thieves that read, "There is nothing in this house worth dying for," and I took that to include their vote. "Not home!"

Some challenges are very region-specific. In the Central Valley, especially in more rural communities, it's very common for people to have barking, unleashed dogs in the yard or even running loose in the street. As I mention in Chapter 15, I can sometimes befriend these dogs by bribing them with dog treats. After throwing them a dog biscuit, I sometimes feel like the Pied Piper, with several now-friendly canines trailing behind me hoping for another morsel. However, if they keep barking, I pass on the house.

If there are "No Soliciting" signs on the door, it's a judgment call. Campaigns encourage us to knock these doors, because it's not against the law and we're not actually selling anything. Their vote is not for sale, and we're there to offer information. I've actually had some good conversations with voters at these houses. Yet if there's anything else that makes me hesitate, I may just leave some campaign literature with a note and move on.

I also pay attention to what other voters in the neighborhood tell me. If they warn me about particular houses or describe recent shootings in the area, I take note and adjust accordingly. If I make a good connection with a voter or they offer to help me out if I need anything, I make a note of their address and might ask for their phone number in case something comes up in the field. I've never had to circle back to them, but it's comforting to realize that people in the community are watching out for me.

Trust Your Judgment

There's a saying attributed to the Prophet Mohammed that goes something along the lines of "Trust in God, but tie your camel first." It encapsulates that balance between taking reasonable precautions – tying up your camel rather than leaving him free to roam – then moving forward with confidence and faith. It's good to be cautious, but not paralyzed with fear.

Each person has to make their own decisions about which risks are worth taking. If my time in the field is any guide, sometimes that algorithm shifts over time as I get more information and gain more experience – both rewarding and cautionary. Yes, there are risks to any action we take, not just those related to election work. Still, it's helpful for me to remember that there are also risks to doing nothing.

Whenever I take just a fraction of the time I used to spend doomscrolling or obsessing about the perils to our democracy and channel that into action, no matter how small, I receive outsized benefits. I no longer feel like a horrified, helpless witness to a slow-moving train wreck. I've been encouraged and sometimes deeply moved by the kindness, strength and thoughtfulness of strangers I've talked with all across the country. That's a redemptive experience I wouldn't trade for anything. I hope you, too, can find a way to connect with that generosity of heart from our fellow Americans.

Summary

- While maintaining your safety, keep in mind the difference between feeling uncomfortable and feeling unsafe. Remember there are also risks to doing nothing.

- Trust your gut, respect your limits, and pay attention to small clues. Each situation is different.
- No action is completely risk-free, but you can take reasonable steps to take care of yourself and reduce your risk.

Chapter 4
Always Say Yes to the Water

There's a certain kind of weather I've come to associate with canvassing – hot, dry, dusty, the kind of merciless heat where I seek refuge in the shade of a skinny tree to look up the address of my next voter. When I started canvassing in California's Central Valley in 2018, many voters offered me bottles of water at their door. I politely turned them down: "Oh, no thank you – I'm good," I'd say cheerfully. I'm a hard-core environmentalist, and hate to contribute more plastic bottles to the waste stream. I imagine that bottle swirling around for decades in the Great Pacific Garbage Patch, and microplastics infiltrating my body. I always come prepared with a CamelBak filled with water, and gallon bottles in the car to top up.

I'm also half Japanese American. Growing up, I saw that accepting gifts often meant indebtedness. When someone died, everyone gave *koden* – monetary gifts to help cover funeral expenses. The family kept a ledger to write thank you notes, and also to record who gave what. When someone in the community experienced a loss, your family was expected to give the same amount back. I learned that accepting gifts came with obligations, which felt more like a burden than support.

But then I started to think about those bottles from the perspective of the people who offered them to me. Many of the voters worked in the fields, planting and harvesting the vegetables, fruit and nuts that help feed the nation. They toiled under that same hot sun, often in temperatures 10 or 20 degrees hotter than what I was willing to brave – and they did it out of necessity, not by choice like I was. Many people in the San Joaquin Valley can't trust the water that comes out of their taps, which may be contaminated with arsenic, nitrate or other harmful compounds. In this part of the country, offering a chilled bottle of water is a gesture of solidarity, of compassion. It's a way of saying, "We know what it's like to be outside in these conditions. We appreciate your efforts, and wish you well."

So every time someone offered me water, I started saying yes. In fact, besides tracking how many doors I knocked each day and how many voters I talked with, I started keeping another metric: how many bottles of water did I receive that day? One was good, two was great, and three was amazing! I drank some of them in the field, and brought others back at night like a hunter bagging game. Feeling the weight of multiple bottles clunking together in my bag was a tangible reminder of the success I'd had, the conversations I'd engaged in, and the way my work was recognized by the people I cared about most – the voters.

Learning to Receive

While many voters offered me bottled water to thank me for stopping by, this gesture transcended political alignment. One man, Jovan, a muscular truck driver who was going silver at the temples, politely informed me that his whole household was Republican.

He said none of them would be voting for my candidate. Yet he was curious about what I was doing. He asked if I spoke any Spanish, since that was the first and sometimes only language of many of his neighbors. I told him I'd been studying it for several years, and was picking up some interesting new vocabulary from talking with people in the neighborhood. One young voter had an undocumented uncle who overheard us chatting, and joked that he was looking for a "*gabacha*" to marry – a *gringa* who could help him gain citizenship. Jovan and I both laughed.

I said, "I'm not going to try to change your mind about how you're voting, but I'm just curious – what appeals to you about the Republican Party?" He said, "I was raised to believe that we shouldn't just give people things indefinitely. It's okay to help people get started – like my parents gave me a beater car when I first started working, but after that I was on my own. That's how I think our government should be – give people an initial boost, but don't coddle them indefinitely."

I thanked him for sharing his perspective. I said I wished there was more dialogue across party lines, where people could have civil discourse and share different viewpoints like we were doing just then. He agreed and said, "Well, thanks for doing what you're doing in the neighborhood. If you need anything, just come on by and ask. Can I give you some water?" Of course, I said yes. He went in the house and came back with not just one, but two bottles of water.

These moments of human connection, when I allow myself to receive hospitality and support even from people I might disagree with politically, are where we start to heal our wounded democracy.

Food for the Journey

Gifts of sustenance went beyond just water. In the breadbasket of the nation, the hands that opened the screen door had often picked grapes or almonds for decades, and sometimes cultivated food at home, in yards enclosed by chain-link fences and vigilantly guarded by vocal pit bulls. I met Conchita in her front yard, which had been lovingly cultivated by her father, an immigrant from Mexico. He grew many vegetables and traditional Mexican herbs in his garden, and was able to stop taking diabetes medications thanks to his plant-based diet. They sold extra herbs and eggs from their chickens to neighbors and friends at church. She told me about how he traveled to Bakersfield three times a week for dialysis, and that he was on the waitlist for a kidney transplant. As we talked, she stood beneath a huge persimmon tree weighed down with more than a hundred gleaming fruit. When we said goodbye, she picked three of them and handed them to me.

When they ripened a few days later, I cut one up and ate it with Greek yogurt for breakfast. I texted Conchita a photo thanking her for the persimmons, and sent her my Aunty Diane's recipe for persimmon pudding. Rich and moist, flavored with cinnamon and brandy, it's my aunt's signature dessert which she bakes every Thanksgiving and Christmas. Conchita wrote back, "You're very welcome. And thank you for the recipe! I will definitely be making this when I get more ripe persimmons!" I felt a warm glow knowing that some vestige of our connection might endure beyond our one conversation.

I met another voter, Lorenzo, an earnest college student hoping to become a teacher. He was concerned about the poor air quality in the Central Valley, and wished there were more jobs that didn't make asthma and other lung problems worse. He said he'd feel more confident voting if he had a little more information about my candidate, since he only saw the ads on television. I was lucky enough to work with a campaign that agreed to follow up with select voters if a call from a staffer might help tip the balance in favor of our candidate. So I took down all of Lorenzo's contact information and passed it along to the campaign.

As we were wrapping up, his dad came out and gave me not just a bottle of water, but a whole bag of sweet potatoes, part of the bounty that one of his neighbors had shared with him. On Halloween, I washed and boiled them, then mashed them with coconut milk and garnished them with dill. Delicious! Those sweet potatoes helped nourish me through the final days of the campaign. It reminded me that while I was pushing hard to track down voters and encourage them to vote, people like Lorenzo's family had my back and wanted me to succeed.

Breaking Bread (or Tearing Tortillas) Together

One of my most memorable canvassing experiences happened when I was least expecting it. It was the end of a long, hot Sunday, edging toward twilight, and most voters weren't home. I was ready to cash it in, but told myself I'd just knock on doors that were directly on my way back to where my car was parked.

The last house I canvassed had two men in their 20s listed as registered voters. The family was in their front yard eating dinner, having a birthday party for their daughter. At first the parents were a bit wary, but when I explained in Spanish what I was doing, the mom said to talk with her sons. Manuel came to the gate and was super friendly.

He had already voted for the Democratic candidate. Then Bernardo came over, but said he didn't follow politics much and wasn't planning to vote. I said, "Tell me more about that." We were talking about the election when his mom called out and asked if I had eaten yet. I thought about it for a minute – lunch felt like half a lifetime ago, I was getting hungry, and I had a long drive back to Bakersfield to eat leftovers from my fridge. They offered to fix me a plate, and after a moment's hesitation, I said, "Oh, thank you so much! That would be wonderful!"

They handed me a plate, and Manuel said I was welcome to join them. I paused for a minute, since I was still being careful about COVID. However, it was outdoors and the food smelled amazing, so I said yes and sat down at their table. I served myself some Mexican rice and green salsa that their dad made himself, and they topped off my plate with chicken and tortillas that they grilled right next to the table. Oh, it was so delicious! I also tried some Duvalín, a prepackaged pudding they said was really well-known in Mexico.

We talked for about an hour, in a mix of Spanish and English. Manuel and Bernardo were bilingual but their parents mostly spoke Spanish. I tried to speak in Spanish so we could all participate in the conversation. Manuel was a teacher, and Bernardo worked in agriculture. They were really friendly and curious. They asked where I was from, what I was doing, how much I paid in rent in San Francisco, if I had siblings, what my ethnicity was, where I'd learned Spanish, where my parents lived, and what I did for a living. The two brothers had gone to Europe the previous year to celebrate Manuel's college graduation. Their mom hoped to get her citizenship within a few years and was studying for the exam. Bernardo earnestly asked me, "So do you have any hobbies, besides talking with voters?" We all laughed, and I told them I loved hiking and dancing.

At the end of the night, they brought out two enormous bunches of grapes. I took a short video of Bernardo explaining that the red ones were a type called Jack's Salute, and the green ones were the Autumn King variety, which were only available that time of year and were quite sweet. He had picked them himself, and held them out to me, saying "This is for my friend Elizabeth."

I texted them photos I took that night, and sent them a handwritten thank you note in Spanish to express my gratitude for their incredible generosity. I thought of them each time I savored the firm sweetness of those juicy grapes when I was out canvassing the following week.

That dinner was truly magical. It was wonderful to break bread (or tear tortillas) with people and feel part of the community. The generosity in the Central Valley reminds me of stories I've heard about the American South and the Middle East, where that spirit of hospitality and welcoming the stranger is part of the culture.

Not every encounter with a voter will involve a meal, nor should it. But I have learned that when a voter offers me a gift from the heart, say yes. Whether it's the generosity of their table, the bounty of their garden, or a cold bottle of water on a sweltering day, these unexpected gestures of hospitality are an invitation to enter into a reciprocal relationship of giving and receiving, no matter how brief. Just as the information I share with them may help them make a thoughtful decision or a plan to vote, what I receive from them can nourish me through challenging work – and remind me that we are all together in this struggle.

Summary

- Accepting hospitality from voters can help move a conversation from transactional to relational.
- Allowing myself to receive gestures of support and solidarity is a way to build community and connection.
- When possible, say yes to offers of water and other gifts in the field!

Chapter 5
80% Them, 20% Me

One of the biggest stumbling blocks to getting started with phone banking and canvassing was the myth that I had to be a policy expert and debate champion to talk politics with strangers. I was afraid that I wouldn't know enough, and that people would argue with me in the toxic tone that has become all too common in the public sphere and on social media. I worried that they would think I was a dilettante or a fraud.

Through actually talking to voters, I started to realize that they are often similar to other people I know: voters appreciate being listened to. It's way more important to be a good listener than a great talker. Most people aren't in the market for someone to mansplain to them about policy details. What they actually hunger for is feeling *heard* – that sense that someone is paying attention to what they are saying, without judgment.

One observation of some of my fellow progressives, and I say this with love, is that we have room to grow in terms of listening to others, especially those who disagree with us. Most of my fellow volunteers are smart, highly educated, well-read, passionate and articulate. In today's hyperpolarized environment, it's easy to feel self-righteous for claiming the moral high ground, and to feel entitled to people's votes just because we're *right*. However, there are few things less appealing than a self-righteous know-it-all. We can do better: talk less, listen more. Don't assume – instead, inquire. Get out of the spotlight, and shine it (with gentle warmth) on the voter.

In talking with voters, I try to focus 80% of the conversation on them, and 20% on me. It's amazing what people will share if you take the time to listen and hold space for them. Resist that urge to immediately jump in with related policy points to try to "close the deal." Sadly, many phone bank and canvass scripts take the exact opposite approach. One oft-used formula is, "Hi, my name is Elizabeth, and I'm a volunteer with the Democratic Party. Can we count on your support for Candidate A?" (I told this to my friend Ajila, and she joked, "Whoa, shouldn't there be a little foreplay first?")

I've found that a more effective approach is to take my time and let my friendly curiosity lead the way. As a former journalist, sometimes I pretend I've been commissioned to write an article for the *New Yorker*. What granular details can I learn about this person's life? What questions can I ask to help me understand what's important to them, the challenges they face, their hopes and aspirations?

As the common advice to writers goes, try to "show, not tell." In other words, I don't want to just stop at "This voter is struggling with economic insecurity." I want to know how that affects their work schedule, their living situation, how they raise their kids, what they worry about at night. Many people are more than happy to delve into the details if I'm willing to take the time to listen.

Though my short-term goal is helping to win the upcoming election, I enjoy the work more (and am more effective) when I broaden my aims. My longer-term goals are helping to build a sense of connection and community with the Democrats, to help people feel heard, and to better understand what people in the community are thinking, feeling and experiencing. Canvassing and phone banking give me a rare opportunity to talk with people outside my normal sphere. It's an amazing chance to find out about another part of the state or country. How often do most of us have the privilege of direct access to a broad swath of humanity beyond our circle of family, friends and co-workers? That's usually the province of physicians and members of the clergy, but voter engagement invites me into that hallowed realm.

For example, I talked for almost an hour with Serena, a young nursing student who was voting for the first time. Her mom brought out folding chairs so we could chat on their front stoop. Before she saved up enough to buy a car, she had to be at the bus stop at 6 a.m. to take a bus to school in Bakersfield. Though her small town is just 30 minutes away by car, the bus ride took an hour. Her class was at 10 a.m., so she'd park herself in the library to study, take class for a few hours, then wait for the bus again. She didn't get home until 4 p.m., making it a 10-hour day for a two-hour class.

To earn money for school, Serena worked at Subway for minimum wage and harvested grapes over the summer. In the fields there was no age minimum – if you looked at least 13, you were hired. She wanted to become a pediatrician, but it took too many years of school, so she hoped to become a pediatric nurse instead. She felt pressure to get a good career to help her family financially and set a good example for her younger siblings.

All of this opened my eyes to some of the challenges that working class people in rural California face, even with high aspirations and an incredible work ethic. Serena thanked me for talking, and at the end showed me her vote-by-mail ballot, which she had already filled out and was ready to send in.

Listen More than You Talk

When I teach voter engagement workshops and get to be a fly on the wall during practice sessions, I notice that participants often have difficulty keeping most of the spotlight on the voter. They pepper the voter with yes or no questions, interrupt, or expound on their own views without delving in to the voter's perspective. Perhaps this stems from anxiety that if we don't keep talking, the voter will lose interest and shut the door in our face or hang up the phone.

My experience has been the exact opposite. We live in an era of ever-shortening attention spans and countless distractions. The online-industrial complex spends billions of dollars to capture our attention and hold it as long as possible. How often have you been at lunch with a friend, telling them a story, when they hear their phone ping and look down at it to see what text message or tweet just came in? Have you ever been two sentences into telling a casual acquaintance about the wonderful vacation you just took, when they jump in and start telling you about the time they went to the same place 10 years ago? Then after telling you all about their experiences for 15 minutes, they say enthusiastically, "It's been so great catching up with you!"

Maybe it's just my experience as an introvert who happens to be a good listener, but sometimes it can be hard to connect in a way that feels like I've been fully heard – even with people I like. How rare (and unexpected) it is when you, a total stranger, offer this gift to a voter.

Earlier I mentioned that we as volunteers are like the backstage crew of "Democracy: The Musical!" Giving people the spotlight (rather than hogging it ourselves) is crucial for earning voters' trust and respect. Why should they listen to me if I haven't bothered to find out a bit about them and their lives?

Skylar the Skeptic might object, "People are busy, and it comes across as fake if I try to make small talk with a total stranger." Trust me, if people don't have a lot of time, they will tell you. (I had one voter say, "No disrespect, but can you cut to the chase?") Far more often, though, jumping too soon to trying to "close the deal" comes across as entitled and transactional. That rushed approach can communicate that they're just another vote to be harvested, rather than a human being to be heard, understood and respected.

I'm not entitled to anyone's trust, but I can work to earn it. The best way I've found to do this is to take my time, show genuine curiosity about the details of their lives, and demonstrate empathy (more about this in Chapter 6). It's amazing what people will share if they sense I really want to know about their experience and opinions.

Coming out of the collective trauma of the pandemic, when we were so isolated for so long, there is a particularly deep hunger to be heard. I've had a number of voters thank me for listening to them, and say it's been longer than they could remember since they talked at length like this to someone. Most people are so busy with work, school, family responsibilities, and other concerns that it's rare to have the chance to really talk about what's important to them, or what kind of world they would like to inhabit. With trust and respect, so much is possible in a conversation.

GATHER INTEL ABOUT THEIR PRIORITIES

A few tactical notes: resist the urge to finish people's sentences for them. Although your intent may be to show empathy, it can feel disrespectful and shut down a promising connection. Ditto for hijacking the conversation. Even if they express opinions or thoughts that are aligned with yours, try not to jump in with all the ways you agree with them. I've canvassed with more than one person who unthinkingly makes these conversations with voters mostly about themselves. I've witnessed how this makes voters clam up, and it really deflates efforts to encourage *them* to open up – especially if they have doubts about Democrats or the usefulness of voting. (I'll discuss this further in Chapter 11 when we talk about high-potential voters – people who rarely or never vote.)

Remember, you're trying to find out more about *their* lives. The best way to encourage voters to keep talking is to listen intently, show empathy, express curiosity, and ask follow-up questions. Later in the conversation you can share more about your experiences; certainly, if the voter asks, you can talk about what's important to you. Just keep in mind that giving voters the spotlight toward the beginning of a conversation is essential to establishing a meaningful connection with them.

So when, you might ask, do I gently pivot the conversation to the original purpose for my visit or call, which is the upcoming election? Actually, the 80% of the conversation that focuses on them isn't just something to endure until I get to my agenda. In addition to building a foundation of rapport, there's a very practical reason for investing so much time in getting to know about a voter's life. It helps me tailor what information I share about the candidate or issue I'm supporting.

People are smart – they know when I'm just rattling off boilerplate talking points to them. It's a lazy way of communicating – and the metamessage it sends is, "I'm too busy to take a few minutes to understand what's most important to you, so I'll just assume you'll be riveted by these one-size-fits-all soundbites that I'm using with everyone, and that you'll be inspired to vote for my candidate."

I had a humbling experience of this once, when I was phone banking and told an elder that the Democratic candidate for Congress supported increasing the minimum wage. He said, "I'm retired – that's not going to help me. What's the candidate doing to make the cost of living more affordable for seniors like me? I go to the store, and basics like rice and beans are so expensive. The price of gas is so high. I'm barely getting by." This voter handed me his leading concerns on a platter, but people aren't always so forthcoming. I learned to ask about their priorities if they don't bring them up themselves.

Getting to know about the details of their lives gives me some clues for which select talking points might be most compelling for that particular person. In the case of this voter, skipping the information about minimum wage and instead focusing on how my candidate was in favor of lowering the gas tax and protecting Social Security was more compelling.

Strategies for Engaging Voters

Skylar the Skeptic might say, "I'm afraid that if I go off-script, they'll say things and I won't know how to respond. Better to just memorize my lines and be consistent." That works great if your goal is to talk *at* voters. However, if you really want to talk *with* voters (which is much more likely to earn their trust and lead to a meaningful connection that will help you earn their vote), here are some concrete tips:

- **Ask open-ended questions.** Open-ended questions can't be answered with a "yes" or a "no," as opposed to close-ended questions, which can. For example, "Have you heard about Candidate X?" is a close-ended question, but "What, if anything, have you heard about Candidate X?" is an open-ended question.

There are many advantages to open-ended questions, especially if your aim is to elicit information about what a voter cares about. By definition, you're posing the question in a way that invites more than a one-word answer. It also can help voters feel like you genuinely want to know what they think, rather than guessing what answer you want to hear from them. For example, "Have you heard about Candidate X?" implies that they *should* have heard about them, and maybe they'll say yes just so they don't appear ignorant. If they say no, that already sets up an unintended power dynamic where you have more knowledge and are about to preach at them.

By contrast, "What, if anything, have you heard about Candidate X?" doesn't imply any value judgment about their level of prior knowledge about that candidate, whether they've never heard of him or her, or they happen to be the candidate's cousin. Equally important, it allows you to quickly assess their overall familiarity with the candidate. Maybe they wouldn't know them from Adam (or Eve), or they've seen some negative TV ads which have raised some doubts, or perhaps they are a huge fan.

After introducing myself and my role as a volunteer for Candidate X, some of my favorite questions try to surface what's most important to the voter. Rather than asking, "What issues are most important to you?" which is technically an open-ended question but might only elicit a short answer like "The economy" or "Gun control," here are some other ways to inquire:

- If you were the president, what two or three things would you change about our country? (This question is inspired by the work of union organizer Jane McAlevey,

PhD, a senior policy fellow at UC Berkeley's Institute for Labor & Employment Relations. When approaching workers, she asks them, "If you were in charge, what would you change about your workplace?")
- If you were in an elevator with the president for two minutes, what would you tell him to change, and why?
- What concerns keeps you up at night?
- If a politician who really cared about the community was elected, what would be different about our country a year from now?

These open-ended questions often yield juicy answers. That opens up a fruitful conversation and gives me a wealth of information about that voter's priorities.

- **Count to 10 (silently).** Sometimes people are initially stumped if you ask them an open-ended question. Don't panic – this can be a good thing! It may indicate that they're thinking about it, or trying to articulate their response. One strategy I learned as a documentary radio producer is to count to 10 (in my head) while they are thinking. To let them know I'm still paying attention, I try to maintain eye contact, and nod and smile slightly if it's appropriate. Sometimes I see volunteers ask a wonderful open-ended question, but when the voter doesn't respond immediately, they ask another one. Be patient. If someone is thinking about what you said, they're unlikely to abruptly end the conversation. Sometimes people are flattered that you care enough to want to know what they think, and that you're willing to wait while they come up with a response.
- **Be patient.** Some people may freeze or draw a blank when they first hear your question. Perhaps just rephrasing your

question may inspire some thoughts. Or switching gears to a different open-ended question may do the trick.

Sometimes when I'm talking with voters, it can be hard to get traction. I may feel like I'm talking with a sullen teenager, who gives me one-word answers no matter what I say. That's okay! The most important thing is to keep them engaged, even if much of that engagement is nonverbal. The fact that we're both hanging in there, staying in the conversation, is just as important as the words being said. As an introvert myself, it can take me a while to figure out what I think, or to formulate the words to communicate those thoughts. I definitely have things to say, if others have the time and patience to move at my tempo.

If they do start talking, I can make nonverbal noises like "Uh-huh" or "Mmmmm," to encourage them to keep going, or say things like "Wow!" or "Really?!" if they share something intense or surprising.

When trying to elicit information from a taciturn voter, I sometimes feel like I'm a safecracker trying to open a combination lock. There can be a lot of trial and error, and it's important to take my time and pay attention to subtle details. I try to act like I have all the time in the world, and to home in on any cues that indicate a voter might have more to say about a particular topic.

For example, I talked with a college student I'll call Elena. A couple of weeks before the election she was still undecided about how she'd be voting, and said she needed to do more research. When I asked her, "If you were the president, what two or three things would you change about the country?" she couldn't think of anything. When I asked, "If you were in an elevator with the president for two minutes, what would you ask him to change?" she drew a blank.

But then when I asked her, "How would Biden's student loan program make a difference in your life?" she told me how she left her house at 5:20 a.m. to work all day harvesting grapes, getting home in the afternoon for a quick shower before going to evening classes, then coming home, eating dinner, studying a little, and crashing, only to get up and do it all over again the next day. She didn't want to get her textbooks dirty in the fields, so she took photos of a few pages using her phone, then tried to read them during her work breaks. She said how it was hard to really focus on her classes and absorb the concepts because her study time was so fragmented.

She hadn't been able to think of anything she'd change at the start of our conversation. However, once we started talking about how lower tuition costs would make her life better, it turned out she had *lots* of opinions. That led naturally to a discussion about why it was so important to elect Democrats in the upcoming election.

- **Dig for details!** As soon as a voter identifies a priority issue, it can be tempting to jump into sales mode, rattling off your candidate's talking points on that topic. Resist that urge. Instead, spend some time eliciting more details from the voter. Ask follow-up questions. (Bonus points if these can be open-ended questions as well!)

    Getting voters to tell you more about how a particular issue impacts their lives helps them concretize what's at stake for them personally in the upcoming election. It also gives you more information about the specific ways a candidate or their positions might make a tangible difference in that voter's life. Rather than talking about abstract policy positions, helping voters articulate the up-close-and-personal ramifications may help them deepen their commitment to vote and to support your candidate or issue, because they've talked through the details. How might a specific policy improve their health, the quality of their kids' education, or how much time they can spend with the people they love?

Here are a few phrases that encourage voters to open up further:

- **"Tell me more about that."** This is one of my all-time favorite phrases, and one that works in almost any situation, including when I can't think of what to say next. It's nonjudgmental, and signals that I'm curious about their experience and want to know more.
- **"How did that ... (impact you/make you feel/affect your financial situation?)"** This is another open-ended question which invites voters to elaborate on what they just shared with you.
- **"That sounds really hard."** This simple acknowledgment of the real-life challenges people face can help communicate that you really heard them. (More on this in Chapter 6, when I talk about empathy.)

By letting your friendly, nonjudgmental curiosity lead the way, you can find out what matters most to a voter. I talked with a middle-aged man named Matthew, who was sitting in front of his house in a wheelchair. He was a registered Republican, though he mentioned that he hated Trump. He was undecided on the Congressional election and said he needed to do more research. He said he thought the Republicans were better on the economy, and that every time a Democrat got in the White House, the economy got worse. He said he was really struggling to make ends meet.

I said, "I'm really sorry to hear that. Tell me more." He'd worked at a big box store for many years, was transferred out of state for his job, but ended up moving back to his hometown because he couldn't afford to pay rent. He'd decided to come back to the family home, which was paid off.

Matthew seemed to be leaning toward voting for Republicans, but I asked if I could leave him some information about my candidate as just one more data point as he was doing his research. He said sure, so I handed him a flyer. He pointed to the line that said the Democratic candidate supported limiting the price of insulin to $35 per month, whereas the incumbent Republican voted for the status quo. "Now *that* hits close to home," said Matthew. "Tell me more about that," I said. He pointed to one of his legs and said, "I have diabetes, and when I was living out of state, my wife got really sick. I had to quit my job to take care of her before she died. I didn't have health insurance, so I couldn't afford insulin for years. And then they had to amputate my leg."

I was in shock! My mouth was hanging open. I said I was so sorry to hear about what happened to him, and that unfortunately, a lot of other people were in the same situation. I said that was why my candidate was running for Congress, to help make sure that didn't happen to anyone else. I didn't say a lot more, but paused to let that sink in. I could tell he was thinking about what we'd talked about. He wouldn't commit to supporting my candidate, but as I was walking away, I could hear him telling the other people in his house about our conversation. And in the following days, when I met other voters with diabetes or a family member affected by that disease, I mentioned Matthew's experience to underscore what was at stake in this election.

Ask Them About Their Passions

Part of getting people to talk about themselves at length is finding out what they really care about. They say the devil is in the details, and my experience is that passion is in the details as well. Pay attention not only to what they say, but *how* they say it. Where do they show energy or strong feelings, whether of fear, anger, hope or excitement?

For example, I spoke with a young woman named Belinda, who initially said she didn't think much about politics. When I asked her what she would change if she were running the country, she said she would protect a woman's right to choose. She shared that she'd had an unplanned pregnancy when she was a teenager, and struggled over the decision of whether to have an abortion or not. She ultimately decided to keep her child, but said, "I'm very pro-choice, and it's important that women get to make that decision themselves."

Belinda talked about how important it was to increase the minimum wage, especially for single moms like herself. She also talked about how concerned she was about climate change. Funny and sassy, she said, "I can't understand how people say climate change isn't real. That's like people on the Titanic saying, 'This ship isn't going down. What iceberg are you talking about?'"

Another way to find out what matters to voters is to observe their environment with a keen eye. Do you see any signs of their hobbies in the yard? Can you see pictures of their grandchildren in the hall? Are they bending down to pet their cat? Ask them about these cherished people, animal companions or activities, and you'll likely be rewarded with a smile and some enthusiastic stories.

For example, I was admiring a beautiful stone wall inlaid with colorful marbles and smooth river pebbles arranged in floral patterns. When the voter emerged from his house, I asked if he was a professional stonemason. He said he was a retired truck driver, but that he, his wife, and his grandchildren spent six years building this wall on weekends. He showed me where his grandkids had signed their names in the cement, and mentioned wistfully that his wife had passed away a few years ago.

Another voter showed me around her lush garden, pointing out the bird of paradise plant, grapefruit tree, and other treasures. She had worked in a commercial rose production facility, and cultivated her own yard with the same care. She said her family thought she was crazy because she talked to her plants. I asked, "What do you tell your plants?" She said, "Oh, that they're beautiful!"

Yet another voter was a veteran and was studying to become a lab scientist with the support of her GI education benefits. She was putting herself through school working in a hospital lab and was passionate about her work. "I *love* bodily fluids!" she exclaimed. I burst out laughing and asked, "What do you love about them?" "Oh, each one can tell you different things – urine, blood, cerebrospinal fluid," she said. "It's *so* fascinating!"

Seek Their Expertise

This also works with phone banking, even if you don't have visual cues about the voter's environment. In fact, taking a genuine interest in their lives can even help prevent them from hanging up. In January 2021, during the height of one of the COVID surges, I was calling voters for a runoff election for mayor in Modesto, a town in the Central Valley. I spoke with Virginia, a registered Republican in her 80s. As soon as I introduced myself, she said, "I can't think about politics right now – I live with my cousin, and both of us have COVID and aren't feeling well." I said, "Oh, I'm so very sorry to hear about both of you, and I'm sorry to bother you when you're under the weather."

Then I paused for just a moment and added, "But actually, that's related to the reason I'm calling. I'm volunteering for Sue Zwahlen, who's running for mayor. She worked as an emergency room nurse for decades and wants to make sure Modesto protects the health of everyone, especially vulnerable people during the pandemic."

Virginia had never heard of my candidate, but did seem impressed by Sue's background and her positions. I also mentioned that Sue had also served on the Modesto City School Board and sent her six children to public schools. I added, "Sue is interested in hearing the priorities of community members. I wonder, if you could share what you'd want to improve in the community, what would you tell her?"

Virginia said that she'd worked as a math teacher in a low-income school. If she were in charge, she'd make free lunch programs available to all children, regardless of income. That would destigmatize the program and ensure that all kids who needed food could access it. I documented that in the notes section, and then asked Virginia if she had any tips about how to make math fun and interesting, since I personally had had so many bad math teachers as a kid. She enthusiastically described a trick to help students remember the 9 times table, and got really excited telling me about it.

At the end of the conversation I said I hoped she'd feel better soon, and thanked her for talking with me. She said, "Oh, I think I'll be all right." Then she paused and added, "And I think you just earned yourself another vote for Sue." I was thrilled! I confirmed that she had received her vote-by-mail ballot and knew how to return it. Virginia also agreed to tell the cousin who lived with her about Sue.

Skylar the Skeptic might say, "Wow, talking about the 9 times table is *way* off topic. There are so many voters to call – how can you waste time talking about things that have nothing to do with the elections?" I would respond that taking the time to get to know more about people's lives and their rich work histories deepens their investment in the conversation. Give them a chance to shine as they share some piece of expertise or lesson learned. My conversation with Virginia went from her initially not wanting to talk at all and likely not voting due to her health, to committing to supporting Sue Zwahlen by the end, and also telling her cousin about our conversation. Talk about the multiplier effect!

Another time I was calling people to urge them to vote against the recall of Democrat Gavin Newsom, governor of California. I reached Carol, a voter in the Central Valley, who was irritated when she found out why I was calling. "I don't have time to talk to you – somebody else just called me about this yesterday!" she said with exasperation. My stomach dropped about six inches, but I responded, "Oh, I'm so sorry to bother you again – but *I* didn't get to hear your response. I'm so curious – what *did* you tell the other person about your thoughts about the recall?" Leading with my genuine curiosity was apparently effective. Carol indicated that she was a strong Democrat, and although she wouldn't come out and say it, implied that she would vote against the recall.

She asked me where I was calling from. I always tell the truth in those situations, so I said I lived in San Francisco. She said suspiciously, "That can't be true – the caller ID was a Los Angeles number." I explained about how autodialers worked, and that I really did live in San Francisco. Sensing that she still thought I was a scammer, I said, "I'm not knocking doors in person right now because of COVID, but I spent several long weekends in your town before the pandemic, and I really liked it – I met some very friendly people and had good conversations!"

I paused for a moment, but she didn't seem impressed. Then I said, "I really hope to go back once things calm down with COVID. Do you have any restaurant recommendations for me when I do? It's always nice to hear where people in the community like to eat." Without hesitation, she said, "Superior Dairy," a family-run business known for its gigantic scoops of ice cream. I asked her, "What's your favorite flavor there?" and she said, "Chocolate." Then we laughed. If you can get people talking about their favorite food, you *know* you've made a connection!

Asking voters for advice or guidance in other areas besides ice cream can also be fruitful. In 2020 I spoke with Velma, a voter in Georgia. She joked that she was a voting "evangelist" at the FedEx warehouse where she worked. She said, "Some of my coworkers, especially these young guys, tell me they're not voting." I asked her, "What do you say to them?" She said, "I ask them, 'Do you have children?' If they say yes, I tell them, 'What you do – or don't do – today might affect your children years from now. It's to your advantage to exercise your right to vote. I'm going to send you this link about where to vote."

By asking voters in the field about their tips for getting out the vote, you can learn more about approaches that might work especially well in a particular community or demographic, such as young dads. It's an invaluable opportunity to glean intel from people who are on the ground, enhancing your own skill set. It also builds rapport to center *their* narrative and expertise in the conversation. They are the leading actors, and I can be a supporting actor by providing an eager and attentive ear.

'Teaching to a Need'

Don't just take my word for it – there are many others who have far more experience talking with strangers. On the first day of my monthlong canvassing stint in the Central Valley in 2022, I met a pair of fresh-faced Mormon missionaries, Cameron and Zach. They were knocking on the same doors I was, carrying copies of *Santa Biblia* and *El Libro de Mormon* – the Spanish versions of the Holy Bible and the *Book of Mormon*. They wore their signature white collared dress shirts, dark khakis, black name tags, and thousand-watt smiles.

They said they enjoyed doing their work in the Central Valley because the people were very friendly. They had both studied Spanish in high school, went through an intensive language and theology immersion at the start of their mission, and spent an hour each day continuing their language study. They were interested in my canvassing work, and asked if I needed anything. I couldn't think of anything, but they said if something came up later, I should just let them know.

On a Saturday night about 10 days later, I was in another town on a busy road. I heard someone call out a friendly greeting. I was a bit wary, since I didn't know anyone there except the handful of voters I'd talked with earlier that day. It turned out to be my friends Cameron and Zach again. We compared notes about our recent experiences, and I asked them the most important factors for being successful in their work. Cameron said, "Making sure that they know that they are cared about and loved as a child of God." Zach added, "Knowing the culture and having good follow-up questions. You should be interested in who they actually are before you pursue your purpose. Make sure that they know that you care about them and that you don't just want something from them. It's a two-way thing."

I asked what kinds of questions they might ask to help communicate their genuine care for those they meet. Zach said, "Getting to know where everyone is from, how long they've lived here and why they came, whether it's for work or family." Cameron said, "Getting to know the details of their life, so you can tie your purpose in and get something to really click with them personally."

Zach jumped in and made a point I'll always remember. "We believe in teaching to a need," he said. "Things that people are struggling with or need in their lives, there is always something that Jesus Christ taught that applies directly to that. Giving them things that are *actually* going to help them, rather than just teaching what *we* believe."

I said that it sounded like they need to take the time to really find out about the lives of the people they talk to – what's hard, what's challenging – before they jump in and start telling them about Mormonism. "Yes, these are people – not numbers," said Zach. "It's easy to get caught up in how many people you need to get registered [to vote] or taught, but the minute that you start putting names to the numbers is when you will have success."

I pondered that for a few moments, then asked them about any rookie moves they'd seen with new missionaries. "Getting too straight to the point, too quickly, is a mistake that a lot of us make," said Cameron. "You want to take your time and show that you care about them specifically, and not just about what you're doing.... There is always room for improvement. Look at why things work or not. Think of ideas that you haven't tried. Be creative with it."

As different as our aims were in pounding the pavement, I had tremendous respect for their approach. After all, they were out in the field for almost two years, knocking on the same doors I was. I thought it was hard enough talking politics with strangers. But that was nothing compared with their work – engaging strangers in conversations about Mormonism in a majority Catholic community.

The proof is in their outcomes: through their respectful, sincere interest in the people they met, they'd built up a cadre of 15 families who invited them into their homes *each week* to do teachings about Mormonism. If we as campaign volunteers were even half as successful, we'd be winning elections in swing districts and states by a comfortable margin!

When Is It Time for '20% Me'?

So far, I've talked a lot about the "80% Them" component. So when do I bust my "20% Me" moves?

I know other canvassing approaches place a lot of emphasis on telling "our story" – describing in personal terms what fuels our passion, what's at stake for us or those we care about in this election, and trying to humanize identities that some groups may have spent a lot of energy trying to demonize as "other." A human-to-human interchange can go a long way toward breaking down those artificial barriers. Those efforts can be highly effective and even transformative in the ways that voters think about otherwise abstract issues.

My personal hesitation with that approach has to do with several things. First, sequencing is very important. Of course, I need to start by introducing myself and why I'm calling or am on their doorstep. But before I can expect others to care about my experience, I need to demonstrate that I care about theirs. The best way I know how to do that is to put in the time and effort to hear their concerns and understand their lives.

This is particularly important because I have mostly canvassed in working-class neighborhoods in rural California. I'm a college-educated, self-employed writer living a privileged life in the bluest of blue cities, San Francisco. Although my maternal grandparents worked as an auto mechanic and housecleaner, and my parents worked in Hawaii's pineapple fields and canneries to put themselves through college, I have very little understanding of the everyday lives of most of the voters I talk with. It's important for me to come with humility and a keen awareness of my own ignorance of their challenges, working conditions, worries, and hopes for the future. I never want to presume that I know what their experience has been, or assume what their beliefs may be on any particular issue. Only after I have a better understanding of what matters most to *them* do I feel able to share something from my own experience that might be relevant to our discussion.

Second, many people's internal motivations are far stronger than anything I could share with them. I can certainly offer them information related to their priorities, and underscore areas of alignment between what they care about and the candidate or issue I am supporting. (I really double down on this approach in the case of "high-potential voters" – people who rarely or never vote – which I'll discuss in Chapter 11.) But I often find that helping them hear their *own* motivations and rationales, and getting them to talk about that in more depth, can be far more compelling than telling them about why an issue means so much to me.

However, there are some circumstances where I *do* talk about what drives me. When a voter named Armando said he wasn't going to vote, I said, "Tell me more about that." He just didn't have time to think about it, and there wasn't anything compelling enough in those midterm elections that would get him to the ballot box.

I said, "Could I share a bit about why I'm out here today, talking with people in the community?" He said sure, so I said, "Several members of my family have preexisting health conditions, and it's important to me that they'll always have access to health insurance. When Obamacare passed, it protected people like my family members. It made sure they couldn't be denied health care insurance or get charged more just because they'd had cancer or heart disease. Unfortunately, many Republicans want to get rid of that protection; they've voted dozens of times to end Obamacare."

Armando told me that two of his children have heart conditions, and that protection for preexisting conditions was also a concern for him. We talked about the Democratic and Republican Congressional candidates' views on this issue, and he ended up committing to vote for the Democratic candidate.

It's thrilling to participate in the metamorphosis of a conversation that starts with disinterest and transforms into a firm resolve to vote, fueled by something important to a voter. It reminds me that beneath the surface of "I'm not voting," there may be more flexibility and room to maneuver than first meets the eye. I try to stay curious and try different approaches. I start with the 80% end of the equation, and migrate to the 20% end if needed.

Sometimes telling my story, no matter how heartfelt, falls flat. I was talking with one young voter in the Central Valley in 2018, who wasn't interested in voting. I asked him what he'd change about the country if he were in charge, and he couldn't think of anything. I asked what worries kept him awake at night, and he said everything was fine.

Finally I said, "Could I share a bit about why I'm talking with voters in the neighborhood? I'm really concerned about the way that President Trump and others are talking about banning Muslims from coming into our country, and wanting to lock other people up. My mom's side of the family is Japanese American, and I had relatives who were sent off to prison camps during World War II, just because they were of Japanese descent – even though they were American citizens like you and me. I don't ever want that to happen again in our country, no matter what someone's background or religion." He listened politely, but still didn't budge on his decision not to vote.

Other times I've had better luck. In December 2020 I was phone banking for Raphael Warnock and Jon Ossoff a few weeks before the Georgia Senate runoff. I reached a young voter, Jesse. He was very courteous and attentive, but couldn't think of anything he'd change if he were in charge of the country. Eventually, though, he did say, "I guess I'd let people vote, whether or not they were citizens." I said, "That's a really interesting idea. I know that some school districts are letting both citizen and noncitizen parents vote for school board elections." I paused for a moment, then added, "But for right now, for most elections you need to be a citizen to vote. That includes you, right?" He confirmed that yes, he was a citizen. I said, "Maybe it's *especially* important for you to vote, to have your voice heard on behalf of other people in your community who can't vote yet."

Finally, I mentioned that part of the reason I was calling was because although I was glad that Joe Biden was elected, we really needed to win Democratic control of the Senate to get anything done. I said that my friends Sarah and Sally were small business owners and had taken a real hit during the pandemic. Biden wanted to extend support for small businesses after it expired, but Republicans had already made it clear that they wanted to end those programs. I told Jesse that this was part of the reason I was calling voters that day.

I asked what, if anything, he thought about that, and he said yes, he thought it would be good if those small businesses could get more help. Then I asked if he might consider voting in this runoff election, and he said, "Yeah, I would." I could hardly believe my ears! I told him that it would be best if he could vote early, just to get it taken care of. I told him exactly where he could go and what hours the early voting location was open. At the end of the conversation, he told me, "Well, I hope things work out for your friends." I was so touched!

It was even more exciting when I called him back on January 5, 2021, Election Day in Georgia, just to see if he had any questions. He didn't have a lot of time because he was at work, but I asked, "I'm so curious – are you still planning to vote?" He said, "Oh, I voted early like you said, a few days after we talked." Jesse and voters like him were part of the razor-thin majority that helped Ossoff and Warnock win their Senate seats – and allowed Democrats to retake the U.S. Senate.

Let Your Nonjudgmental Curiosity Lead the Way

If you think you might not have the perfect words for every voter encounter, don't worry. Remember, you don't need to be a brilliant orator or a policy wonk to engage in meaningful conversations with voters. In fact, it can be off-putting if a voter feels like you are talking at them, spouting lots of factoids and policy positions.

Instead, harness the power of your nonjudgmental curiosity. Find out more about what *they* care about and what their lived experience is like. Ask about what they find challenging in their lives, and what hopes they have for their future, their family and their community. Take your time, ask open-ended questions, and then ask follow-up questions to elicit more details. By focusing 80% of the conversation on what's important to them, you not only build rapport, but also glean valuable information that helps you tailor what information you *do* share with them later in the conversation. If needed, you can share a personal story about what motivates your passion for this work, but try to keep the spotlight on them most of the time. Many people feel honored that a stranger cares enough to want to know about their lives.

Summary

- Listen more than you talk.
- Ask open-ended questions, then count to 10 (silently!)
- Dig for details about voters' lives, challenges and hopes. This builds rapport and allows you to identify which tidbits of information will be most compelling for that voter.
- Remember the advice from our Mormon friends: "We believe in teaching to a need. Take your time and show that you care."

Chapter 6
Empathize, Empathize, Empathize

One of the things I love most about canvassing and phone banking is that it gives me a little window into the lives of people I would probably never otherwise meet. It's a tremendous privilege to get a glimpse into other worlds, and to connect with fellow citizens about things that matter.

It goes without saying that it's a challenging time in our country and our world. Growing wealth disparities, the loss of lives and livelihoods due to the pandemic, the increasing effects of climate change, the many threats to our democracy – the list goes on. I've learned that one of the most essential components for doing voter engagement work is empathy. Many people are struggling with hard things right now.

I met José in Bakersfield the day before the 2022 midterm elections. When we first started talking, he seemed very cynical about voting, and described everything that wasn't going well in the community. He told me about all the people who had been shot and killed in the neighborhood, showed me the hole in his garage door from the stray bullet that had whizzed by his head, and pointed out the house of the older couple down the street who were raising their grandkids after their parents died of COVID.

From the way he was talking, I was pretty sure he wasn't going to vote. But then he shocked me by saying, "Of course I'm going to vote for the Democrats – I have to!" He thought it was especially important for young people like him to get out and vote. When I asked him to tell me more, he said, "We need to get our voices out there. If we don't vote, nothing is going to change. We need to put the right people in office. Things here in California are expensive, and we really need to fix that. It's not the American Dream if you're struggling."

I asked him what he'd say to someone who said, "My vote doesn't matter." José said, "If you don't put your vote in, you can't complain about the outcome. Everyone needs to stop arguing and just fix the country. Put the screws back that fell out. Our kids are going to be left after us, so make it better for them. It's horrible that Bakersfield has the highest murder rate in California. I don't want that for the town I grew up in. It's scary to want to raise a family here. But I don't want to leave it – I love Bakersfield. It's my home, but we aren't taking care of it. I'm about to cry, thinking about it. People just need to vote."

At the end of our conversation, he assured me that he would vote for all the Democratic candidates, and he also agreed to make sure other voters in his family got out to vote. He seemed a bit surprised that he'd gotten so emotional talking with me. All those feelings were just under the surface, waiting for someone to ask him what he thought. I didn't need to do anything except listen with compassion and invite him to tell me more. He wasn't asking me to fix his problems, give advice, or tell him everything would be fine. Sometimes, just taking the time to let people know they are seen and heard can be powerful for both of you. And that experience can also help people articulate their *own* reasons for why voting is so important.

Take the Time to Listen

Of course, it's not always that straightforward. That same month I also spoke with a voter, Daniel, in his 60s. He was missing several teeth, smelled strongly of cigarettes, and had trouble standing due to weakness in his legs. Even with the hardships he'd endured, he retained a wry sense of humor. He hadn't voted for many years, and didn't plan to start now.

He told me that decades ago he'd had a great job driving a backhoe in the oil fields, making $20 per hour. Tragically, he was exposed to coccidioidomycosis, the soil fungus that causes Valley fever. It's an illness that afflicts many people in the Central Valley who work on the land, and can sometimes be fatal. He developed a 107 degree fever, had never been so sick in his entire life, and nearly died. Even when he was hospitalized for COVID a few years ago, it was nothing compared with that. While he was deeply grateful to the doctors who saved his life, he became permanently disabled and was never able to work again.

I told him I was so sorry to hear about his ordeal, and that it sounded like a difficult situation. Daniel said that he and his wife had a hard time making ends meet, and added, "When I was growing up, a dollar used to be able to buy a pack of cigarettes, some gum and some candy, with change left over – but now, a dollar doesn't even buy hard times." He said his wife worked for minimum wage cleaning motel rooms. When I mentioned that the Democratic candidate for Congress voted to raise the California minimum wage and asked whether that had made a difference in their lives, he said, "It didn't help us get ahead, because everything is so expensive." And when I told him that I was volunteering in part because I wanted to maintain health care access for family members with preexisting health conditions, he agreed that everyone should have access to health insurance, but then said, "Things will stay the same no matter what we do, so I'm not interested in voting at all."

Although he didn't budge on his decision to not vote, I learned so much from talking with him. And as I was leaving, I thanked him for talking and said I didn't want to hold him up any longer. He said, "Oh, you're not holding me up – the wall is."

Our conversation calls to mind a quote attributed to Mother Teresa: "I am not called to be successful – I am called to be faithful." Sometimes witnessing the hardships and joys of other human beings doesn't always translate into earning votes or winning elections. Yet taking the time to listen and let people know that they matter, no matter what they choose to do with their vote, is part of how we start to reweave the ties that bind us together as a country.

An Empathetic Witness – Not a Therapist

Some of what people share with me can be hard to hear – at times, even heartbreaking. That can feel like a lot to take in as a volunteer. Try to remember that they aren't asking you to fix their problem for them. It can be a form of service just to witness their experience and let them know they are seen and heard. In fact, jumping too quickly from them sharing a vulnerable part of their experience to how that relates to policy issues can feel jarring – like you're trying to sell them something. Instead, try spending a little more time acknowledging the depth of what they have just shared with you.

In one of the voter engagement workshops I taught, I observed a practice session between two volunteers. The person in the canvasser role, Jenny, asked the person in the voter role, Sarah, what she'd change if she were running the country. Sarah said, "I'd make sure that we had universal health care. My dad got a kidney transplant, but then he lost his insurance and couldn't afford his immunosuppressant drugs anymore. He ended up having to go back on dialysis, and then rejected his transplanted kidney and ended up dying."

Jenny said, "Sorry to hear that. So can we count on your vote for Mark Kelly for Senate?" I called a time out and asked if I could give some feedback. I said, "Whoa, Sarah just shared a really hard thing that happened in her family. It would be great if you just paused the conversation there and spent a minute acknowledging the intensity of what she just told you. You could say something like, 'Wow, that sounds so hard. I'm very sorry for your loss,' and then count to 10 and see how Sarah responds. It feels kind of callous when someone tells you something so personal and then you just jump ahead to trying to 'close the deal.'"

Then I asked Sarah, "What was your response to that part of the conversation? What would you have wanted to hear?" Sarah said, "Actually, that was a true story. I didn't have the energy to make something up for this role play, so I told you what actually happened to my dad – he got a kidney transplant, lost his health insurance, couldn't afford his meds, and ended up dying." We all sat in stunned silence for a minute. Sarah said, "Yeah, it would have been nice if you acknowledged that loss before moving ahead with your agenda. It kind of felt like I couldn't get in a word edgewise, because you just kept talking."

Sarah wasn't asking Jenny to be her therapist, her best friend, or her grief counselor. Just slowing down enough to acknowledge the challenges that another human being has faced can go a long way toward earning their trust and respect. And sometimes giving them the opportunity to elaborate on how a difficult experience affected them or shaped their perspective yields helpful information. Later in the conversation, you might gently allude to some of the specific concerns they shared with you, bringing the conversation back to what's at stake for them in the upcoming election.

The Language of Empathy

There are many ways to show empathy. Asking open-ended questions and acknowledging difficult experiences that the voter shares with you are important ways to use language to express compassion. There are other tools you can employ as well. Slowing down and allowing spaciousness in the conversation can communicate that you're not in a hurry and have time to hear what they have to say, even if it's hard for them to talk about and challenging for you to hear.

"Backchanneling" is a linguistics term that refers to the way that conversations are co-created between two people. The speaker uses the front channel to do most of the talking, whereas the listener uses the back channel to indicate that they are paying attention and want to hear more. Listeners can backchannel by using short phrases like "Mmm-hmm," "Seriously?" and "Wow!" and to express agreement, surprise or amazement, without interrupting the flow of the speaker's narrative.

Another key element is your body language. If you are canvassing, try to make direct eye contact. Nodding can let them know you are listening and following their story. Letting your facial expressions communicate surprise, concern or sympathy helps provide nonverbal feedback that you really heard what they had to say and are acknowledging the depth of what they shared.

Even while phone banking, it's possible to express empathy. Sometimes I overemote a bit, opening my eyes wide or raising my eyebrows to express surprise, or furrowing my brow when I hear something sad. Obviously, they can't see my facial expressions, but combined with my verbal responses and "Uh-huhs," that slight exaggeration helps transmit my intent across the phone line. When I canvassed during the COVID era, I wore a mask; I tried to exaggerate my facial expressions, especially with my eyes and eyebrows, since the rest of my face was covered up. It sounds cheesy, but that did help project my intention of empathy and attentiveness even through a barrier.

Two Conversations

Communicating empathy when someone shares about hardships is one thing, but I find it more challenging when a voter's belief systems differ from mine. I met Isabella during the 2022 midterms. She'd recently moved to California from the Southwest, and was shocked at how expensive everything was. She wasn't enthusiastic about voting, because in her words, "Nothing changes." In 2016, she actually voted for Trump, because she thought he might shake things up in a good way. Yet she wasn't happy with how things turned out. "I feel kind of bad about voting for him," she said. "My husband is a DACA recipient, and my dad would hardly speak to me after I told him how I'd voted."

I said, "Well, a lot of people voted for Trump in 2016." I was trying to peel away some layers of shame that might prevent her from voting again, and suss out how her remorse over voting for Trump might inform future voting choices. Isabella was impressed that the Democratic candidate for Congress was born and raised in the area, that he'd worked in the grape fields and in construction, and had fought to increase the minimum wage and get overtime pay for farmworkers as a state assemblyman.

She sheepishly admitted she hadn't voted since 2016. I said, "It's understandable that you've been turned off by politics – but now would be a great time to get back into voting." By the end of the conversation, she said that she'd look into voting again, and I could tell she was really thinking about it.

Sometimes when I talk with voters, it almost feels like I'm in a comic strip where I can see two conversations in my mind. When

Isabella said she voted for Trump in 2016, there's a thought bubble with the words, "You did WHAT?!" next to my head. Still, I tried to reflect back the *best* interpretation of what I heard her say when I responded, "A lot of people voted for Trump in 2016."

When Isabella said she hadn't voted for years, I might be thinking, "How can you not vote when so much is at stake?" But instead I said, "Now would be a great time to get back into voting." Because I tried not to criticize or judge her past actions, she seemed to feel freer to express her opinions, rather than feeling boxed into a corner of shame and defensiveness, or giving up and saying that she wasn't going to vote.

Of course, this is a lot of information to take in. Sometimes what people share can bring up a lot of feelings inside me. This is perfectly normal, and probably most people motivated enough to canvass or phone bank have strong opinions that diverge from those held by some of the voters we talk with. However, venting my own opinions directly at voters I disagree with can torpedo my efforts to connect with them. Getting into a debate with people at their doorstep or on the phone sets up an adversarial dynamic that I'm almost certain to lose. Most likely, they'll just close the door in my face or end the call.

It's important to avoid getting into a verbal arm-wrestling match with a voter. Instead, I try to bring my nonjudgmental curiosity to the conversation. I affirm the very real challenges they are facing in their lives, try to better understand what is important and why, and try to gently guide the conversation in a positive direction. I can file away some of my own strong feelings about these conversations for when I debrief with a canvassing buddy, other volunteers over dinner, or at the end of the phone bank. It's important to find an outlet for all the emotions and unspoken responses that build up in my internal thought bubbles, especially during particularly challenging conversations with voters.

EMPATHIZE, EMPATHIZE, EMPATHIZE

In 2018 I once spent a weekend training a bright, articulate new volunteer how to canvass. She was initially shy about talking with voters, and was scared to even ring the doorbell. However, she quickly gained confidence and soon was marching up to doors ahead of me. Then we encountered one young Latino voter who bluntly declared that he was a Republican. She launched into him, saying, "How can you do that, after everything Trump has done? You're voting against your own interests!" I could see his expression harden and the walls go up. I tried to divert the conversation, but she was dogged in her determination to get him to see it her way.

Over lunch, I tried to explain to my canvassing partner how telling the voter that he was voting against his own interests would probably alienate him and make him double down on his beliefs. Nobody likes to lose face or to have a total stranger tell them what to think. On the other hand, asking open-ended questions about what was most important to him, in a spirit of nonjudgmental curiosity, might be a more effective method of sounding out any possible openings. I mentioned how we humans are complex creatures, and may have conflicting motivations. What might look like acting against our own best interests might actually align with other values we hold, such as self-sufficiency or playing by the rules. For example, I pay more for produce because I try to buy my fruits and vegetables from the farmers market rather than the supermarket, when possible. Someone could say that I'm acting against my own interests by needlessly paying more than I have to. However, it's worth it to me to shell out a little more to support small farmers. She listened and considered what I was saying, but didn't seem convinced.

After lunch I said, "I'm going to head to the bathroom before we hit the road." She nodded and said, "I'll be on the other end of the park, smoking a cigarette." I smiled but tried not to laugh. I'm not sure she realized the irony in her statement. After she'd just upbraided the young voter about being a Republican and voting against his own interests, she just shared that she was going to smoke a cigarette – which pretty obviously went against *her* best health interests! I didn't say anything, but it was a reminder of how easy it is to judge other people from the outside. In reality, many of us are full of contradictions like that. We humans are a complicated bunch! Shaming and judging others doesn't usually help change behavior, but engaging with empathy, respect and curiosity can sometimes help other people come to their own conclusions about how they might want to proceed.

CAN YOU OBSERVE THE VOTER LIKE AN ANTHROPOLOGIST WOULD?

Skylar the Skeptic might say, "But there's so much at stake in this election! And some of the things they say are dead wrong. I can't just let that slide – that's part of how we got into this whole mess, with the facts being up for grabs. How do we bring truth to the Fox News watcher?"

I hear you! It's so frustrating to hear people tell you that up is down, or that the Earth is flat. Yet honestly, if people are spouting distortions, misinformation, or outright lies they've heard on Fox News, the internet, or attack ads, it's usually not very effective to try to argue with them. Often these beliefs are grounded more in emotion than facts. Trying to get them to change their minds by correcting them or landing a zinger might work in a debate match or a jury trial, but doesn't tend to go over so well in these kinds of conversations.

In a conflict with a teenager or aging parent, how often have you pointed out an inaccuracy in something they've said and heard them say, "Oh, wow – you're so right! Thanks so much for taking the time to set me straight!" There are other ways to move a conversation in productive directions, some of which I'll outline later in this chapter and the ones that follow.

When I encounter these situations, I try to slow down the conversation. I take a deep breath, and imagine I'm an anthropologist studying a fascinating culture completely different from my own. Instead of trying to prove them wrong, can I get curious about them and their beliefs? What if I've just been given an amazing opportunity to learn more about how someone with a very different perspective thinks? After all, most of us only get to read about these folks in the paper, all filtered through a reporter's lens, which often is geared toward highlighting the most controversial elements. If it bleeds, it leads – points of connection and thoughtful reflections tend to not sell newspapers or generate ad clicks.

Most people want the best for themselves, their families and their communities. We might disagree about the best way to get there, and that's okay. If I can set my burning passion to save democracy on the back burner for just a bit, it frees me to consider the possibility that I might gain a better understanding of how others see the world. That can help me tune my approach, increasing the chances that I might connect with this voter or others like them – even if we don't agree on everything.

The Importance of Reflective Listening

I'll admit, some conversations challenge me to tap into deep reserves of active, nonjudgmental listening. In these moments, I try to presume good will, and work hard to reflect back the best interpretation of what a voter tells me.

One hot afternoon in October 2022, I hesitated before knocking on the door of a voter I'll call Iliana. She was listed as a registered Republican, and I wasn't sure how I'd be received. Also, I was tired, getting hungry, and sweat was rolling down my back. However, I wanted to knock on one more door before I took a break for lunch.

Iliana turned out to be quite friendly and cordial, and talked with me for more than 30 minutes. When I asked what two or three things she'd change about the country if she were in charge, she talked about fixing supply chain issues in the grocery stores, because it had been harder to find basics like foil wrap and the kind of bread she likes to eat.

Then she said she was also concerned that her school district was teaching about nonbinary gender to her son, who was in elementary school. I could feel my hackles rise. This was one of those wedge issues – like bathroom bills, critical race theory, and book bans – that Republicans have leveraged to divide us from each other. They're throwing some of the most vulnerable kids under the bus, using them as a smokescreen to cover up their own lack of productive work around the economy, health care, or any other substantial issue. I thought about my LGBTQI+ friends, and how many of them were bullied in school and have dealt with homophobia or transphobia.

That was what was in my thought bubble. But I took a deep breath, remembered my intention to listen really hard and bring friendly curiosity to the conversation, and said, "Tell me more about that." Iliana was upset, because she thought parents should have more options about how and when that particular topic was taught. She didn't think it was age appropriate to talk about nonbinary gender to young children. However, she said she didn't have a problem with them teaching this to high school students, who were old enough to understand.

I could have argued that waiting until high school was too late, given how many kids are bullied and may even commit suicide because of their gender identity. However, she was actually giving me an opening. She wasn't denying that nonbinary gender existed or that it was morally wrong, but instead had concerns about *how* it was taught, and at what age.

Iliana was particularly offended that the school district took a hard line on the issue. She said she first learned that her son was being taught about this when she asked what he'd learned in school that day, and he started telling her about the class on nonbinary gender. "When I complained to the school district, they told me, 'If your child is enrolled in this district, they're going to learn about it, and that's that,'" she recalled with anger. She bristled at this top-down approach.

I tried to reflect back the best interpretation of what I heard her say. I said, "It sounds like you think that educating kids about this issue should be a partnership between the parents and the school." Iliana said, "Yes, they should give parents *options*. Parents should be able to opt in and decide whether they want their kid to go to a training about this topic, or if they could go to a study hall or other activity instead."

I said, "It sounds like you think it would be better if parents had choices about whether and how this issue is discussed with students." She said, "Yeah. Young kids often get confused when they hear something but don't totally understand it. I only happened to hear about this when I asked my son what he'd learned in school that day, and he mentioned nonbinary gender. As the parent, I should be the one to raise the issue with my son. That way I can answer follow-up questions or explain more if he has questions or is unclear. I don't like this top-down approach from the school district, which doesn't leave any room for choice or dialogue. It was their way or the highway."

As I was taking that in, she added, "I think would be great to educate the parents, not just the kids." I asked, "What do you think would be a good way to do that?" Iliana said, "You know, like they had a webinar on Zoom for parents about how to prevent bullying.

They could do something similar for this issue, so parents could learn more." I said, "Wow, that's a *great* idea!"

I was genuinely impressed! And she's right – educating the whole family rather than just the student would probably be more effective, if the parents were willing to participate. It also helped me see that she was thoughtful about this issue and had creative ideas about how to improve the process. Although I had initially labeled her as intolerant and bigoted, I saw that that was my own bias. Her idea about a webinar, as well as her openness to teaching students about nonbinary gender at an older age, made me realize that there was more nuance and openness to her thinking than I had originally assumed.

As we were wrapping up, she thanked me several times for listening to her. She mentioned she had voted for my candidate in the past when he ran for state Assembly, and would probably vote for him this time for Congress. Her husband and adult son were out, but I asked if she'd tell them about our conversation and ask them to vote for my candidate as well, and she said she would. This experience challenged me to dig deep into my toolbox and my professed allegiance to nonjudgmental curiosity, but had the potential to touch not just one voter, but three!

Strategies for Navigating Challenging Conversations

From my conversation with Iliana and others like her, I've learned several important strategies for navigating challenging interactions:

- **Presume good will.** Don't judge someone for their beliefs. Don't assume that they're wrong and you're right. Assume that they really do have the best intentions at heart, and want the best for themselves, their family and the community.

Try to bring nonjudgmental curiosity to the conversation. With Iliana, I tried to consider the possibility that she wasn't necessarily biased against nonbinary kids, and just wanted the best for her own child's education.

- **Seek to understand their point of view, rather than have them understand yours.** I aspire to set aside my own judgments, opinions, fears and anxieties – like how nervous I am to be talking with strangers, or how wound up I am about what's at stake in the election, or how many more doors I need to knock before the end of the day. Try hard not to project all that stress onto voters. It's not their job to do what I tell them, or to assuage my anxiety about this election. I am there to listen, to learn, to gain some new perspectives, and most of all to try to show empathy, compassion and respect to those I meet, whether they plan to support my candidate or not.

In my conversation with Iliana, I had plenty of my own biases that I was bringing to the party – being hot, tired and hungry, and feeling angry at Republicans for using gender identity issues (among others) to create controversy and scare people away from Democratic candidates. I tried to see that those were my issues, and to learn more about what Iliana really believed and why. Sometimes when people really feel heard, it can de-escalate tense situations, and they are more open to hearing what I have to say once I've earned their trust.

If I'm flummoxed, some handy phrases that can buy me time and help me better understand them include:

- Tell me more about that. (Yes, you've seen this one before, but it is especially handy in fraught situations and is a way to express nonjudgmental curiosity.)

- What concerns you most about _____?
- What would be a better way to address that situation?

- **Try to reflect back the best interpretation of what you hear.** People usually want to think of themselves as fair, open-minded, intelligent and thoughtful. If you reflect back the most positive or optimistic version of what they shared with you, they will probably be flattered. More importantly, it may move the conversation in a positive direction.

    When I told Iliana, "It sounds like you think that educating kids about nonbinary gender should be a partnership between the parents and the school," it allowed her to claim some agency about how her child should be educated. It also reframed the issue away from *whether* to teach students about the issue to *how* it is done. That was a subtle shift that moved the conversation into a more solution-focused direction, while acknowledging her concerns about the status quo.

- **It's not your job to change their mind.** As activists who want to change the world, this may sound like heresy. Yet as passionate as I may be about an issue, people are entitled to their own opinions. As Helen, one of my activist friends, says, "Free will, baby!" I can engage with respect, which sometimes builds a foundation of trust that allows me to share my viewpoints and perhaps even find some points of agreement. But at the end of the day, no matter what I say or do, I cannot make other people change their minds or their behavior.

    Instead of going into a conversation with the mindset of "How can I get them to agree with me?" it can be helpful to bring different questions:

    - What can I learn from this person?
    - What new viewpoints can I discover?

- How can they help me understand what's most important to them, and what's at the root of the concern they mentioned?

Admittedly, these are aspirational goals. I'm better at them on some days than others. (In Chapter 16 I share suggestions for self-care to improve the odds that I'll bring my best self to these challenging conversations.) But ironically, trying to listen with empathy often creates an opening in my conversations with voters. It helps me earn their respect, and they in turn become more open to what *I* have to say, even though I'm not trying to convince them – perhaps *especially* because I'm not trying to convince them.

Skylar the Skeptic might say, "What if they just want to complain, and are stuck in negativity? How do I respond?" If I've allowed them to vent for a while and it starts to feel like we're stuck on repeat, one approach that Bonnie Dobson, deep canvass manager at Down Home North Carolina, shared with us is to say, with genuine empathy, "I *hear* you," or "I've heard that from some other people, too." Then, after a short pause, you can gently redirect the conversation by saying, "You know, what I'd *really* like to hear more about is your thoughts about ____," and then introducing a topic that might lead in more positive directions.

In many of these more emotionally intense conversations, I hit a point where I ask myself, "Am I wasting my time listening to this?" But I encourage you to keep going for longer than feels comfortable. If they're still engaged with you, ride it out and see where the conversation takes you. If nothing else, you may provide a little comfort to someone going through a hard time. And sometimes that connection you build can lead to amazing places. When people feel heard and seen, they're more likely to be willing to hear you out as well. It's the give-and-take of any relationship, just in microcosm.

SUMMARY

- Bring friendly, nonjudgmental curiosity to the conversation. What can you learn?
- Even (or especially) if you disagree with someone, try to presume good will.
- Listen hard, and reflect back the best interpretation of what you hear.

Chapter 7
Talk with the One in Front of You

One of the big challenges with canvassing is that people may not be home, they're busy, or they've moved. It can be frustrating to knock on door after door, but hardly talk with any voters.

In the spirit of the song "Love the One You're With," if you can't talk with the person listed in your voter contact app, talk with the one in front of you. Being in the field is a golden opportunity to connect with voters and community members. Take advantage of every chance to talk with live humans, even if they're not officially on your list.

Probably a quarter of my conversations are with just these kinds of people. Skylar the Skeptic (and some campaigns) might say, "But I need to get through all the names in my turf! There are so many, and I can't waste time talking with people who aren't even in the app." I understand the need to reach out to voters whom the campaign has identified as priority contacts. Still, if I have a choice between talking with a real human or just leaving a door hanger for someone else, I'll take the real human every time.

Someone who has just moved in, is visiting their sister, or turned 18 last month is a potential supporter; their vote counts just as much as someone listed in the app. Even if they're too young to vote or aren't yet citizens, they likely know eligible voters. These random conversations may also be the only way we'll ever contact some voters who have recently moved, changed their phone number, or never answer their phone. Given how close some of these races are, taking the time to talk with the people in front of us may make the difference between winning and losing.

Also, connecting with people in the field is far more satisfying for me as a volunteer than just marking dozens of names as "Not home" in the app and feeling like I'm spinning my wheels. I remember early in my canvassing life, driving almost two hours each way out to the Central Valley for a three-hour shift, and only talking with about three voters the whole day. The return on investment felt low, and left me feeling tired and unproductive. Having meaningful conversations with whomever crosses my path keeps me motivated and can help prevent burnout. That's important at the beginning of an election cycle, when it makes volunteers want to come back for more. It's also important toward the end of a long campaign, when both volunteers and voters are worn out and in need of inspiration.

I met two brothers, Fred and Jake, on the sidewalk in front of their house. Fred was the only voter listed for that household. Although he said he didn't know anything about politics, by the end of our conversation he had committed to voting for my candidate.

Then I turned to his brother Jake, who had listened in on our whole conversation. I asked him, "If you were the president, what two or three things would you change about the country?" Jake said, "The same things my brother said – I'd want to help people in the community, especially people who are poor." I told him how my candidate supported making health care more affordable and limiting the price of insulin, and mentioned how close the election was going to be – that just a few people's votes could determine the outcome.

I asked Jake if he thought he'd support my candidate, and he said yes. Then I asked him if was eligible to vote, and explained that the only requirements were being 18 or older and a U.S. citizen. Jake said he was 21 and a citizen, but wasn't registered to vote and had never voted. I registered him on the spot using my phone to fill out the form online.

Because he didn't have a signature on file with the DMV, I knew he'd probably need to reregister in person, but I wanted to help cut through as much red tape as possible. I printed out his voter registration receipt and application and went back a few days later to drop it off. I wanted him to be able to bring the completed paperwork with him to the polls, almost like a talisman as he navigated this brave new world of voting. I also saw it as another opportunity to talk with him to firm up his plan to vote and help him feel more invested in the process, rather than just sending him off to wrangle the bureaucracy by himself on Election Day.

When I returned, he and his two little sisters answered the door. I handed him the paperwork, and we talked through his plan to vote. He said he could go right after work, and we confirmed where his polling place was. I said, "Don't forget – Election Day is next Tuesday." He said earnestly, "I won't forget." Then I added, "It would be great if you could bring Fred with you as well!" He offered me a bottle of water (which of course I accepted), and I talked with his little sisters, who had been listening to our entire conversation. I joked with them and said they could join their big brothers in voting a few years from now.

Although Fred was originally the only registered voter in the household, by talking with the one in front of me, I was able to register Jake to vote, and likely secured another vote for my candidate.

I also helped raise awareness about the importance of voting for Jake and Fred's two little sisters. Building a culture of engagement with voting isn't just about one-on-one conversations. It can really be a family- and community-wide affair, if I take advantage of the opportunities that chance hands me on a platter when I'm out in the field.

Talk with the Neighbors

Another time I was looking for a voter's house, and asked one of the neighbors if I had the right address. He said I did, but his neighbors had been away all week. He asked what I was doing, and when I explained I was talking with people about the upcoming election, he said, "Oh, my mom needs information about voting."

So I went next door, and spoke with his mother, Graciela. Their whole household had recently moved from a nearby town and she needed to reregister to vote, which I helped her do on the spot as we stood in their laundry room. She was a distant relative of Dolores Huerta, the iconic labor leader and civil rights activist who co-founded the United Farm Workers.

Because Graciela only spoke Spanish, I was able to help her navigate the bureaucratic hurdles on the website and to request that she receive future voter information pamphlets and ballots in Spanish. I told her where her polling place was and the hours it was open, since it was too late for her to get a vote-by-mail ballot for this election. Although she was the only eligible voter in the household, I could hear her entire family buzzing with talk about the election and how I was helping their mother reregister to vote. Since they had moved so recently, no canvasser would ever have known to knock on her door. And while I never was able to talk with their neighbor – the voter I'd originally been looking for – I helped Graciela get a step closer to casting her ballot.

I had similar experiences with many other voters who had recently moved. This was particularly common in housing projects with many units, which seemed to have higher turnover rates than single-family homes. Although the person who answers the door may tell me that the voter listed at that address has moved, I always say, "Thanks so much for letting me know – I'll make a note of that. Hey, are *you* eligible to vote, by any chance?"

Often I can provide useful information, whether it's telling them where their ballot drop box or polling place is or how to reregister to vote at their current address. I can also find out about their priority issues and share information about my candidate that's tailored to their interests. These always feel like fruitful encounters. Since many people don't answer calls from unknown numbers, and because these voters have not yet reregistered, these serendipitous conversations are likely the only one-on-one contact a campaign will have with them. Even though these encounters won't be documented in the app, the most important thing is that they may help turn out additional voters who are particularly hard to reach.

Take Advantage of Chance Opportunities to Connect

I met Leticia one evening as a Technicolor sunset was fading into embers above her house. Her husband and daughter were the voters on my list, but they weren't available. Leticia told me she got her ballot delivered at a relative's house a few blocks away, so it was just a fluke that I got to chat with her. We talked for about 30 minutes, and she told me how she thought there should be more support for social service and mental health programs, since some of her family members struggled with mental illness and homelessness. She also thought caregivers should be paid a living wage, and that there should be more funding for schools, particularly to educate students, families and teachers about how to prevent bullying. Tragically, one of the children across the street had taken his own life after being bullied at school, and the whole community was in shock.

I didn't have any information about her party affiliation or propensity to vote, since she received her ballot at another address and wasn't listed in my app. So I was surprised when she mentioned, almost sheepishly, that she was a registered Republican and usually voted for Republicans. I said, "Oh, interesting! Tell me more about that." She said, "I just registered to vote when I was in high school, and picked a party kind of at random. But I don't really know the difference between Republicans and Democrats." I explained that Democrats tended to be much more in line with the priorities she had talked about, like investing in social services, mental health programs, paying workers a living wage, and funding for schools. I told her how my candidate stood on some of the issues that were most important to her, and that if he were elected, he'd work to improve those areas.

Toward the end of our conversation, Leticia tentatively asked me, "How would I go about reregistering as a Democrat?" I asked for her phone number and texted her a link to the California Secretary of State's website where she could reregister online, and she said she would think about it. As we said goodbye, she thanked me for coming by and listening to her concerns. This was another example of how talking with the person in front of me might not only have earned us another vote, but might have helped a voter change their party registration from Republican to Democrat.

Prioritize People over Checklists

In late October 2018, dusk was falling on a Saturday night. It felt like a suburban ghost town – apparently everyone was out having way more fun than I was, since the houses were dark, the driveways were empty, and nobody was answering their door. Before it got completely dark, I wanted to make contact with one more voter. I saw a dad playing catch with his three young kids in the street, so I called out, "Hi! Are you eligible to vote, by any chance?" The dad, Arun, said he was, so I introduced myself and explained what I was doing.

He listened to what I had to say, then told me, "I wasn't quite sure how the ballot worked." I asked if he'd already received it in the mail, and he said yes. I said, "Why don't you go get it and I'll show you? It's pretty easy once you know how it works." So he went in his house and came back out with his ballot. He turned on the light in his garage, and we spread out the pages of the ballot on the trunk of his car. His three kids all gathered around, their eyes wide.

I got a piece of scratch paper, and drew a mockup of a sample race between Candidate A and Candidate B. "See, you fill in the middle of this arrow next to either Candidate A or Candidate B's name, whichever one you want to vote for," I said, demonstrating on the piece of scratch paper. I also showed him how to sign and date the vote-by-mail ballot envelope, and explained how to return it in time to be counted.

I told him why I was supporting the Democratic Congressional candidate. Arun seemed to resonate with his priorities, and mentioned he wasn't a big fan of Trump. Toward the end of the conversation, he said with a trace of embarrassment, "I haven't voted since I became a citizen 12 years ago, but I was thinking I might vote this year." I said, "This would be a great time to start voting. Do you think you could fill out your ballot this weekend and get it in the mail on Monday?" He said he could probably do that. Then I turned to his three kids and said, "It's great that you got to see how voting works. In a few years, all of you will be old enough to vote, too!"

Arun wasn't on my voter contact list, perhaps because he had never voted before. But instead of knocking on three or four more doors where nobody was home, I was able to spend 15 minutes helping a random voter get one step closer to casting their first-ever ballot. I also got to show three future voters how elections work. And in that Congressional election, the Democratic candidate eked out a victory, flipping the seat from red to blue with just 862 votes – perhaps with the help of Arun's very first ballot.

Workers Are Voters, Too

During GOTV weekend in 2022, I was looking for three voters whose address was listed in a commercial district. It was a bit weird, because the area didn't look zoned for residential units; yet the household had three registered Democrats, so I really wanted to find them. I went into a store because it was the closest location I could find to the voters' address. I asked the two employees, a young man and woman, if they could help me find the address.

They both whipped out their phones and tried to help me, but no luck. I thanked them for trying, then asked, "So… are either of *you* eligible to vote, by any chance?" It turns out they both were, but neither had paid much attention to the upcoming elections, partly because they'd both been really sick. The young man, Eduardo, said he would probably vote, but needed to do some more research. We talked about his priority issues, and I offered him a flyer about my candidate.

Then I turned to the young woman, Alicia. She was very nice, but said, "You know, I just try to stay out of politics. Half of my family is very pro-Trump, and the other half hates him. We just have to agree to disagree, or better yet, not talk about politics at all." I said, "I totally get that – it sounds really stressful to be in the middle of that." Then I paused for a moment and said, "Setting aside politics, if *you* were running the country, what two or three things would you change?"

As the mother of young children, she was very concerned about tolerance and treating people well. She said how farmworkers deserve to earn more money because of how hard they work, and I mentioned that my candidate fought to raise the minimum wage and to get overtime pay for farmworkers during his time as a state assemblyman.

Then Alicia talked about how important abortion rights were, and that she'd want to reinstate Roe v. Wade to protect a woman's right to choose. She mentioned that she had recently experienced an ectopic pregnancy. Her doctor said if she'd come in a few days later, she might have been in danger of losing her life. I said, "That sounds so scary! I'm *really* glad you're okay. Your kids need you." I paused for a moment, then added, "It's really lucky that you don't live in a state like Texas, where it would have been really hard to get the care you needed under these new laws."

We talked about how life is complicated, and it's not always black and white. I told her that my candidate was pro-choice, and that there was a ballot initiative to amend the California Constitution to protect a woman's right to choose. "Since you have such strong feelings about this issue, voting would be a great way to make your voice heard," I said.

By the end of the conversation, Alicia said she was thinking more about voting. She said, "I recently moved out of my family's house, and my ballot is still at their place." She seemed reluctant to stir up a hornet's nest by going back and retrieving her ballot, when politics was such a contentious issue in her family. I said, "You know, whether you vote and how you vote are your business – nobody else needs to know about that. You can actually go to the polling place this Tuesday, and reregister to vote at your new address. By chance, have you gotten any mail at your new place – like a phone or electricity bill?"

She said she had, so I said, "Great! Just bring that, along with your driver's license or California ID, and then you can reregister and also vote on the spot." I told her where the polling place was – just a few blocks away from where we were – and the hours it would be open on Election Day the following week. I also asked if there was anyone she respected who she could talk with about the issues on the ballot. Alicia said, "Yeah, my brother is very liberal. He can be kind of preachy, but he's really smart." I said, "I get it – I don't like being preached at, either. But since he's smart, maybe he would have some interesting information about some of the candidates and issues, and would at least give you some food for thought." At the end of the conversation, she said, "Yeah, I know I should probably vote. I'll think about it."

I never did manage to find the three voters listed in my app. However, by asking for help and then engaging the ones in front of me at their workplace, I was able to have in-depth conversations with two other voters, completely by chance!

Vote Tripling and Expanding Your Reach

If I've invested time in a conversation with a community member – whether or not they're a voter – and they're supportive of my candidate, I try to leverage that enthusiasm. The easiest ask is "vote tripling." No, this is *not* asking them to vote three times – something that's obviously illegal, not to mention immoral. Instead, it's a great way to get like-minded people to vote. I ask strong supporters to name three people they can personally talk with to encourage them to also vote for my candidate. (Asking them to name specific people they know – family members, friends, co-workers, neighbors – helps them visualize actually doing it, and is more effective than a general suggestion to "tell everyone you know.")[13]

Sometimes I try to frame this in a way that underscores the voter's deep roots in the community. I might say, "Thanks so much for talking with me, and your support of Candidate X. This election is going to be so close, and we need everyone to get out and vote. I'm wondering if you can think of three people you can talk with to encourage them to vote for Candidate X as well."

If they seem open to the idea, I might say, "Could you tell me their first names and how you know them?" (Like making a plan to vote, having them specify who these people are and how they know them helps to solidify the intention to spread the word to these individuals.) Then I might say, "You know, it will mean so much more for you to tell them about Candidate X, since they know and trust you, rather than just me, a random stranger. Thank you so much for getting the word out there!"

If they are enthusiastic and friendly, I may also invite them to share intel about the neighborhood. If I say something like, "What are your neighbors like?" they might offer me information about who just moved in, who's friendly, who's away for a month, and which houses have people or dogs I need to watch out for. In the rare situation where I do encounter a problem while canvassing, it's good to have a possible ally in the neighborhood. I've had more than one voter, usually an older man, tell me, "If you run into any problems, just call me or knock on the door, and I'll help you out."

Everyone Is a Potential Ally

When you're talking to the person in front of you, cast your net wide. Every single person in the field has the potential to share valuable information with you, if you demonstrate respect and ask the right questions. Don't underestimate the help that children or non-citizen household members might be able to offer. Even though they aren't yet eligible to vote, they probably know eligible voters and can help you connect with them if you take the time to acknowledge them and build rapport.

I was trying to reach Cristina, but her son, Samuel, said that she was out. "What's this about?" he asked me. Samuel looked about 10, and was incredibly precocious. I explained that I was a volunteer for the Democratic Congressional candidate in the upcoming elections, and said I had some information for her and wanted to make sure she knew how to return her ballot. I asked if there was any way he could contact his mom so I could talk with her. He whipped out his tablet, called Cristina, and succinctly repeated all the information I'd told him – including the candidate's name – as efficiently as an executive assistant briefing a corporate CEO.

I asked if I might be able to speak with Cristina directly, so he pointed the tablet in my direction, and I spoke into it, explaining more about why I was there. Through the tablet, I was able to confirm that she had received her ballot, that she was a strong supporter and would be voting for all the Democratic candidates, and that she'd be sure to mail in her ballot before Election Day. I was able to note all that information in the canvassing app, and to get it from the horse's mouth – even if it was through a tablet rather than in person.

Samuel had been so helpful with connecting me with his mom that I asked if there was any way he could help me contact his neighbors. I had been trying to reach a voter next door, but there were barking dogs in the yard, and I didn't want to risk their wrath by opening the gate. So Samuel used his tablet to call the grandmother next door. Like magic, she came out to the sidewalk to chat with me a minute later. Although she wasn't eligible to vote, she understood how important the elections were. She went back inside and pulled her grandson, Vicente, away from watching the football game to talk with me. Leveraging the power of neighborly and familial connections allowed me to overcome the barriers of snarling dogs and the lure of an exciting football game so I could talk directly with Vicente. That's something I could never have done on my own!

Just down the street, I was trying to reach yet another voter, but nobody answered the door and the house was dark. I spoke with one of his neighbors, Delia, who was doing yardwork. I explained what I was doing and why I was supporting the Democratic candidate. Delia said she herself was not yet eligible to vote because she was a resident, not a citizen. Even so, she was a big supporter of the Democratic Party, and she enthusiastically agreed to pass along some information to her neighbor about my visit.

I handwrote a note to the voter, attached it to some campaign literature, and gave it to her. She promised to give it to her neighbor the next time she saw him. I'd like to think that a personalized note, hand-delivered and accompanied by Delia's endorsement of the Democratic candidates, might have a bigger impact on her neighbor than me just leaving a door hanger on his gate.

TALK TO THE DOORBELL

A quick word about smart doorbells like Nest or SkyBell. I personally tend to dislike them because I associate them with more upscale neighborhoods that use them as a sort of electronic butler to avoid talking with riffraff like me. However, sometimes they can help me connect with voters or gather important information.

If the voter is not home and the ring automatically forwards to their phone, it allows me to make voice-to-voice contact with the voter, even though they aren't on site. (It's a bit like a reverse phone bank, where I am there in person and they are remote!) Talking with a voter via their doorbell has allowed me to have the entire conversation that I would have had if they'd opened the door in person. Occasionally, this real-time conversation has also helped me find out that the voter I'm trying to reach has moved away without leaving any contact information. I note this in the app to save future canvassers from a wild-goose chase.

When I am curing ballots, I may spend all day tracking down five or six voters who had a signature mismatch or forgot to sign their ballot. My mission is to get them to sign an affidavit confirming that they did indeed vote and that their ballot should be counted. Once I was trying to reach a voter named Jessica. I could hear someone inside the house, but nobody came to the door. I rang again, and the doorbell forwarded the ring to her husband's phone while he was out driving. I explained why I was at their house. He assured me that his wife was home, but was in the shower. I took a deep breath, parked myself on her front stoop for about 10 minutes, then rang the doorbell again.

This time Jessica came to the door wrapped in a towel, still slightly dripping, and cracked open the door an inch. "Can I help you?" she asked. We both laughed a little at the awkward situation. I averted my eyes as I explained that there was a small problem with her ballot, but that it was really easy to fix. All she needed to do was sign and date the form I had brought. She opened the door another inch and I slid the clipboard through. Jessica signed the form, then told me that she had registered to vote more than a decade before when she was in high school, but her signature had changed since then. That's why her ballot signature didn't match the one on file with the DMV.

Another time when I was curing ballots, I had an entire series of interactions with Ronald, a voter I never met in person. He was a strong Democratic supporter who had a signature mismatch on his ballot. I first came by his house when he was out running errands, but his doorbell forwarded the call to his phone. I explained the situation, and he appreciated that we were making a house call to help him cure his ballot. He enthusiastically mentioned that all four voters in his household voted for our candidate.

While I had him on the line, I also asked him if I might be able to get his direct phone number in case we needed to contact him with any questions. He gladly gave it to me while we were still talking through his doorbell. (The campaign often doesn't have a voter's current phone number; some people have gotten new cell phone numbers since they registered years ago, and many others have cancelled their landline and now only use a cell phone. That's why volunteers like me show up unannounced to try to cure ballots, since sometimes the only way to reach people in a timely way is to come in person.)

After we spoke, I left a cure form at Ronald's door. I attached a Post-it note with the campaign office's phone number, and asked him to call or text us after he'd filled it out so we could pick it up. A few days later, he called the campaign office to let us know the form was ready. Since I had written down his cell phone number when we talked, I texted him directly. Here's an excerpt from our exchange:

Elizabeth:

Hi Ronald! This is Elizabeth, a volunteer with Rudy Salas. I spoke with you through your doorbell a few days ago about your ballot form. 😊 *I heard that your form was ready to be picked up. Would you consider putting it under your doormat and I can pick it up sometime this evening? If you'd prefer, I can ring the doorbell and you can hand it to me personally. Thank you so very much!*

> Ronald:
> Absolutely! We're heading to the movies at 5:30…I'll leave it in the door like you left it…thank you again for helping to save democracy….you guys are amazing & I celebrate you

Elizabeth:
Wonderful! A million thanks to you. I so appreciate your kind support. And my colleague at the campaign office said your message made her day!

> Ronald:
> Oh that's fantastic

When talking with a voter or their household member through a doorbell, I try to smile at the camera and look as friendly as possible, since they might be able to see me via their video camera. Just like phone banking, making an extra effort to be respectful, warm and appreciative can help overcome voters' suspicions and increase the chances that they'll hear me out before hanging up. With ballot curing, telling them I'm there to help make sure their vote counts usually gets their attention and allows me to move forward with getting that form signed.

Don't Be Afraid to Ask for Help

Talking with the one in front of me is invaluable, even when I really need to speak with a specific voter. One day the campaign asked me to pick up a cure form for a young voter, Javier. I arrived at his house at the appointed time, but his father told me that Javier had just left a few minutes before with his buddies for a long weekend away. I was hugely disappointed – I was so close, yet it would be at least three days until we could get this resolved!

Thinking quickly, I asked Javier's dad if he would call his son on my behalf. He agreed, and after chatting with his son for a minute, he handed the phone over so I could explain why I was there. I asked Javier if he'd consider coming back to take care of this paperwork. Luckily, Javier said yes.

While we were waiting, I asked Javier's dad about his life. He told me about coming to California decades ago from Mexico and working on various farms. I admired their adorable white puppy, who was chained up in their yard. About 10 minutes later, a big pickup truck pulled up at the house with Javier and his buddies, and Javier jumped out. He said he'd already signed the form, and went in the house to retrieve it. Getting this cure form was a team effort: Javier was willing to talk with me, his buddies agreed to turn around and delay their weekend getaway by a few minutes, and his dad went out of his way to call his son and ensure that Javier's vote would be counted.

By the way, asking a voter's family member to use their own phone to contact an absent voter is probably the best approach. It avoids putting them in the awkward situation of having to decide whether to share the voter's phone number with me or not. (If they're doubtful about my intentions, they'll probably just say no, which cuts off the possibility of real-time contact with an offsite voter.) It's also much more likely that the voter will pick up a call from their family member rather than my phone, with its unknown phone number from a different area code. Once I've made voice-to-voice contact with a voter, I can always ask them directly for their phone number, and they can choose to give it to me if they're comfortable.

Accept Invitations for Respectful Dialogue

One of my most moving experiences of talking with the one in front of me happened in November 2018. I was curing ballots after Thanksgiving in the Central Valley for the district's Democratic Congressional candidate. One morning I visited a house looking for a voter, Timoteo. His sister said that he worked the night shift and recommended that I come back at 1:30 p.m.

When I circled back that afternoon, one of Timoteo's neighbors approached me. In this majority Latino neighborhood, the neighbor was one of the few white people I'd seen. My heart sank. He looked like the stereotypical Trump voter – white, heavyset, suspicious of what I was doing. I admit, I was jumping to conclusions based on my biased read of the situation, but my first thought was, "Oh boy, it's on!"

I didn't own a car, so I'd rented a Zipcar to drive down for the long weekend. The neighbor called out, "Hey! Can I ask you about that Zipcar?" I was wary of where this conversation might be going, but figured it would be rude to ignore him. So I said, "Uh, sure. What do you want to know?" He said, "Is that like Uber?" I said, "Well, kind of – except it's more like a rental car, and I'm the driver rather than having someone drive me around."

Then he asked me what I was doing in the neighborhood. I told him that I was with the Democratic Party, helping people who had a small problem with their ballot make sure that their vote was counted. He said rather scornfully, "How much are you getting paid?" I said, "Nothing! I'm a volunteer. This work is pretty stressful for me, actually, and you couldn't pay me to do it. But this election is so important that I'm going out of my comfort zone to help out." He seemed impressed that I was there on my own dime, but saw the Oregon plates on the Zipcar and said with disbelief, "You came all the way from *Oregon* to help people fix their ballots?"

I said, "Oh, no – I'm from the Bay Area." I couldn't quite bring myself to say "San Francisco," since it's the supposed hometown of latte liberals. However, now that he'd wondered if I was a true fanatic who had crossed state lines to cure ballots, I figured that driving a mere four hours from the Bay Area looked relatively tame.

I braced myself for blowback, but instead he asked, "So why is this election so important that you'd drive all the way from the Bay Area to help people fix their ballots?" Now it was my turn to be a bit astonished. I said, "Wait – you want me to give you my pitch for why I'm supporting the Democratic candidate? But the election is over. I don't need to convince you of anything." He said, "Yeah, I'm curious what would make someone come all this way to volunteer to do this."

He seemed sincere – not sarcastic, but genuinely curious and a little surprised. I took a deep breath and told him that some of my family members had preexisting health conditions, and it was really important to me that they would always be able to access health insurance. Obamacare provided that protection, but I was worried that the Republicans would get rid of it, since they'd been trying for years to do away with Obamacare.

Then he said, "I actually agree with you on that point." (That was really not what I was expecting to hear next from him.) He said, "I actually voted twice for Obama. But then I voted for Trump." (In my head, I thought – I'm actually talking with one of those Obama-to-Trump voters I've read about in the *New York*

Times – this is amazing! I was so curious to hear about his thought process behind that pivot.)

Then he surprised me even more when he added, "Yeah, I voted for Trump, but I *really* don't like how divisive he is." I said, "Yeah, I know what you mean. The things he says are dangerous – people are going to get hurt." He nodded, then said, "But what *you* need to understand is, oil drilling is a huge part of the local economy here. Under Obama, it all went to shit. It's the same thing across the country. I have family in coal country who are miners, and Obama tried to take away their livelihood." I said, "I totally get that people need to make a living. These issues are complicated. I guess my perspective is, on balance, the Democrats are looking out more for the little guy than the Republicans are."

Then he mentioned disdainfully that he hadn't voted for the Democratic candidate because he'd seen the television ads saying how the candidate was actually from the East Coast and didn't even live in California. I said, "Actually, that's not true. His wife is a doctor, and she was getting her master's degree in public health at Johns Hopkins in Maryland for a few years. He stayed in California with their kids – kind of like a military spouse holds down the fort while a servicemember is deployed." He said, "Oh, I didn't know that." I said, "Yeah, there were a lot of negative ads that weren't true in this election, unfortunately."

Then he started telling me about the different people in the neighborhood, including the household I was there to visit. He said, "They work nights – so don't knock on their door, because they're probably sleeping right now." I said, "Actually, I have an appointment to meet with the voter. I was here earlier today, and they told me to come back at 1:30. I don't mean to be rude and cut our conversation short, but I should probably get going – I don't want to be late."

I was a little annoyed with the neighbor for lecturing me about the neighbors and why Republicans were champions of the working class. If I was honest, though, I was also impressed by how astutely he had deduced my mission and where I was from just by asking a few well-placed questions. I respected how he wasn't just trying to yank my chain about the Democrats, but shared his lived experiences of how politics affected the economy and his family members. It was also interesting to hear how he regretted his vote for Trump in 2016. And debunking the attack ad was important – in two more years, if our candidate ran again as an incumbent or a challenger, we'd need votes from people like him.

So as I was getting ready to head to Timoteo's house to cure his ballot, I said, "I really appreciate you taking the time to talk with me. My name is Elizabeth. What's your name?" He said, "Wayne." I stuck out my hand and he shook it. I said, "It's nice to meet you, Wayne." He said, "Nice to meet you, too."

Even though Wayne was not on my short list of ballots to cure, I'm so glad I took the time to talk with him. I learned a lot from our conversation, and got to challenge some of my own stereotypes. I'd like to think that I gave him a few things to think about, too – whether it was to question the accuracy of attack ads, or perhaps just having another data point in his ideas about Democrats. In this current climate where we are all led to view people with different viewpoints with suspicion, mistrust and even hatred, there is no substitute for unmediated dialogue. When it's possible, I believe these kinds of conversations are part of the healing that needs to happen to understand other people's perspectives and start to mend the deep rifts in our country.

Talk with the One Who Answers the Phone, Too

Talking with the one in front of me also applies to phone banking. In 2020 I was calling Texas in support of Democratic Senate candidate MJ Hegar, and I got in a long conversation with Rebecca, a friendly woman with a strong Southern accent. She mentioned that she'd been a lifelong Republican, but that year had decided to vote for all the Democratic candidates. I said, "Wow, that's a big shift! What made you change direction?" She shocked me by saying, "Oh, the Republicans' opposition to same-sex marriage was the last straw. I just couldn't stand how prejudiced they were on that issue." So much for my stereotypes of Southerners.

When I started to tell her more about MJ Hegar and the other Democratic candidates in Texas, Rebecca stopped me and said, "Wait – why are you telling me about Texas? I've never lived in Texas, and I live in Alabama now." Neither of us could figure out how she ended up on this call list, but we'd had such a good conversation up until that point that I didn't want to let it go to waste. I asked if she happened to know anybody in Texas, and it turned out she had quite a few friends there. I said, "There are some really great Democratic candidates this year, including some very smart and courageous women. Would you consider encouraging your friends in Texas to vote for them? Maybe you could post links to the candidates on social media." She enthusiastically agreed, so with her permission I texted her links to the website for MJ Hegar as well as the Democratic candidate who was running to represent northern Dallas in the Texas House of Representatives.

I've also turned many other "wrong number" calls into an opportunity to talk with voters, especially since they are likely unreachable any other way if the campaign doesn't have their current phone number. If they say, "You've got the wrong number," I'll say, "Oh, sorry about that. Are you eligible to vote in [name of their state], by any chance?" If they say yes, I continue the conversation as if they were the one I was assigned to talk with. I've shared information about my candidate with many people that way. I've also helped a number of voters confirm their polling location and hours, and answered other questions about voting.

When calling in October 2020 to Georgia, I was trying to reach a middle-aged woman and ended up talking with her 17-year-old daughter who said her mother wasn't home. I told her why I was calling, and asked if she'd pass along the information about the upcoming election to her mom. She said yes, and then I asked a bit about her. She said she was going to community college, and I asked what she was studying. I also asked if she was eligible to vote, and she said she would turn 18 a few days after Election Day in November. I said, "It's possible that one or both of these U.S. Senate races in Georgia might go to a runoff in January, which could decide who controls the Senate. If you get registered to vote on your birthday, you'd be eligible to vote in that election, which would be really important!"

It's never too early to start laying the groundwork for the next election, or the next generation of voters. We need to be playing the long game. Wrong numbers, leaving messages with household members, and engaging with other people we encounter along the way are all tiny steps in this direction. Talking with the one in front of you can also help you connect with those you originally set out to find. Take advantage of these opportunities to widen your scope of awareness and increase your effectiveness in the field!

Summary

- Take advantage of opportunities to talk with household members, neighbors and others you meet – even if they aren't on your official list.
- If the voter isn't home, ask their household member to call the voter from their own phone. This avoids putting the family member in an awkward position of disclosing the voter's number to you, and also increases the chances that the voter will pick up the call.
- For phone banking, anyone who picks up the call is a potential voter or ally. Ask if they're eligible to vote or know others who are, and continue the conversation as far as you can take it.

Chapter 8
Seize the Day (and the Night!)

Some people, especially high-potential voters (those who rarely or never vote), may have good intentions about voting. However, they might just need a little help getting over the hump. Life is complicated and busy. So many people are juggling work, school, child care, elder care, health issues, and much more. There are also many structural factors which can impede someone's ability to vote, such as lack of transportation, inability to afford taking time off work to vote, and language barriers. Some obstacles are intentionally designed to make voting harder; these voter suppression tools include (but aren't limited to) requiring a voter to present specific types of photo identification, reducing or eliminating early voting options, and purging people from the voter registration rolls if they've missed several elections.

If I meet a voter who expresses enthusiasm for the Democrats or my candidate but faces obstacles, I do what I can in the moment to get them one step closer to actually casting their ballot. Because people are often making hard choices between competing priorities, striking while the iron is hot decreases the chances that "later" becomes "never" when it comes to voting.

I met Jaime when I was canvassing his household. He was a strong Democratic supporter, but had just become a citizen a few months ago and wasn't registered to vote. After working for decades in the fields, he was now retired and joked that he'd become a bus driver, shuttling his four grandchildren around to all their activities. I registered him to vote on the spot using the California Secretary of State's webpage on my phone. Unfortunately, because it was so close to the election, it was too late to get a vote-by-mail ballot. He didn't have email, so with his permission I had the voter registration form and receipt sent to my email address. That night I printed it out and brought it back to him the next day so he would have paperwork to show the poll workers if they needed to see it on Election Day.

Skylar the Skeptic might say, "But that's so time-consuming! It's not really my job to register people to vote – we're just supposed to be turning out registered voters by this point in the campaign." I agree, some of these stories describe labor-intensive interactions. By all means, you are the best judge of how to most effectively spend your time. Personally, if I'm already talking with a voter and they're a strong supporter, I'll do whatever I can to remove as many barriers to voting as possible, even if that's not in my "job description."

This isn't just about the current election, but all those to follow. If I can help someone get registered, or to vote for the very first time, they are that much closer to voting in subsequent elections and hopefully becoming a consistent voter. If I don't take the time to do this, there's no guarantee that someone else will in the future. My bias is to seize those golden opportunities and make the most of them.

Concierge Follow-Up

For the 2022 midterms, I volunteered with the Rudy Salas for Congress campaign. Because I was there for a month, I got to know the staff pretty well, and developed good relationships with them. I asked if they would be willing to follow up with select voters. These were the ones whose main hesitation about committing to vote for Salas was wanting to do more research about specific policy positions that were beyond my knowledge base. The campaign staff were great, and said they'd be happy to help with that.

I tried to be judicious, but perhaps two or three times a day I encountered these kinds of voters. For example, I spoke with Alejandro, a first-time voter and college student. When I asked him what issues were most important to him, he said, "Support for public education and looking out for the little guy." Using a tool from Motivational Interviewing (see Chapter 11 for more information), I asked him, "On a scale from zero to 10, how likely are you to vote, with zero being not very likely, and 10 being very likely?" He said, "Oh, probably a five." I said, "What might boost your 'five' to a six or a seven?" He said, "If I could do more research, I'd feel more comfortable making a decision."

I offered him some campaign literature, but also said, "I'm just a volunteer, and I don't have all the details about Rudy Salas's policy positions. But I'm in touch with his campaign staff, and they're much more knowledgeable than I am. Would it be helpful if someone from the team reached out to you and answered any questions about public education funding and taking care of the little guy?" Alejandro said, "Yeah, that would probably help me feel more confident about voting for Rudy."

I wrote down his cell phone number, noted the best days and times to reach him, and asked if it was all right to leave a voicemail or send a text. He said yes, and outlined his availability. I texted all this information to the campaign staff, and one of the members reached out to him.

Make Voters Feel Special

Similarly, I talked with Santiago, a thirtysomething go-getter who had been an economics major in college. He hadn't had a chance to do much research about the Congressional race and was still undecided. He had some conservative positions, like believing that earned income should not be taxed as much as it was, but also believed we needed to invest more in infrastructure. I found it hard to get traction in our conversation. Maybe it was my own sensitivity, but I felt like he was mansplaining to me about how the economy worked. I got the vibe that he might be more convinced if he heard the same information coming from a man rather than from me.

I tried to play to his ego. I said that he had some pretty astute observations on the economy and wondered if it might be helpful to talk with a campaign staffer who was more knowledgeable about those specific issues. Sometimes framing it as the equivalent of "Would you like to speak with my manager?" helps voters feel important and special. I said, "I'm sure you're really busy with work, but maybe you could just talk with them for a couple of minutes as one more data point in your decision-making process?" He gave me his cell number and said that the best time to reach him was at 10 a.m., any day of the week, and that people could text him first and he'd call back if he was available.

Obviously, this arrangement only works if the particular campaign you are working with has the bandwidth to make a few follow-up calls. So it's worth asking at the beginning of your shift if someone is willing to be available for this kind of occasional, tailored outreach. It's one way to provide that additional touch to an on-the-fence voter, which in some cases could help us earn their vote. So many people feel cynical about campaigns only coming around at election time; sometimes they feel flattered that their concerns are important enough to merit a personal call from someone higher up the food chain than I am.

The other advantage is obtaining current contact information for the campaign database, which hopefully can be folded into their record. Many voters are unreachable for phone banking because they've changed their phone number. This is one way to facilitate meaningful follow-up with voters who actually *want* to be called, and are primed to hear from the campaign.

Become a Taxi Driver for the Day

On Election Day, I was trying to find another voter who lived in the back unit of an apartment complex. I was too scared to go back there alone, since there were some loudly barking dogs guarding the building. As it started to rain, another resident of the building, a young man named Craig, came out to see what all the noise was about. When I explained why I was there, he called off the dogs and escorted me to the back unit to talk with his neighbor.

That voter was busy on the phone and couldn't talk with me, so I started chatting Craig up about the elections. As his girlfriend came out to join us, Craig talked about how important voting was, especially for young people. However, he mentioned that he hadn't actually had a chance to go vote himself. His girlfriend, Maria, was less enthusiastic and had never voted, but was listening to our conversation. I asked Craig, "What, if anything, might make it more likely that you'll be able to vote today?" He said, "Oh, I'll walk over to the polling place as soon as the rain lets up."

I knew it was forecast to keep raining until the polls closed, so I asked him, "What are you doing in 10 minutes? Can I give you guys a ride over there?" It was now or never – they were available, I was right there, and my car was a block away. They agreed, so I got my car and picked them up a few minutes later in the pouring rain. I gave them Democratic slate cards, which they read as we drove over there. Maria asked whether Melissa Hurtado, the Democratic candidate for State Senate, was a good person to vote for. I agreed enthusiastically.

It was my first time ever giving people a ride to the polls, and it was one of the most exciting experiences I've ever had as a canvasser. I knew they were both a bit nervous about voting, so I sat in the observer section of the polling place (next to some older Republican women decked out in red, white and blue) and waited for them while they cast their ballots. I wanted Craig and Maria to see that I was there for them through the whole process. I wasn't going to abandon them or make them find their own way home in the downpour. Afterward, I took a picture of the two of them in the parking lot next to the "Vote Here" sign, each of them wearing their "I Voted" stickers. It was only the second time Craig had voted, and the very first time for Maria. When I dropped them off, we gave each other hugs, and they thanked me for the ride.

These were two young voters who weren't on my list and who I happened to meet just by chance (remember "Talk with the one in front of you"?) I found out later that although there was a volunteer who was driving voters to the polls, people had to wait several hours for a ride. By then, Craig and Maria might have gotten busy with something else. Try not to let that happen! Instead, ride their wave of enthusiasm (or at least their ripple of willingness), and do what you can to help them get to the finish line.

By the way, State Senator Hurtado won her race for reelection by only 20 votes – out of more than 136,000 ballots cast. It's possible that Craig and Maria helped put her over the top that day.

Accompany Voters On That 'Last Mile'

Later that day, I met another voter named Ana. She was in her late 80s, was visually impaired, had mobility issues, was recovering from a bad cold, and only spoke Spanish. She also said she and her husband had never received their ballots in the mail. Ana was a committed Democrat, but didn't think she was up for voting in person because of all her health issues, especially because it was raining and she'd been sick. I assured her that I could drive her to the doorway of the polling place and could wait for her while she voted, but she didn't think it was a good idea. As late afternoon edged toward nightfall, I could feel her vote slipping away.

Her husband, Arturo, came home. He wasn't very friendly, and bluntly told me he wasn't going to vote. Still, I sat on their front porch for about 20 minutes in the pouring rain, looking up options on my phone and calling the voter hotline to explain Ana's situation. The hotline volunteer told me that unfortunately, it was too late for Ana to register for remote access voting, since she would have had to request that at least a week before the election.

Talk about a "last mile" problem: it was so frustrating to be at the house of two registered Democrats who were less than a mile from the polling place, yet would not be voting – one because of health limitations, and the other because he had decided he wasn't voting. But Ana and Arturo probably heard me talking with the voter hotline on their porch, because I had the volunteer on speakerphone while I looked up possible resources on my phone.

Maybe I wore them down by spending so much time on their porch, because eventually Arturo came out again and gruffly said, "All right, I'll vote – but I don't know where to go." Ana still didn't feel up for voting, but he was willing. I tried to explain where the polling place was, but he didn't seem to recognize the name of the site or understand my directions. I thought about having him follow me in my car. However, because the route included some left turns onto busy streets on that rainy evening, I asked if I could just drive him there in my car. He agreed, so I drove him there, waited for him in the observer area, and drove him home. When I dropped him off, he thanked me and shook my hand.

Demonstrating persistence and a willingness to pull out all the stops can inspire other people to step up as well. Or maybe Arturo just wanted me off his porch! But whatever the reason, that was one more vote for Democrats. And while we lost Ana's vote that day, one out of two was better than none at all.

EFFECTIVE IS BETTER THAN EFFICIENT

In November 2022, I was trying to cure the ballot of a young voter, Yesenia. Her home address was listed as a store in a commercial district, and it was closed the weekend afternoon I stopped by. I taped a Post-it note to the door with a request for her to call the campaign office, and also took a picture of the store's hours so I knew when would be a good time to circle back.

A few days later, I went to the store again and talked with the owner. He said that Yesenia was his granddaughter. They'd gotten my note but hadn't had a chance to follow up yet. I asked if he might be able to give her a call with his cell phone so I could talk with her directly. She picked up the call. He handed the phone to me, and I explained why I was there. Yesenia said, "I'll be at home most of the afternoon – do you want to just come by later?" I said, "How far are you from your grandfather's store?" She said, "Oh, about 10 minutes." I said, "Can I come by in about 15 minutes?" She said that would be fine.

Even though I would have to drive across town and had other ballots to cure that were closer by, I decided to go for it, since she was available at that moment. We got the cure form taken care of right away. Yesenia was a community college student, and I was glad to cure her ballot before she got pulled away by other responsibilities. I also explained the importance of having her signature match the one on her state ID, which hopefully she'll keep in mind for future elections.

Sometimes the most efficient route is not always the most effective one. If someone is available right now, I do my best to jump on that opportunity before the trail goes cold.

Take Your Time

Sometimes seizing the day (or night) means slowing down. It was dinnertime, and I was trying to cure yet another ballot when I knocked on the door of a Spanish-speaking elder named Joaquin. He answered the door, but seemed a bit suspicious at first. However, after I explained why I was there, he warmed up and invited me in. He seemed intimidated by the form. (Of course, it was only available in English, even though a sizable chunk of the district's electorate is monolingual Spanish-speaking.) I did a rough translation of the bureaucratic language for him, and showed him how to fill it out.

He had a rather long name – first name, middle name, and two last names – and seemed to have some difficulty with writing. He kept making mistakes as he was signing his name, and apologized with some embarrassment about how long it was taking. I told him, "Don't worry. I have plenty of time, and lots of extra blank forms. If you make a mistake, we can just throw it away and try again. It's no problem."

As we sat in the dim light of his kitchen, a clock ticked away loudly during the 15 or 20 minutes it took for Joaquin to complete the form correctly. I tried to slow my breathing, not worry about time passing, and just be present with him as he put all his effort and focus into the task. When he finally filled out the form to his satisfaction on the fourth try, we were both relieved. He shook my hand warmly, and mentioned how other canvassers had come by his house during the campaign but were at his door for just 30 seconds before leaving. He seemed to appreciate my patience and the time I spent with him.

I was touched by the effort that he invested to get this right, and grateful that he allowed me to sit with him through a challenging and somewhat stressful process. I wrote down my name and phone number, just in case he had any election-related questions in the future. He folded up the paper and put it in his wallet for safekeeping, which felt like a huge honor.

Late the next day, I received a phone call from an unknown number. No, it wasn't Joaquin. It was actually a campaign staffer I'd never met who had been redeployed from another part of the district to help with ballot curing. Unfortunately, there was a glitch with our app; voters who had already cured their ballots were being asked to fill out the form again. Apparently Joaquin had tried to explain that he'd already taken care of this, but the staffer wanted to confirm this was accurate. Joaquin pulled my number out of his wallet, which is how the staffer was able to call me to iron this out.

After I finished explaining all that, I asked if I could speak with Joaquin. The staffer passed the phone to Joaquin, and I thanked him again for his time and support, and told him not to worry – his cure form had already been turned in, and he was all set. Joaquin seemed reassured, and it was an unexpected gift to talk with him again and see that he trusted me enough to reach out.

As I was writing this book a year and a half later, I got a call from an unknown number. It was Joaquin! He had just filled out his ballot for the 2024 primary election, and wanted to make sure that he was signing his name correctly. He had kept my number and taken me up on my offer to call any time for questions related to the elections. I was able to look up the picture I took of his cure form and confirm that it matched the way he had just signed his ballot. And again, I was humbled and honored that he would think to reach out to me to make sure his ballot was signed correctly.

One other note: when working with elders, it's especially important to slow down. (I've learned about this from interviewing geriatricians for my day job as a medical writer.) Older adults might need a bit more time to think or respond to you. They may have hearing loss or vision impairment, arthritis, or shortness of breath. They may also feel some shame that they're moving slower than they used to, or that they're having to correct a mistake on their ballot. Sit down if you can, especially for ballot curing, which is hard to do just using a clipboard. Remember that their fine motor coordination and arm strength may have diminished with age, so letting them sit at a table makes the process easier. This is especially important when ballot curing, because you want their signature to be legible – it's the whole point of getting a signed affidavit!

Just as important, sitting down with them communicates that you're not in a hurry. It also puts you at the same level as them; you're not a scolding, impatient teacher, tapping your foot while a slow student takes up your precious time. Instead, your body language can help communicate that you are fellow human beings in this endeavor together. Your patience, compassion and appreciation can help transform a bureaucratic transaction into another slender thread in the beautiful web of democratic engagement that we are all weaving together, in community.

Seize the Night, Too

It was already dark when I went to Liza's house to cure her ballot. Her parents said they were all strong Democrats, and that Liza would be home from work in half an hour. I left a cure form and a Post-it with my phone number on it so she could call me to pick it up after she signed it.

I had already tried to contact most of the other people on that day's ballot cure list, and was getting cold, tired and hungry. Instead of trying to squeeze in one more house or revisiting another voter, I sat in my car across the street and ate a snack. When I saw a car pull up in front of the house, I got out of my car. I tried to sound as friendly and apologetic as possible as I called out, "Hey, is that Liza? I'm sorry to bother you. My name is Elizabeth, and I'm a volunteer with the Democratic Party. There was a small issue with your ballot, but it's really easy to fix, and I have a form you can sign to take care of it. I already talked with your parents and they mentioned you'd probably be home around now, so I thought I'd just wait for you."

Liza looked a little startled, but understood what I was there for. She signed the form on the spot, before she had even gone inside her house. That felt like a victory. If I know someone is due home soon, sometimes staying put and waiting for people to come to me can be more fruitful than running around trying to connect with other voters who may or may not be available.

For canvassing and ballot curing, there's a golden window of opportunity between about 5 p.m. and 7 p.m. when people are actually home from work, before they go to bed or when it veers into the rude zone to knock on their door. If I've already established friendly contact with the household, it can be more acceptable to stake out their house or reinitiate contact a bit later than I would for a house I haven't had any contact with yet.

SEIZE THE DAY (AND THE NIGHT!)

THINK LIKE A SOCIAL WORKER

Phone banking also provides opportunities to seize the day. In October 2020 I was calling Wisconsin, and talked with a registered Democrat named Marcela. She faced so many obstacles to voting: she had recently moved from Milwaukee out to the suburbs but hadn't reregistered to vote, so she never got her vote-by-mail ballot. She was also legally blind, and couldn't use the internet because she couldn't see well enough to read the screen. Obviously, she didn't drive. She relied on her 18-year-old son to help her with getting around, but he didn't have a car, either. She also shared that she was really tight on money, so taking a cab, Uber or Lyft was out of the question.

I could have just given Marcela the number for ride assistance. However, since she'd just told me that she was visually impaired and couldn't use the internet, I knew she probably wouldn't have the capacity to follow up. I asked if I could get back to her, so I wrote down her phone number. Then I researched the voter ride assistance programs in the area. Milwaukee had several programs, but out in the suburb where she now lived, the only resource available was a ride service run by the county. I called up the county ride scheduler, and while I had her on the phone I called Marcela back and patched her in on a three-way call. That way, all three of us could talk at the same time. (More information about the logistics of three-way calling in Chapter 15.) Marcela and the scheduler agreed on a day and time when she could get a ride to City Hall to vote early, but the scheduler said she'd need to call back to confirm.

A few days later I followed up with Marcela to see if her ride had been nailed down. She said the ride was confirmed, but then said that she needed her son to accompany her to help her navigate. She'd never been to City Hall before and was legally blind, and she was sure she'd get lost between the car and the registrar's office.

I kicked myself for not thinking of this earlier. But while I had her on the line, I initiated *another* three-way call to the county. We talked with the same ride scheduler we'd spoken with the first time. I asked if Marcela's son could also get a ride to City Hall, since he was 18 and also eligible to vote. The case worker said no – the ride program was only for people with disabilities.

Invoking the power of the Americans with Disabilities Act (with the friendly-but-firm implication that it would be much easier for her to say yes rather than risk the hassle of us filing a complaint), I said, "But since Marcela is legally blind and won't be able to find the registrar's office on her own, wouldn't a reasonable accommodation be to let her son accompany her to vote?" The scheduler paused and said, "Okay, that's a good point. Her son can ride with her in the van."

Marcela's son didn't have a driver's license or state ID, so unfortunately he wouldn't be able to vote himself, since Wisconsin is a voter ID state. I did have information about VoteRiders, a nonprofit that helps low-income people obtain a photo ID. But Marcela said, "He's busy playing video games and doesn't have time to talk." Even though I asked a few times if I could talk with him directly, she declined to put him on the phone. Sigh – you can't win them all.

However, when I checked back a few days later, Marcela had indeed voted! Even though her son hadn't voted because he didn't have a photo ID, I was thrilled that together, Marcela and I were able to navigate the hurdles of disability and transportation scarcity to get her all the way to the polls and back. Marcela's vote was one of 20,682 that put Wisconsin's 10 electoral votes in Biden's column – a razor-thin 0.6% margin of victory that made all the difference in the 2020 presidential election. That was worth every minute I spent on securing this one vote!

There are other ways to maximize voter contact on the phone. Using the same three-way calling approach, you can call the voter ride assistance number or voter hotline so you and the voter can navigate the bureaucracy together. That eliminates the need for a voter to write down the phone number and find the time and energy to make the call on their own later on. It also allows you to be their advocate, asking follow-up questions or helping to clarify what the government employee or volunteer is saying if there's any doubt. For voters who have cognitive impairment or whose first language is not English, having you on the line may make the difference between them voting or not.

BUILD ON A GOOD CONNECTION

Another way I've tried to leverage a good phone bank conversation with a voter is to ask if I can text them the candidate's website, or other useful information such as the address and hours of their polling place or early voting location. I have also asked if they'd be willing to post that information to their social media accounts. Sometimes I'll appeal to their strengths and connections by saying, "I so appreciate your support of Candidate X! *(slight pause)* This election is going to be so close. If I texted you Candidate X's website, would you be willing to post it to Facebook or other social media and urge your friends and family to vote for them as well? I'm doing my best as a volunteer to get the word out, but it would mean so much more to people who know and trust you if *you* recommended that they vote for Candidate X."

If the voter agrees, I send a text with the information. I usually cut and paste the same basic message, but customize it using their name and referencing something we talked about, so they know it's not a canned message. (See Chapter 15 for some technical tips.) Here's an example:

Hi Juliana! Thanks so much for talking today, and for your support of Candidate X. Please encourage your friends and family to vote for Candidate X as well. Her website is www.CandidateXForCongress.com. Thanks for being a voter! Respectfully, Elizabeth

If we've had a good phone conversation, sometimes I ask voters if it would be all right for me to check back in a few days or weeks to see if they had any other questions. Usually people say yes. I confirm their phone number and write it down in my elections notebook, along with their name and a few notes about the things we talked about. I loop back to them closer to the election. Most of the time, people remember me right away, and we can pick up the conversation where we left off without having to go through the whole spiel again. I'm able to find out if they've voted yet or not, and can use that as another opportunity to thank them for their support and ask them to remind three friends to vote.

I also try to casually reference something they mentioned in our first call, whether it's asking how their son's basketball game went or saying I hope the rest of their game night was fun. (This is where writing down a few notes about what we talked about in my notebook can help jog my memory.) It's a way to distinguish myself from the slew of other calls they might be getting about the election. It also signals that I remember our previous conversation and see them as a whole person with a full life, not just another vote to chase down. It's subtle, but helps shift the vibe of the call from telemarketer to friendly acquaintance. Not surprisingly, people tend to appreciate this concierge approach.

In addition to providing one more reminder to vote or an additional opportunity to answer any last-minute questions from voters, it's incredibly rewarding to follow up and hear when someone has actually cast their ballot. It gives me useful feedback if these conversations are actually helping turn out voters. That boosts my energy, and makes me want to keep calling and knocking on doors!

To recap, many people really want to vote, but face a lot of hurdles. Take advantage of the shining moment! Whether you're at their door or on the phone, help them overcome some of those obstacles and cut through the red tape. Even if you spend extra time driving across town, waiting around, or wrangling the bureaucracy, it's worth it. Every vote counts!

Summary

- Strike while the iron is hot! Help the voter get to the finish line, whether that's registering them to vote on the spot, driving them to the polls, or waiting 15 minutes in front of their house to cure their ballot. A little extra effort can make the difference between almost voting and *actually* voting.
- Take your time, and remember that it's more important to be effective than efficient.
- For phone banking, offer to text them follow-up information. Utilize three-way calling to help nail down assistance with rides, obtaining a photo ID, or other follow-up tasks that might otherwise fall by the wayside.

Chapter 9
Help Them Visualize Voting

One staple of get-out-the-vote efforts is helping people make a plan to vote. Studies have shown that helping voters make a specific plan to vote can increase turnout.[14] Will they vote early or on Election Day? Will they vote by mail or in person? If they're voting in person, what day and time will they vote? Where will they be coming from, and what will they be doing before they go vote? Walking the voter through all these logistics is a rehearsal for actually voting. Even if they face obstacles, like bad weather, a busy work or school schedule, or transportation challenges, thinking out loud about their plan ahead of time increases the chances they will follow through.

Take a Picture

Building on this idea, in the 2022 midterms I started thinking about other ways to help people visualize voting. I began making the polling place and the ballot drop box site my first ports of call when I started a canvassing shift. I took pictures of each with my phone, and noted local landmarks. If a voter had recently moved to town or had limited literacy, they might not know the name of the church or street, but when I showed them a picture, they recognized places right away. I could also tell them, "It's right across from City Hall," or "It's next to the Vallarta supermarket," since I had gone in person and seen what was around there. When I led a small team of other canvassers, I texted them these images the night before our canvass so they'd have them on their phones, too.

Sample photo of polling place

Because the ballot drop boxes were relatively new in the county where I was canvassing, I could use the picture as a visual aid to explain how they worked. I might say, "They're open 24/7 through Election Day. If you're busy or worried about your ballot getting delayed in the mail, you can just drop it off any time. You can do it at 6 a.m. on your way to work, or at midnight when you're getting off your shift." Many people thanked me, since they weren't familiar with how drop boxes worked.

HELP THEM VISUALIZE VOTING

Sample photo of ballot drop box
(white box at left of building entrance)

Because some drop boxes were a bit hidden, I could enlarge the photo and show them exactly where they were located. "This drop box is on the left side of library entrance – it's this big white metal box. Just put your ballot through the slot and you're done voting!" Even if some voters were hesitant to talk with me at first, I helped establish credibility by offering useful, nonpartisan information. That made them more willing to open up about what issues were most important to them in the upcoming elections.

CREATE A MAP

This works for phone banking as well. Some well-funded phone banks may conveniently provide information about the polling place on the screen for each voter you talk with. You can type those addresses into Google Maps and quickly find cross-streets and nearby landmarks to help voters visualize where to go, if they aren't already familiar with the site.

Sadly, other phone banks – especially those for downballot races like state assembly – usually run on a shoestring and have the bare minimum of information about the voter. Sometimes they don't include basic information like where they can go vote. However, there are workarounds. You can look up the secretary of state or county recorder's listing of early voting places and polling places online, and bookmark those websites for easy reference when talking with a voter.

When I was calling Spanish-speaking voters in Milwaukee to encourage them to vote early for the 2020 presidential election, I took it a step further. I knew that most of the voters we were trying to reach that week lived on the South Side of Milwaukee. Using the city registrar's listing of early voting centers, I created a Google Map with a pin for each; the purple pins were the ones on the South Side. (You can see the map here: *https://tinyurl.com/MKE-EarlyVote*)

If we had the address of the voter, we could type it into the search box on the map and see which early voting centers were closest to their home. If we didn't have a current address, I would ask them to tell it to me so I could look up their closest early voting centers, and zoom in to find the nearest cross-street and local landmarks. I also included notes for each early voting center that would appear in a popup box. That way I could quickly identify what days and hours they were open (since each site had a different schedule), whether voters needed an appointment to vote early there, and the final day to vote early at that location.

For that particular phone bank universe, almost none of the voters I spoke with knew where or how to vote early. They truly appreciated receiving this information, and it gave them more options for casting their ballot if work, illness, or other obstacles might have deterred them from voting on Election Day.

Even though it was a fair amount of work to set this up, it felt worthwhile. I also led a couple of pop-up Spanish-language phone banks for some of the volunteers I'd helped train through our Spanish for Activists online workshops, so we were able to share this resource with another 20 phone bankers.

'Every Vote Adds Up'

Another variation on the theme of helping people visualize voting is inviting them to talk about *why* they're voting, and why it's so important. I found this especially effective with young voters who were passionate about voting. If they were strong supporters and said they were definitely going to vote, I asked if I could use my phone to make a short video or audio recording of them. (You can make video recordings using your camera app; for audio recording, you can use the Voice Memos app on an iPhone, and the Recorder app on Android phones.) If you're social media-savvy, with the voter's permission you can share the recording online and tag them so they can share it with their networks.

Some questions you could ask them:

- Why are you voting?
- Why is it so important to vote?
- What would you say to someone who tells you, "My vote doesn't matter?"

- What's one thing that you wish more people knew about voting?

I was inspired by the thoughtfulness and insight of these young voters. I met Rosa when she came out to check the mail. When I told her why I was there, she rolled her eyes and told me, "I've been getting so many calls and postcards about the election!" She showed me the postcard that she'd just pulled out of her mailbox, reminding her to mail in her ballot. She also showed me the phone log on her phone. Every recent call (besides those from her mom) was from a phone banker!

Even though she found all this a bit annoying, she said she would be voting, partly because her mom was making her. I asked her, "Can I make a short recording of you talking about why it's so important to vote? Then if I meet people who say, 'My vote doesn't matter,' instead of them having to listen to me, I can just play them your recording." Here's part of what she said:

> *There is a movie I saw about voting. There was one specific voter who didn't vote, and it was his vote that counted, because it was a tie. I've heard from the callers who have been calling me that it's really going to be a close one. So… if me and my family don't vote and they're just missing that five votes to get ahead, our votes do count. Everything adds up. Just like they say every penny adds up, I think every vote adds up. (laughs)*

I also talked with Gissel, who was especially motivated to vote because of the recent overturning of Roe v. Wade. She told me:

> *I think it's very important to vote because there are a lot of things going on. Especially right now for me, it's the abortion laws. We have moms, we have sisters, we have cousins, we have aunts… I think it's important for them to have the choice.*

> There are so many medical emergencies that we truly don't understand. And sometimes an abortion is the best option. I truly believe in it, so you have to vote.
>
> This little thing helps. It's for the future, and not just my future or your future, but your kids' futures. They need a better world, because it's not so great right now. We need to help them. We need to guide them. If voting for someone helps, then that's what we should do.

People are often honored that a stranger thinks what they have to say is worth documenting and sharing with others. Recording voters' thoughts about the election doesn't just inspire other people. It also helps them articulate their own reasoning, and may strengthen their commitment to following through so they can live up to the advice they're giving to others!

Summary

- When canvassing, take a picture of the closest ballot drop box, polling place and early voting location, and make a note of local landmarks. You can show these pictures to voters on your phone to help explain where to vote.
- When phone banking, if the computer program doesn't provide you with a voter's polling place or drop box, bookmark the secretary of state or county recorder's listings on your web browser so you can look up this information for voters. If you're phone banking to a particular city, you can also create a Google Map and "pin" the city's early voting sites or polling places. By typing in the voter's address, you can provide directions to the closest one.

- If you meet enthusiastic voters, especially young people, ask if you can record and share a short video or audio clip of them talking about why voting is so important. This reinforces their intention to vote, and can help motivate others.

Chapter 10
Embrace Your Inner Detective

In addition to cultivating "soft" skills like empathy, compassion, and focusing 80% of the conversation on the voter to draw out their concerns and hopes, I've also honed my detective skills when trying to connect with a voter. Sometimes this requires asking lots of questions, paying attention to clues, and jumping through hoops to finally reach my goal.

If nobody answers the door after the first knock, I usually wait 20 or 30 seconds, then knock again. I respect people's right to privacy, but sometimes being politely persistent has gotten voters to open their door.

I always tune my ears for signs of life. Is someone using the weed whacker in the back yard and can't hear the doorbell? I'll follow the sounds and give them a friendly wave, and sometimes we'll chat over the fence. One time in Chesterfield County, Virginia, the house and yard were quiet, but I heard a lot of noise in the garage. It turns out the voter had converted her garage into a childcare center. Although she was harried with half a dozen toddlers running around her, at least I was able to give her some campaign literature and my 30-second spiel about the candidate.

While channeling my Sherlock Holmes persona takes persistence and attentiveness, being honest, respectful and friendly with everyone I meet often makes them more willing to help me get in touch with a voter. One Saturday morning in November 2022 I was curing ballots in the Central Valley. I was trying to find Gilberto, but nobody answered the door. I knocked on the doors of his neighbors on both sides of his apartment. They told me that Gilberto and his brother worked until 10 p.m. Then they pointed out Gilberto's car at the curb and said that since it was there, he was probably home, but might be sleeping after working late. I asked the neighbors to let him know I'd come by, and also left a note at the door.

As I was getting ready to leave, the door opened. It was Gilberto's identical twin brother, and I explained why I was there. Finally, he went to the back of the house and got his brother to come to the door, and we were able to complete the cure form. Although I had to talk with three other people first, I finally connected with Gilberto – mission accomplished!

Keep Going Until You Hear 'No' – or 'Yes'!

I was curing another ballot in 2022 when I pulled up at the listed address. At first I thought I had the wrong building. It was next to the hospital and looked like clinic office, but turned out to be a nursing home. The front desk felt as unwelcoming as Checkpoint Charlie – the famous (or infamous) militarized crossing point in the Berlin Wall during the Cold War. I told the staff person, "My name is Elizabeth Chur, and I'm a volunteer with the Democratic Party. I'm here to help Juanita Reyes fix a small problem with her ballot." The staff person eyed me skeptically and said, "Are you authorized to speak with her?" With as much confidence as I could muster, I said, "Yes, I am!" She said sternly, "Who authorized you?" I said, "The Rudy Salas campaign."

That seemed to satisfy her, so she rather reluctantly told me to go down the hall, turn right, and walk to the end of the hallway. "Talk with the nurse at the nursing station," she said. "*If* she approves your request, she'll tell you how to find Juanita." (A friend who is a geriatric social worker later explained that if the voter is not conserved due to mental incapacity, *they* get to decide whether they want to speak with you – not the staff. This is the voter's residence, not a prison.)

I marched down the hallway, trying to look as official as possible with my clipboard, and braced myself for another interrogation. When I got to the nursing station, I explained why I was there and asked if I could speak with Mrs. Reyes. Without hesitation, the nurse pointed to a beautiful elder in a wheelchair a few feet away. "That's her," she said. "Really?" I said with some disbelief. I was prepared to field more hard questions, but the voter was right there.

Juanita was in her 90s, sharp as a tack, and wearing a vibrant maroon sweatshirt with a star-shaped design on the front. I explained in Spanish why I was there. She nodded and said, "My hands don't work so well anymore because of my arthritis, so that's probably why there was a problem with my signature." I could only imagine how much work those hands must have done in her lifetime. I imagined them sowing seeds, weeding, and harvesting from dawn to dusk, year after year – not to mention changing diapers, making thousands of meals, and folding mountains of laundry.

I showed her the form and pointed at where she needed to sign her name, which she did. Then I pointed at the section where she needed to print her name and address. I didn't know how to say "Print your name" in Spanish, so I asked her, "¿Cómo se dice 'print' en español?" She said, "Con la letra de molde." I will never forget that phrase, or the fact that she taught it to me as I knelt by her wheelchair in the corner of that nursing home. I was able to use it every day for the rest of my week of ballot curing.

Juanita had trouble writing her address because of her bad arthritis. We were told that the voter needed to complete the form without us filling in anything for them. Then the activities director came by and asked if she could help me. I explained the situation, and she said, "Staff are authorized to fill out paperwork for residents." So she wrote in the address on the form. Just in case there was any question by the county clerk about why there was handwriting from two different people on the form, I asked the activities director to sign her name and add her phone number at the bottom of the form.

Although I had to interface with a few different staff members before I connected with Juanita, I was determined to keep talking with people until I hit a brick wall – or, happily in this case, got that cure form signed. It was truly an honor to help this elder make sure her vote would be counted.

By the way, for every cure form I completed, I also attached large Post-it notes with the date and time I obtained the signature, the voter's name and phone number, and any other background information that might be helpful. This can be helpful in case the campaign staff or their lawyers have to advocate with the county recorder for the form to be accepted, or need to get back in touch with the voter. (Depending on how close the election is and how polarized the supposedly nonpartisan county recorder's office is, I can imagine that the election results might hinge on this contextual information that only volunteers like us can provide.) It's always better to have too much documentation than not enough!

For example, I wrote down that Juanita had developed arthritis, which is why her signature didn't match the one on record. I also note if a voter tells me they signed their ballot envelope in a hurry when they were on the bus, if they have different ways they sign their name (for example, sometimes using their middle initial, other times with their full middle name), and include contact information for additional household members if they share that with me.

Learn Something from Everyone You Meet

While I helped Juanita cure her ballot, she taught me how to say "print lettering" in Spanish – a gift I will always treasure. I find that asking voters and others I meet for advice or tips not only enriches my knowledge base, but can help them feel seen and honored for some of the rich life experience they possess.

Everyone in the field is a potential teacher or helper. One time while canvassing in Virginia, I found myself knocking the same doors as a young man selling cell phone service plans. I asked him how he determines the most efficient route in a convoluted turf, since this is an issue I wrestle with in the field. He told me how his company actually runs trainings on how to do this, and let me take a picture of that day's route, which he had sketched out by hand before getting it approved by his supervisor.

Many times when I'm having trouble finding a residence, I'll flag down the postman or delivery truck driver and ask for their help. I figure they know the street numbers better than anyone, and usually they are glad to help me.

Some large housing complexes, like the ones built for farmworkers and their families, are labyrinths. Oftentimes the central building has a map of the complex posted on a billboard. I try to make that my first stop, and take a picture of the map. That helps me navigate the buildings more efficiently, since there are usually multiple voters I want to talk with in that community. If I'm with a canvassing buddy, I text them the map as well. The map can be especially useful if I'm canvassing after dark, when it's harder to read the apartment numbers and figure out where each building is in relation to the others.

My friend Sheila taught me another trick. When we were in a large housing complex and needed to find a voter whose apartment number wasn't listed in the app, she went to the manager's office and found out which unit he lived in. (Because your mileage may vary with how welcoming apartment managers may be, it's probably best to make their office your last stop in case they ask you to leave the premises instead of helping you locate a voter.)

If someone is passionate about voting, as I mentioned in Chapter 9, I may ask them what they'd say to someone who isn't planning to vote. It's always helpful to glean tips from others, especially if those approaches are particularly relevant to the specific community or culture you are working in.

Skylar the Skeptic might say, "I don't have time to have all these side conversations with people! I just want to reach as many people as possible." I agree, it can take more time to broaden my focus beyond just the questions I need to answer in the voter contact app. However, my goal is not necessarily to reach as many voters as possible. While that's important, I also want to keep honing my craft and building my toolkit of voter engagement skills. Staying teachable and picking up new ideas, resources and strategies from people I meet makes me a more effective and knowledgeable canvasser and phone banker. To me, it's worth the investment of time.

Invite People to Help You

When I went to cure the ballot for Felicia, she was initially suspicious. I said I understood, and told her she was welcome to mail in the form herself if she wasn't comfortable having me take it to the campaign to deliver in person. Perhaps because I wasn't pushy, she eventually warmed up to me and signed the form. I invited her to take a picture of it, and also to take my picture for her records.

Then I asked if by any chance she happened to speak Tagalog, since her name and accent sounded Filipino to me. Felicia said she spoke Tagalog and two other languages spoken in the Philippines, and explained more about the origin of each. I told her I was really impressed. Then I said, "It's possible I might need to help some Filipino voters who don't speak English fix their ballots. Would you consider interpreting over the phone if I need help communicating with them, since now you know how ballot curing works and could explain it to them?"

Felicia said, "Yes, I could do that." She gave me her phone number, which I programmed into my phone. Then I asked if I could call her right then to make sure I'd entered it correctly. She agreed, so I called her. She answered the call, had me type my name into her contacts list, and saved my number. That way she'd recognize my number and know to pick up if I called her from another voter's doorstep. During this conversation, our connection blossomed from skepticism, to me helping her, and ultimately Felicia being willing to help me in the future. We went from strangers to allies in just a few short minutes.

She was all dressed up to go out to dinner and apologized for having to run, but I thanked her profusely. She seemed flattered that I valued her linguistic superpowers, and was more than willing to assist if needed – just because I asked.

Wait for Your Moment

Occasionally, timing is everything. I was trying to cure the ballot for Alejandro, and arrived after dark. There was no response when I rang the doorbell, but I knew someone was home – the lights were on, there was a lot of banging in the kitchen, and the stereo was blasting. I knocked as hard as I could – twice – but still no response.

Then the song on the stereo changed, and I realized I'd missed my three-second window of audibility. So I waited another four or five minutes for the song to change again. (Luckily Alejandro wasn't rocking out to electronic trance music or Wagner's Ring Cycle – I would have been waiting a lot longer!) I positioned myself next to the kitchen. When the song changed again, I rapped "shave and a haircut" on the kitchen window, really loudly. I wanted him to hear me, but also wanted to communicate that I was friendly and not the police or ICE.

Alejandro lifted the curtain and peered out at me. He was shirtless, and looked surprised and a bit taken aback. He made a gesture asking me to wait. A minute later he opened the door, fully dressed and quite friendly. He seemed a little embarrassed, and said, "Sorry, I was cleaning out the fridge and didn't hear anything." He invited me into his house and I sat beneath a crucifix on the wall while he filled out the form. That experience taught me the importance of choosing my moment – and being ready to pounce (or knock) when it arrives.

Summary

- If a voter doesn't answer the door, look and listen for clues that might lead you to where they are.

- Don't be intimidated by gatekeepers – stay respectful and polite, but keep going until someone actually tells you "no." (Or they might eventually say "Yes"!)
- Invite people to help you, and learn something from everyone you meet.

Chapter 11

Making 'I Don't Vote' the Start, Not the End, of a Conversation

(written with Jacqueline Tulsky, MD)

One of the most frustrating things I hear in a close election is voters who tell me, "My vote doesn't matter," or "I'm not voting – nothing ever changes." What can you even say to that?

Quite a bit, it turns out. In fact, as I was wrestling with this challenge, I connected with Jaqueline Tulsky, MD, an amazing doctor at Zuckerberg San Francisco General Hospital. She has developed a wealth of experience navigating difficult conversations with her patients. I'll tell you more about Jackie in a minute, but together we developed an entire workshop devoted to helping people explore changing their behavior around voting, entitled "You and the 34%: How to Have Meaningful Conversations with High-Potential Voters." This chapter is adapted from that training, which helps volunteers become more effective in connecting with people who rarely or never vote.

High-Potential Voters: (At Least) 34% of the Electorate

We all know how close the 2020 elections were. Less than 43,000 voters in Arizona, Georgia and Wisconsin decided the outcome of the Electoral College.[15]

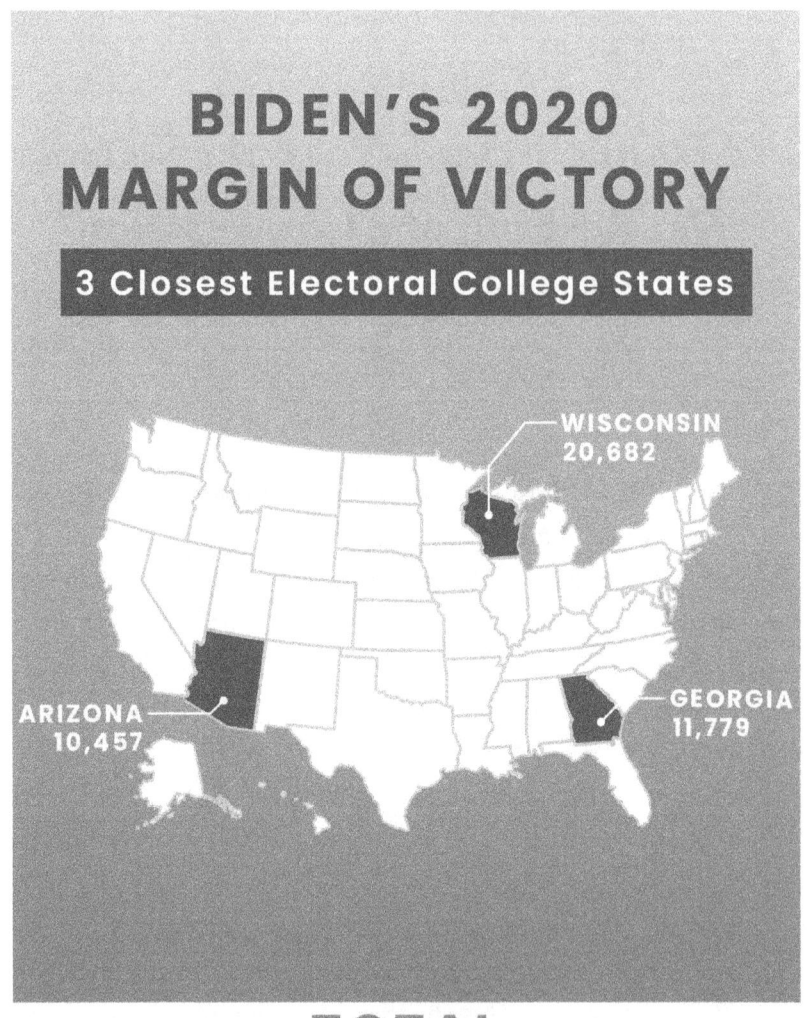

Perhaps equally mind-boggling is considering the popular vote in 2020, when you include *all* eligible voters.[16,17] (The number of eligible voters is determined by Census data. It includes citizens age 18 or older who aren't barred from voting because of past felony convictions, depending on the laws in their state.)

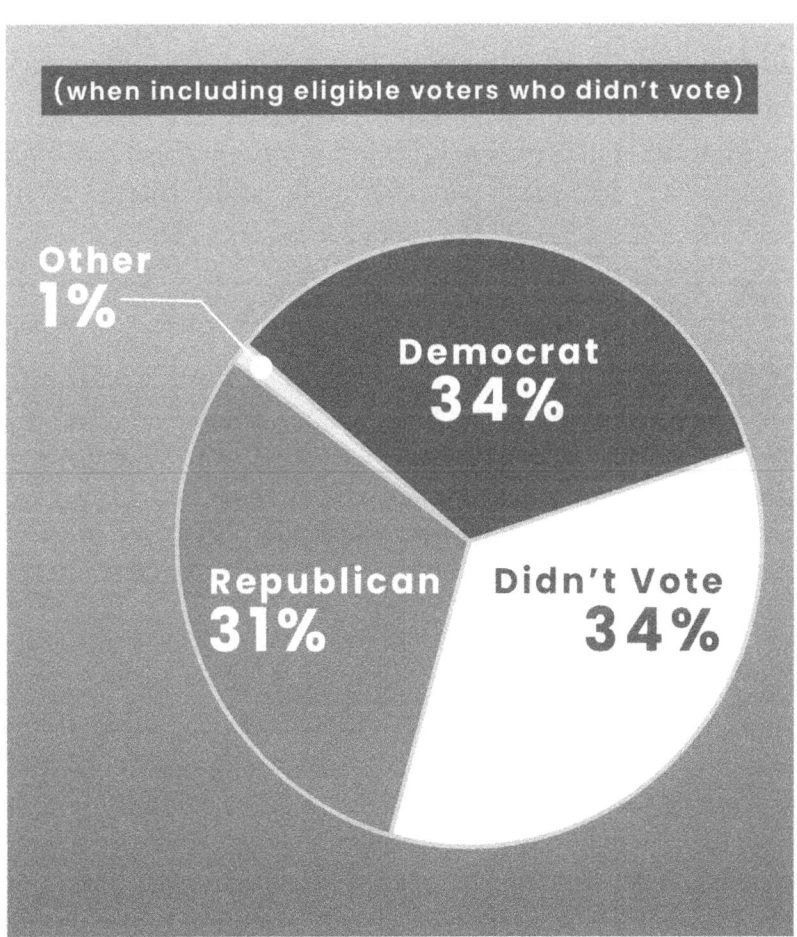

VOTE SHARE: 2020
(when including eligible voters who didn't vote)

- Other: 1%
- Democrat: 34%
- Didn't Vote: 34%
- Republican: 31%

As you can see, in 2020 the Democrats got 34% of the popular vote, and Republicans got 31%. The tiny sliver of "Other" represents third-party voters,[18] which includes some of those elusive "swing voters" we hear *so* much about.

But perhaps our greatest opportunity for impacting the election are eligible voters who didn't vote at all. In 2020, a year when we saw the highest turnout in over a century, *34% of the electorate* still did not cast a ballot. Many in that group were young people, people of color, and lower-income voters – people who may be inclined to support progressive priorities.

Of course, some of these people had their votes suppressed. Others just need help navigating logistics, like confirming their polling location or how to request an absentee ballot. But there is some portion of this 34% that flat-out is not interested in voting, or only votes occasionally. (Midterm elections historically have lower turnout. In 2018, 51% of eligible voters didn't vote, and in 2022, 54% of eligible voters didn't vote.[19])

People who rarely or never vote are often labeled "low-propensity voters." But I like a term used by Anat Shenker-Osorio, a Democratic communications strategist. She calls them "high-potential voters." It focuses on their strength and their power. If we could encourage even a fraction of these "high-potential voters" to get out and vote, it could have a big impact.

Three Types of Voters

Engaging with voters isn't a one-size-fits-all process. Instead, I try to tailor my approach based on how the conversation unfolds.

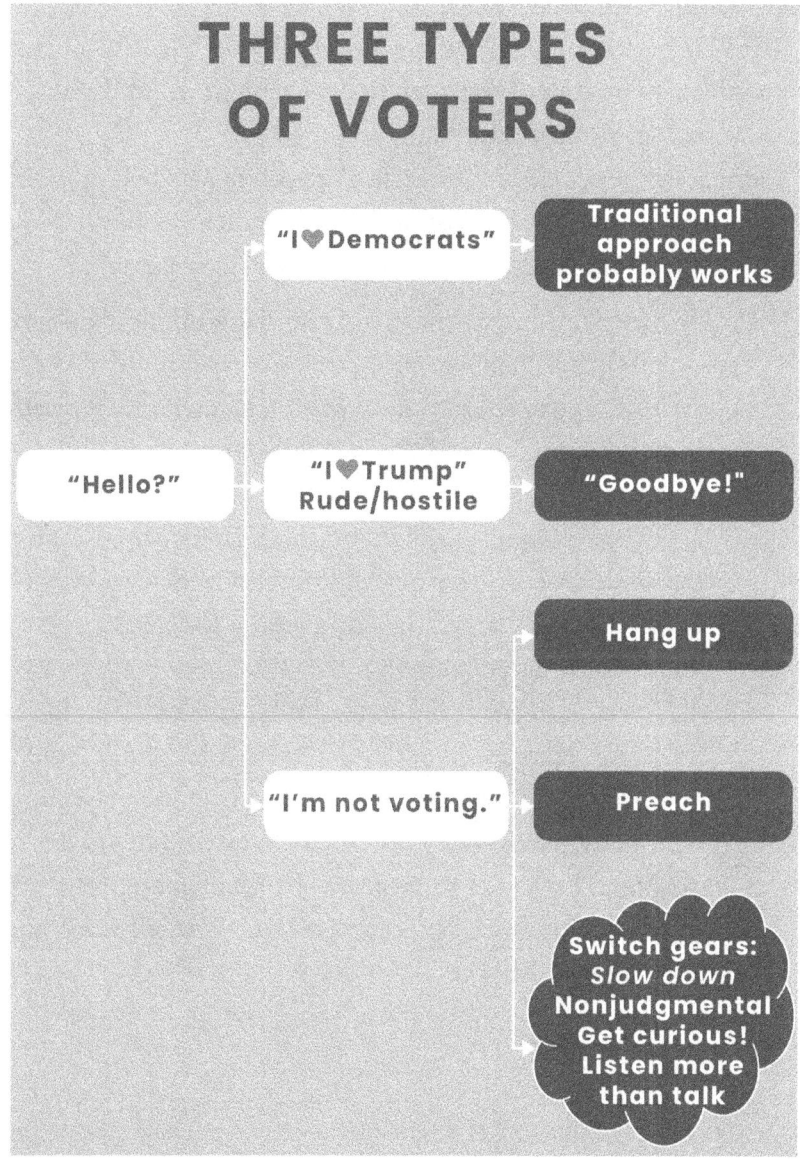

THE JOY OF TALKING POLITICS WITH STRANGERS

If they're a strong or likely Democrat, the traditional approach of mentioning a few of the candidate's talking points and making a plan to vote probably works great. This is essential to any campaign, and helps ensure that our strongest supporters have all the information they need to vote.

If I encounter someone who would *never* vote for a Democrat, or happens to be rude, I don't try to change their mind. I politely say, "Have a great day!" and hang up.

But at least once each shift, I talk to someone who tells me, "I'm not voting." Bingo! I've just connected with a member of the 34%! But… how should I respond? There are three pathways:

- The first is to just thank them and hang up. Some phone bank scripts actually say to do this! Perhaps they think it's a waste of time to engage with people who aren't enthusiastic about voting. However, this is a lost opportunity.
- The second path is to *preach* at them: you know, recite the talking points and tell them *all* the reasons why this election is so crucial. That usually doesn't work very well. It feels bad to talk at people, and it really feels bad to be on the receiving end of that.
- The third path requires me to shift gears and slow down. Try to get curious. Show empathy and be nonjudgmental. Listen more than you talk, especially at the beginning. Ask open-ended questions, then silently count to 10 to give them a chance to respond. It's challenging, but this approach can make the conversation more effective and satisfying for the voter – and for you!

Helping Voters Find Their Inner Motivation to Vote

Let me tell you about one of these high-potential voters. In December 2020, I was calling Georgia for the Senate runoffs and spoke with a voter I'll call Ofelia. She was really stressed out and didn't know there was another election in January.

She said, "I don't have time to think about politics, and just try to tune them out." She couldn't even remember the name of the president, but she said she didn't like him. She described how hard things were with her elderly mother, who had lots of health issues. Although Ofelia got laid off during the pandemic and her unemployment had run out, she still helped her mom financially.

This went on for about 20 minutes, and I wondered if I was wasting my time. After all, there were so many voters to call, the runoffs were in just a few days, and Ofelia just told me she tried to tune out politics. Was she really going to show up for a runoff election she hadn't even heard about? But she seemed to really need to talk. Also, some of the other people I'd reached that day either hung up on me, had already voted, or didn't have time to talk. I wanted to make the most of having a live voter on the line, so I said, "I'm so sorry to hear about your situation. It sounds really hard. My mom also had a lot of health issues in her later years, and I know it can be so stressful to be a caregiver."

Ofelia told me more about her worries about her mother. Then she paused and asked, "So are you a Democrat?" I wasn't sure what political affiliation she might have, if any, so I cautiously responded, "Yes, I am." She said she leaned that way, too, but said she hadn't voted in November. I said, "Oh, interesting! Tell me more about that." She said, "I figured Trump was going to win again, so what was the point?"

I said, "I'm really glad Biden will be our next president. But it was a really close election, and it showed that we needed every voter. You know, it would be tragic if Biden can't get anything done because the Republicans still control the Senate. They've blocked Democrats for *years*. In the latest pandemic relief bill, the Democrats wanted to include money for things like extended unemployment benefits, but the Republicans refused. If they keep control of the Senate, that'll probably continue. But if the Democrats win these two Senate seats in Georgia next week and gain control of the Senate, we can help people who really need it during the pandemic."

Something clicked for Ofelia. She said, "Okay, that's it! I'm going to go vote and make sure my family does, too!" I said, "That's great! Could you spread the word to three people you know?" She said, "Yeah! My husband works in construction and has close to a hundred coworkers. Most of them didn't vote in November either, but we'll tell them that now that we have a new president, we want to make sure he can get things done. So get out and vote on January 5th! We're Hispanic, and we're going to get this going. We'll tell them, 'Get out and vote, and then come to the cookout!'" I said, "Wow, you are really connected to the community. You and the people you know could decide the outcome of the runoffs!"

Toward the end of the conversation, I helped her make a plan to vote. She was out of town but would get back before Election Day. We discussed the options for early voting and voting on Election Day, and what time she could go vote.

I asked if I could send her information about early voting, and text her a reminder on Election Day. She said sure, so afterward I texted her. This is what she wrote back:

> *God works in mysterious ways. You made my day. Yes, I will take all my friends [to the polls]. I can literally imagine [the poll workers'] faces when we walk in. Unfortunately I don't*

have a [loud]speaker. I would go around town announcing it ha ha.

That's just one example of how eliciting a voter's concerns, trying to respond from the heart, and connecting what *they* care about with what's at stake in this election can help them draw their own conclusions about voting.

MOTIVATIONAL INTERVIEWING: A TOOL FOR MAKING POSITIVE CHANGES

One way to do this is to incorporate some tools of Motivational Interviewing, or "MI." This approach was initially developed by clinical psychologists William Miller, PhD, and Stephen Rollnick, PhD, to help clients change addictive behavior. Since publishing their first book on the topic in 1991, there have been more than 1,000 clinical trials of MI demonstrating it can help people make positive changes in their life.[20] (If you want to do a deep dive into the topic, you can check out their book, *Motivational Interviewing: Helping People Change and Grow*.)[21]

MI has been applied broadly across many areas, such as smoking cessation, diet and exercise. Today, MI is widely used in fields such as psychotherapy and social work. However, you don't have to be a psychiatrist or a social worker to incorporate some of these approaches to your conversations with voters.

In 2021, I was fortunate enough to interview Jackie Tulsky, MD, as part of my day job as a freelance medical writer. She's an HIV primary care physician and addiction medicine specialist. She worked for decades at Zuckerberg San Francisco General Hospital and Trauma Center's Ward 86, one of the world's first dedicated HIV clinics, before retiring recently. Over the years, many of her patients have had HIV, substance use disorders and mental health issues. And yet, even with these huge challenges, some were inspired to make big life changes, like taking a step toward reducing their drug use.

She has used MI to engage with compassion, drawing out her patients' intrinsic desires to change, and helping them align their actions with those desires. For many years, Jackie also worked as an MI trainer. When I saw that on her biography, I invited her to collaborate with me to develop a workshop to help volunteers to use some of these tools in our conversations with voters – especially high-potential voters. Happily, she said yes. To date, we've trained more than 1,100 volunteers from across the country through our online, interactive workshop, "You and the 34%: How to Have Meaningful Conversations with High-Potential Voters."

Some readers may already have a lot of background in MI. While the tools we suggest are inspired by MI, we've taken liberties to adapt these approaches to voter engagement in a *very* applied way. This chapter is just scratching the surface, but we hope you'll still find a few useful nuggets. With that caveat, I'll hand the mic (or the pen) over to Jackie to explain some key elements of MI in the next few sections.

THE SPIRIT OF MOTIVATIONAL INTERVIEWING

MI is a method of communicating which seeks to draw out someone's own motivation, to help them sort out their own ambivalence for change. Ambivalence is something most of us are familiar with: feeling two ways about something at the same time. I want to eat healthily, but that bag of open chips knows my name and is calling me. And though many people are not happy with their elected leaders, life doesn't seem to change much no matter who's in office, so why bother voting?

There are some specific skills and tools that we can use to have MI-consistent conversations, but learning MI starts with a philosophical approach to communicating. The "Spirit of MI" has four principles with the acronym of PACE. Interestingly, all four are woven through Elizabeth's conversation with Ofelia, helping Ofelia resolve ambivalence about voting:

- **Partnering:** We try to take the attitude that what the voter thinks and has to say is as important as what we have to say. We ask questions that are open and invite them to tell us more. We listen, seeking to understand what they are ambivalent about, what they wish would change and why. We learned that Ofelia had too much to do, and so much felt out of her control. But she didn't like Trump. And there were things that were very important to her, like taking care of her mother.
- **Autonomy:** We honor a person's control of their own decisions. We recognize and respect the right *not* to change. Maybe Ofelia will "vote her interests" and maybe she won't. When we acknowledge and accept another person's autonomy, they have space to move forward, rather than feeling backed into a corner, defending their initial position.
- **Compassion:** We have empathy for how hard it is to change ourselves or the world. We express genuine curiosity about what motivates a person's actions, and what might help them do something different. When Elizabeth listened to Ofelia's troubles and said, 'I know what it's like to care for a family member,' she showed compassion for how hard it is to be human. That sharing is not meant to shift the focus away from Ofelia, but to simply acknowledge that "It would be hard to add one more thing like voting to your very busy life – and yet you manage to do so much."

"SPIRIT" OF MOTIVATIONAL INTERVIEWING

PACE

Partnership: *We help voters hear themselves*

Autonomy: *Voter gets to decide*

Compassion: *Life is hard. Change is hard!*

Evocation: *Draw out their desires and hopes*

- **Evoking:** Drawing out the person's own ambivalence and helping them explore reasons why they might want to change. Ofelia talked about her life, and Elizabeth said, "Tell me more… about your family, your work." Evoking means asking the person what they want to change: "If you elected a person that listened to you, what three things would you want them to know?" or "If an honest person was elected, what two or three things might be different a year from now?"

We use PACE, the four principles in the Spirit of MI, to support all our other MI skills.

A Different Way to Communicate

Communicating with MI helps the people we talk to, but it also helps *us*. We may see people in a different light, and MI supports our ability to engage. Many of you have done hours of phone banking and canvassing. Perhaps you've felt a little discouraged between people hanging up on you, and those who are adamant that they don't vote. It's really common to feel frustrated with important but difficult work. Maybe some of you have thought, "If they would only listen and understand why they need to change!" more than once.

I know that feeling. After 15 years at San Francisco General, I loved the job of caring for people, but most of my patients had problems that never seemed to improve. I was frustrated and on the edge of burnout. A colleague was trying to help me, and thought I should look into this communication thing called Motivational Interviewing. So I took an introductory course, and it was such a revelation! It turns out that making people change was *not* my job. My job was to help them find their *own* reasons or motivations to change.

Soon after the course, I saw a patient I'll call Joe. We had a 10-year relationship. Some of his medical problems were better, but it was clear that his heavy drug use, not his HIV infection, was going to be the cause of his death. But the more I tried to tell him how dangerous it was, the more he dug in his heels. According to Joe, cocaine was *not* the problem, and he was very turned off by my lecturing approach. With MI Spirit in mind, I was ready to try something different when I knocked on the exam room door.

I smiled at him and said, "Hi, Joe. Thanks for coming in today. Can we take two minutes to talk about your lab results?" He nodded gruffly. I said, "You're doing terrific with your HIV meds, and your virus is under control. But the drug test showed cocaine again. What do you think about that?"

Joe just looked at me and said, "Hey, Doc, I know what you always have to say." Instead of launching into my usual speech about how dangerous his cocaine use was, I tried a different approach. With sincere and nonjudgmental curiosity, I said, "Tell me more about crack cocaine. What do you like about using it?"

He looked me right in the eye, and without skipping a beat, he said, "You feel like you're riding a rocket ship. You have energy, ideas – you feel so good, like you can do anything! My back pain disappears. You just never want to stop."

I was surprised, but channeling my recent MI training, I asked him, "Oh, wow. So what, if anything, is not so good about using?" Joe thought about it for a few seconds, and I bit my tongue to keep from saying anything. He said, "The rocket ship falls to earth. You crash and you're wrecked." I said with feeling, "Wow, 'The rocket ship crashes.'" He said, "Yeah, and you're broke. Nothing for food or bills for the rest of the month."

Joe seemed surprised to hear himself say this, and frankly, I was stunned. It never occurred to me that he would have such rich things to say about using, or why he might want to not use. Pain relief, wasted money, feeling bad afterward – all these were things we had never talked about.

That conversation marked a big change in our relationship, as well as how I saw Joe and other patients like him. It started with me listening – and Joe hearing – what he had to say. After we had that talk, I was no longer the one bringing up reasons to stop using. His cocaine use decreased significantly, and he eventually planned to stop. It turns out that his life and health goals did not include cocaine. And me, I spent many more happy years at San Francisco General until I recently retired.

MI reminds me that I am not driving the bus. I just have to help people figure out where they want to go, and maybe the best route – though often they know the roads pretty well.

MI-guided conversations like the ones you heard with Ofelia and Joe can be learned. It's not a "natural gift" that you're either born with or not. There are tools and skills that you can develop. There are even ways to give information so you are not "the sage on the stage" taking over the conversation, but a partner helping expand the person's engagement in democracy.

How to Start a Conversation – and Keep It Going

Let's look at a few of those MI tools and skills. A handy way to remember three ways to start a conversation and keep it going is the acronym of OAR, which stands for **O**pen-ended questions, **A**ffirmations, and **R**eflections:

- **Open-Ended Questions:** These can't be answered with a yes or a no. They are sincerely curious and nonjudgmental. People may need time to answer them, so remember to wait – you may even need to count to 10 (in your head) if there's no response. If they start responding, you can encourage them to keep talking without interrupting them by making sympathetic sounds like "Mmmm" and "Uh-huh" and "Wow."

You heard some examples from Joe and Ofelia's stories (the boldface text indicates useful starting phrases that can be used for conversations with other voters):

- **"What's not so good about** crack cocaine?"
- **"Tell me more** about not voting last November?"

There's one special type of open-ended question called the Ruler. It can be especially helpful for assessing a voter's motivation level. For example, you could ask them, "On a scale of zero to 10, how likely are you to vote, with zero meaning very unlikely and 10 being very likely?" If they say "Three," then you could ask them, "Oh, why isn't that number a zero or a one?" and they may share some interesting information about why they *might* be interested in voting. Then you could follow that up by asking, "What might boost your 'three' to a four or a five?" That could open the door for them to share things that could help them take the next step toward voting.

(One note: Not all closed-ended questions are bad. Those can be answered with a yes or a no, and can be very useful in specific situations, such as asking, "Have you received your ballot yet?" or "Have you had a chance to vote yet?" But for building rapport and helping people feel comfortable opening up to you, consider using an open-ended question such as, "What, if anything, have you heard about Candidate X?")

- **Affirmations:** This reminds someone that they've made changes in the past. It acknowledges previous actions that demonstrate strength or effort, based on specific things you've heard them mention.

Again, here are some examples from Joe and Ofelia's stories:

- **"You're doing a terrific job with** your HIV meds, and your virus is under control."
- **"It can be so hard** to take care of a family member."
- **"You are really** connected to the community."

• **Reflections:** By repeating or interpreting what the voter said, you can help them hear themselves. It also shows that you're really listening. This is probably the hardest part of OAR. Some examples from Joe and Ofelia's stories:

- When Joe says, "The rocket crashes," I just simply repeat his words: "The rocket crashes."
- When Ofelia tells Elizabeth, "I figured Trump was going to win, so what was the point?" Elizabeth chooses to interpret a little and says, "The election was really close, and it showed that we needed every voter."

OAR – Open-ended questions, Affirmations, and Reflections – is a very useful MI tool that can help someone talk about their frustrations as well as their priorities.

Sample Dialogue: OAR in Action

To help you see some of OAR in action, here is a sample dialogue between a voter, played by Jackie, and a phone bank volunteer, played by Elizabeth. This is just the first few minutes of a conversation, to illustrate how you might start to engage a high-potential voter. You might want to underline any examples of Open-ended questions, Affirmations, and Reflections in this dialogue to help you start to tune your ear to how these can be used in a real conversation.

Elizabeth: *(Ring, ring)*

Jackie: Hello?

Elizabeth: Hi, my name is Elizabeth Chur. May I speak with Jackie Tulsky, please? *(listens)*

Jackie: *(pauses)* Uh, yeah, that's me. What's this about?

Elizabeth: I appreciate you taking my call. I'm a volunteer with Nevada Senator Jacky Rosen. I'm not calling to ask for money – this is just a one-minute check-in call about the upcoming election. We're just trying to find out –

Jackie: I'm sorry, I'm really busy.

Elizabeth: Oh, it sounds like you've got a lot going on right now.

Jackie: Yeah, and I really hate these kinds of calls.

Elizabeth: I hear you. I actually don't like making these calls either – *and* at the same time, the upcoming election feels *really* important. It would be so valuable if you could just give me a minute to share some of your thoughts about where things are heading in the country.

Jackie: *(a little annoyed)* Oh, I don't vote.

Elizabeth: Oh, interesting. Tell me more about that.

Jackie: It's just a waste of time. All those campaign promises, then nothing changes. I'm so tired of it. I've got enough to do without that. *(pauses, then sighs)* I've voted before, but *my* life sure didn't get any better.

Elizabeth: You voted when you thought it would impact you.

Jackie: Well, yeah. When I thought it would make a difference, but nothing happened. *(pause again).* Look at things now. I take care of my granddaughter, and her asthma gets worse every year with all these wildfires. And prices have gone up so much lately. My daughter and son-in-law both work full-time, but they can barely make ends meet. And my daughter just got a second job at Home Depot down in Las Vegas, and it costs more than $50 to fill up her car.

Elizabeth: You're a really strong person with a hard-working family. *(brief pause)* I'm wondering, if you had a chance to talk with Senator Jacky Rosen, what two or three things would you want her to put at the top of her to-do list?

Jackie: I have no idea. *(pauses)* I really don't know.

Elizabeth: I'm wondering, if you could change two or three things about Nevada, what would they be?

Jackie: Two or three things about Nevada… Well, I'd raise the minimum wage so maybe my daughter could just work one job. And it just seems to be getting hotter every year.

Elizabeth: Wow – it sounds like you have some great ideas. Tell me more about minimum wage and the climate.

We're going to pause the dialogue here, but hopefully this gives you an idea of how you might start to talk with a high-potential voter and keep them on the line, even if they're reluctant to talk at first. We'll talk more about where to go from here in the next section, but we'd like to make one suggestion. At this point in a conversation, when they've mentioned some priority issues, it can be tempting to try to "close the deal" by reading them some talking points. Instead, we encourage you to dig deeper about the topics they bring up, like minimum wage and the climate. Find out more about what they care about, and why. (For more ideas, see Chapter 5, "80% Them, 20% Me" and Chapter 6, "Empathize, Empathize, Empathize.")

Hopefully you noticed some examples of OAR in the dialogue, such as:

Open-ended questions:

- "If you had a chance to actually talk with Senator Jacky Rosen, what two or three things would you want her to put at the top of her to-do list?
- "If you could change two or three things about Nevada, what would they be?
- "Tell me more about that." (Okay, technically it's not a question, but it invites the voter to elaborate on what they've mentioned, and is one of the most useful phrases to have in your toolkit.)

Affirmations:

- "You're a really strong person with a hard-working family."
- "You have some great ideas."

Reflections:

- "You've got a lot going on right now."
- "You voted when you thought it would impact you."

MAKING 'I DON'T VOTE' THE START OF A CONVERSATION

CHANGE TALK VS. SUSTAIN TALK

When we switch gears into MI mode, we bring our nonjudgmental curiosity to the conversation. We try to listen more than we talk. As this flow chart shows, Open-ended questions, Affirmations, and Reflections are all tools for helping elicit something called "change talk."

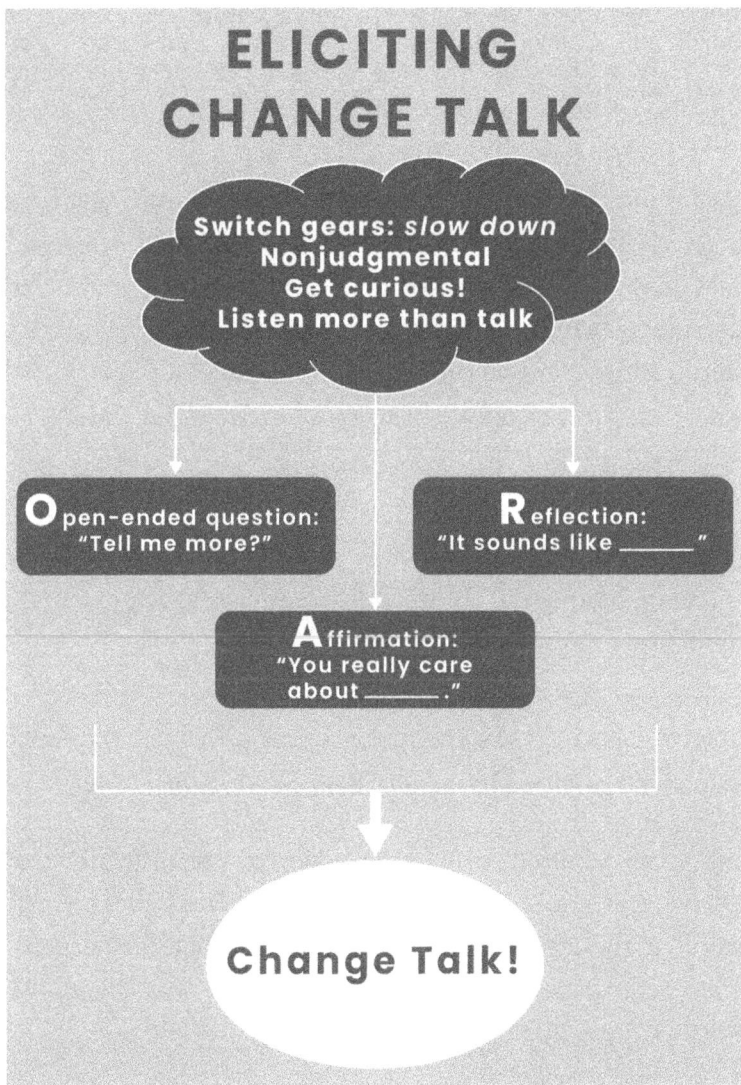

The heart of MI is the skill of listening for and amplifying change talk. This is any expression of reasons to change behaviors or opinions. It may be a comment about what a person did in the past, or how things were better or different, or something about what concerns them now. The goal is to have the person talk about their *own* motivations to change, and to help them hear themselves.

Here are some examples of change talk from Joe and Ofelia:

- "The rocket falls to earth. You're broke, no money for the rest of the month."
- "I don't really like Trump."

But remember we said that people often feel ambivalent about changes? What we might hear most when we start a conversation is "sustain talk." These are comments that support the status quo, or statements that argue for keeping things the way they have been. It's the "Just go along to get along" approach.

Here are some examples of sustain talk from Joe and Ofelia:

- "You feel like you can do anything using crack cocaine."
- "I don't have time to think about politics. I just try to tune them out"

Now I'm going to hand the mic (or the pen) back to Elizabeth to share some tips about change talk and sustain talk.

'Name the Hidden Hope, the Buried Yearning'

Often, a conversation with a high-potential voter isn't divvied up 50-50 between change talk and sustain talk. Many times, they'll say nine things about why they're not voting, but then they'll mention one little thing that indicates they might have other thoughts or feelings about voting.

Milk it! If you listen hard, people sometimes give you this opening. This little shred of change talk is the crack in the wall of the status quo. That's what you want to focus on, reflect back, and invite them to talk more about. You know how mice are so talented at finding food? They don't need you to leave the pantry wide door open – if there's a crack in the wall, they can squeeze themselves through it to get to the good stuff. That's what we want to do if voters give us an opening.

One of my activist colleagues and friends, Charlie Varon, told me that MI invites us to "name the hidden hope, the buried yearning." Sometimes voters don't serve up their change talk on a platter. They may make negative comments about elections or the state of the country. Still, if you bring your curiosity and empathy to these statements, you might be able to gather more intel about what they care about.

For example, they might say, "Politicians make lots of promises, but nothing ever changes." You could say, "Sounds like *you* have some ideas about how the country could improve. Tell me more about that!" Or they might say, "I haven't voted for decades." You could say, "You have a track record of voting. What inspired you to vote the last time you did?"

One time in 2020, I was calling for Amy McGrath in Kentucky, the Democratic candidate for Senate running against Mitch McConnell. I talked with someone who said he wasn't going to vote, but mentioned that he thought U.S. senators should have term limits. I said that Amy McGrath supported term limits, and asked if he'd consider voting for her, since he seemed so passionate about this issue. He said no.

Then I asked, "Is there *anything* that would motivate you to vote?" He thought about it for several seconds, then burst out laughing. He said, "If Amy called, or even left me a voicemail, I *swear* I'd vote for her! We need new people and ideas in government. It's like an old car that keeps breaking down – sometimes you just have to buy a new one." I asked for all his contact information, including his cell phone number and the best days and times to reach him, and what he'd want Amy McGrath to leave on a voicemail if she couldn't reach him. I passed all that information on to the campaign and asked them to follow up with him if they could.

By asking him that question, he gave me way more information, and even committed to vote, if he heard from Amy. That was a long way from "I'm not voting." And oftentimes, engaging with high-potential voters is a journey of many small steps. It's not up to me to singlehandedly transform someone's relationship with voting. Instead, I can help a voter reexamine their views or consider a different perspective. I trust that other volunteers and people they meet may help them continue that conversation over the long haul.

Dig Deeper

Change talk is the beating heart of MI. If someone says things like, "*I wish that*...gas prices weren't so high," or "*I don't like that*... we can't afford health insurance," or "*If*... I didn't have to work two jobs, *then* maybe I could coach my daughter's soccer team," you've really unearthed some valuable information!

As we mentioned earlier, it can be tempting to jump right into trying to close the deal. But try to *dig deeper*. Keep using Open-ended questions, Affirmations and Reflections to elicit more details. Often, the voter will share more change talk, helping you better understand what they care about, and why. Imagine that you're getting paid a dollar for every word the voter says. By using open-ended questions and reflections to encourage them to keep talking, you can increase your "commission."

ELICIT EVEN MORE DETAILS

Dig Deeper!

Open-ended questions:
"If someone who listened got elected, what would be different?"

Reflections:
"It's important to support candidates with integrity."

Change Talk!

"I wish ____"
"I don't like ____"
"If ____ , then ____"

Offer strategic info, then invite reflection

"Jacky Rosen supports Biden's student debt relief plan. What do you think of that?"

Once you've uncovered that information, you can offer strategic tidbits of information that directly relate to their priorities, and ask them to reflect on what you shared. If someone tells you they're worried about student debt, you could say, "Senator Jacky Rosen supports Biden's student debt relief plan and wants to make college more affordable for everyone. What do you think of that?"

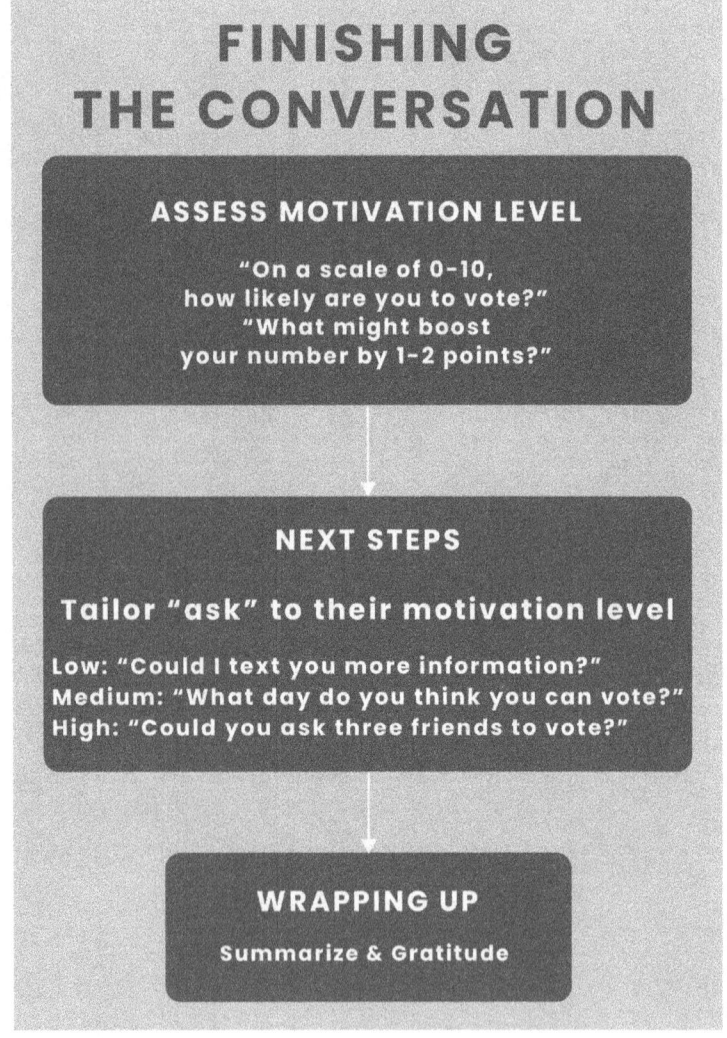

Finally, as the conversation winds down, you can use the Ruler to assess how motivated they are to vote, or to support your candidate. Then you can make an ask that's tailored to their level of enthusiasm. If someone says they're a "Two," it might not make sense to say, "Can we count on your vote?" But we can help them take the next step by offering to text them the candidate's website.

Incremental progress is fantastic, especially with the 34%! You're laying the groundwork for the next conversation they have with a volunteer. Of course, if the voter is more motivated, you could help them make a plan to vote, or ask them to vote triple by saying, "Could you make sure three friends or family members vote to reelect Senator Jacky Rosen?"

End on a positive note by summarizing any next steps, like "I'll text you that information in a minute," and thank them for their time.

For more tips and suggested phrases for navigating conversations with voters, please see Appendix B.

SAMPLE DIALOGUE: ELICITING CHANGE TALK

Now we'll show you another sample dialogue, this time of an entire conversation between a volunteer and a voter. We encourage you to underline examples of change talk and sustain talk. Pay attention to ways that the Jackie, as the volunteer, digs deeper to draw out even more change talk from Elizabeth, the voter.

Jackie: (*Ring, ring*)

Elizabeth: Hello?

Jackie: Hi, I'm trying to reach Elizabeth Chur.

Elizabeth: Uh, who's calling?

Jackie: My name is Jackie Tulsky, and I'm a volunteer with Nevada Senator Jacky Rosen. I'm not calling to ask about money. This is just a one-minute check-in call about the upcoming election, and she's asked us to call every voter in the state to find out –

Elizabeth: *(interrupts)* Oh, I'm not interested in politics – I don't vote.

Jackie: Tell me more about that…

Elizabeth: I just graduated from college. I don't consider myself a political person.

Jackie: *(sympathetically)* Congratulations! That's a huge accomplishment. It takes a lot of persistence to get a college degree these days.

Elizabeth: Yeah, I sure hope it's worth it.

Jackie: Sounds like you're wondering if it was worth it.

Elizabeth: I made some good friends and learned a lot, but the tuition was more than I was counting on.

Jackie: You got a lot out of it, but now you're wondering how you're going to tackle all that debt when you're just starting out.

Elizabeth: Yeah, I had to move back home after graduation, and I'm working part-time for a friend while I look for a real job. This isn't exactly what I was hoping for once I got my degree.

Jackie: What were you hoping to do after you graduated?

Elizabeth: Well, I love working with older people, and there was this job at Meals on Wheels. They helped my grandparents out a lot in the last few years, but the

	starting pay was just too low. So I might have to just get a job at some big company.
Jackie:	You really want to give back, but your student debt is getting in the way.
Elizabeth:	Yeah. *(sigh)*
Jackie:	Elizabeth, I'm curious – what, if anything, you've heard anything about the government's student loan plan?
Elizabeth:	Yeah, I saw some stuff on Facebook about it, but I haven't really had time to look at the details.
Jackie:	Would it be OK to share a bit about the details and how it would help people like you?
Elizabeth:	Okay, but I only have a couple more minutes. I'm actually heading to work right now.
Jackie:	I'll make this quick! In his first term, President Biden approved billions of dollars to forgive student loan debt for graduates who work in nonprofit and government jobs and have already made a certain number of monthly payments. What do you think about that?
Elizabeth:	Well, that would be really great.
Jackie:	Senator Jacky Rosen definitely agrees with you, but unfortunately, a lot of the Republicans have worked to overturn the plan. It's important to have people like Jacky Rosen in Congress who believe in making college affordable for everyone. *(brief pause)* You know, this election is going to be really close. I'm wondering, on a scale of zero to 10, how likely are you to vote in this election, with zero being, "I'm

not interested," and 10 being, "I'm ready to vote today!" What number would you be?

Elizabeth: Hmm, I guess a two.

Jackie: Oh, why not a zero or a one?

Elizabeth: Well, my best friend was a political science major, and she thinks voting is important. *(sighs)* I don't know, I guess I should vote, but I'm so busy with everything.

Jackie: Someone you respect thinks voting is important, especially if it would improve things like student debt relief and affordable education. *(pauses)* What would help you get to a three or four?

Elizabeth: I've never voted before. I don't know how it works.

Jackie: Oh, I think you'd find it pretty easy, especially because you should be getting your ballot in the mail within the next couple weeks at the address that you put on your voter registration form. I can text you the link where you can double-check your voter registration information. And if you have any questions, you could talk with your friend, the political science major.

Elizabeth: Yeah, OK.

Jackie: Great! I'll do that right now. It's terrific that you're considering voting in this election. I really hope that Jacky Rosen can earn your support.

Elizabeth: Yeah, I'll think about it. I've got to go now.

Jackie: Thanks so much for talking. Have a great day!

Hopefully you were able to hear some examples of change talk and sustain talk, such as:

Change talk:

- "I sure hope it's worth it."
- "I love working with older people."
- "That would be really great."
- "My best friend was a political science major, and she thinks voting is important."

Sustain talk:

- "I'm not interested in politics – I don't vote."
- "I just graduated from college. I don't consider myself a political person."
- "I guess I should vote, but I'm so busy with everything."
- "I've never voted before. I don't know how it works."

'You Just Asked Questions and Listened'

If you're curious about how these techniques work out in the real world, you might be interested to hear this report-back from August, one of our workshop alums. He's a superstar phone banker, and a few weeks after taking our training he sent us this email:

> *I just finished up my phone bank. My last call was a classic "You and the 34%" call. I can't get over how effective the perspectives, tools and techniques are from your training. The call began with "I don't vote any more. I don't even watch the news," and the call ended six or seven minutes later with the woman on the call taking down the website to request an absentee ballot for the upcoming primary and general elections in Wisconsin.*

That result alone would have made my shift, but seeing the woman's journey from feeling overwhelmed by events and being cut off from any political engagement to requesting a ballot was like watching a time-lapse of a flower opening. Pretty incredible.

To wrap up this chapter about creating meaningful connections with high-potential voters, I'd like to leave you with one last story of my own. In October 2020, I called Dallas for Joanna Cattanach, a Democratic candidate for state legislature. I spoke with a 30-year-old named Juan. He told me, "Oh, I'm not voting."

I said, "Oh, interesting! Tell me more about that!" He said he wasn't a political person, he'd never voted, and wasn't voting this year, either. I tried to stay curious and nonjudgmental. All of my friends vote, so this "not voting" thing is something I only read about in the paper. Yet here was a live person who could give me more insight into what goes into that decision.

I asked Juan whether his friends voted. Some of them did, and they were all over the map from conservative to liberal. They all got along, but they didn't talk much about politics. I asked if he were in charge, what he might change about the country. He said everything was fine – he still had his job, and his family and friends hadn't been affected by the pandemic. I said I was glad to hear they were doing okay.

And then, almost as an afterthought, Juan mentioned that he didn't really like President Trump. My ears perked up. "Oh, really? What don't you like about him?" I asked. "I don't like the way he talks about Mexicans," Juan said.

I said, "Yeah, he's said some pretty intense things." I paused for a moment, then added, "You know, it's possible that Texas could flip blue this year. The presidential race is going to be really close, but if Texas went blue, that could decide the whole election!"

He still wasn't interested in voting, so I asked him, "Would it be okay to text you information about how to vote by mail? It might give you more options if you decided you *did* want to vote. And if you didn't want to vote, you could just throw your ballot away." Juan said yeah, I could send him information. I also asked if I could call back in a few weeks to check in, and he said sure. I thanked him for his time – we'd talked for over 20 minutes – and said goodbye.

I knew it was a long shot, but at least he hadn't hung up on me. On Election Day I called Juan back. He picked up and totally remembered me. I said, "I'm so curious – did you end up requesting an absentee ballot?" Before I could even finish my sentence, he said, "I already did it – I voted!" I almost fell out of my chair.

He said, "A couple of Saturdays ago my friend and I didn't have anything better to do, so we looked up the early voting place, and it was five minutes away. We went there – there was no line – it took less than 10 minutes. And I voted for all Democrats – including that local candidate you told me about."

I was blown away. I said, "When we talked, you weren't interested in voting. What changed?" Juan said, "Honestly, our conversation got me thinking." I said, "What about it?" He said, "The fact that it went on for so long. Other people had called before, but when I told them I wasn't going to vote, they just hung up. You seemed interested in my reasoning, without trying to persuade me. You just asked questions and listened. Later I was frustrated with the crazy things Trump was saying, and I told my friend, 'Come on, let's do this!'"

I said, "That's amazing! What would you tell someone else who had never voted?" He said, "It's easy. It doesn't take a lot of time." I asked if he thought he'd vote again. Juan said, "Uh – I guess so. Well, probably. Yeah, definitely – now that I know how it works." I could almost see his thought process evolving as he heard himself speak.

This is our future. This is how things are going to change for the better, one voter at a time, one conversation at a time. Right now we have a precious window of opportunity to up our game when engaging with at least 34 percent of the electorate: voters like Juan and Ofelia, and the many other high-potential voters like them.

So many elections are decided by a handful of votes. Until now we've left a *lot* of votes on the table. Just think what we could accomplish if we had full participation in our democracy – including many members of the 34%. Let's reach out to every single eligible voter in this year's elections. Let's engage the power of their hidden hopes to transform our country, together!

Summary

- High-potential voters make up at least 34% of eligible voters, and could decide the outcome of the next election. Take the time to engage with them.
- The MI spirit of Partnership, Autonomy, Compassion and Evoking (PACE) can help you build a foundation of respect and empathy.
- Open-ended questions, Affirmations and Reflections (OAR) can help you find out what's most important to high-potential voters and explore ambivalence they may feel about voting.
- Elicit change talk to help high-potential voters identify internal motivations to vote, getting them a step closer to casting their ballot.

Chapter 12
Navigating the First Minute of a Conversation

One of the most common challenges I hear about from other volunteers is how difficult it can be to get through the first minute of a conversation with a voter, without them hanging up or closing the door in your face. This is a delicate moment: it's that period when they have the least investment in talking with you, and you haven't yet had a chance to earn their respect or pique their interest.

I sometimes think of this fragile first minute the way I imagine a hostage negotiator might. Even if my conversation partner starts out suspicious or irritated, the most important thing is to keep them on the line, talking with me.

I don't have a foolproof method, but I've developed a few approaches that seem to keep more people in the conversation than when I started this work. I've found that these initial moments can be more challenging when phone banking than canvassing. Somehow, it's easier for people to hang up the phone rather than slam the door in your face. However, the suggestions below can be helpful for both situations.

- **Lower your expectations.** Especially for phone banking, more people than not will probably hang up on you before you can even introduce yourself. It's not personal. People are busy and might be getting a lot of calls like this, so take this as an opportunity to try out some of the following approaches and see if any of them help.
- **Channel respectful warmth from the get-go.** So much of what I'm trying to communicate right at the beginning is conveyed through my tone as much as my words. I try to sound pleased and enthusiastic that they've picked up the call (which I usually am, after hearing a lot of answering machines and disconnected phone numbers). I strive for a tone that's respectful, friendly, and upbeat but not pushy. If I'm canvassing, I try to maintain eye contact and smile earnestly.
- **Rehearse your opening lines.** For phone banking, I like to write out what I'm going to say so I can jump right in as soon as they pick up (especially since some of the dialers include a few seconds' delay between when they answer the call and when I'm connected to the voter.)

    I usually start by saying, "Oh, hi! May I speak with *(name of voter)*, please?" This allows me to verify whether I'm speaking with the person who's listed in the calling app. It also lets me get in a sentence where hopefully they can hear my warm, respectful tone of voice.
- **Introduce yourself and why you're calling or knocking on their door.** If they ask, "Who's calling?" or "What's this about?" I say, "My name is Elizabeth Chur, and I'm a volunteer with Candidate X. I'm not calling to ask for

money." I try to say all that in one breath, before they cut me off. At the same time, I try not to rush or sound like some kind of fast-talking auctioneer. Instead, I aim for a pace and tone that's energetic yet relaxed. (I like to use my last name if possible, to sound more professional, but use your discretion.)

Depending on the phase of the campaign, I might use one of the following opening lines:

- "This is just a two-minute check-in about the upcoming election."
- "Candidate X wants to make sure she/he knows what's most important to people in the community right now, and has asked us to reach out to every voter in the state/area to ask – if you could change two or three things about the country, what would they be?"
- "I'm just calling to ask – what, if anything, have you heard about the candidates in the *(fill in name of office)* race?

- **Break the telemarketing mold.** The beauty of being a volunteer is that this is a human-to-human interaction, not dictated by some corporate behemoth. Many people initially rebuff my introduction. I try to stay friendly and engaged; if they haven't hung up or shut the door on me, there's still a possibility we can continue the conversation. I strive to acknowledge their irritation without defensiveness – and perhaps even relate to it with gentle humor. When I respond with authenticity, and try to sound like a regular person instead of someone trying to make a sale, the tide often turns. Here are some common voter responses and things I've said that have actually worked:

THE JOY OF TALKING POLITICS WITH STRANGERS

Voter says…	**I respond…**
"I hate getting these calls!"	*(say with empathy and feeling):* "I *hear* you! I actually hate making these calls myself. I'm a really shy person – but the upcoming election is so important that I'm forcing myself to go out of my comfort zone to talk with other Americans about what's at stake."
"You're the third person who's called/knocked on my door this week to ask me about that!"	*(say with an apologetic tone, then genuine curiosity):* "I'm *so* sorry to bother you again. But *I* didn't get to hear what you told the other people about *(fill in name of Candidate X/issue.)* I'm so curious – what *are* your thoughts about that?"
"Oh, I don't vote."	*(say with nonjudgmental, friendly curiosity):* "Oh, interesting! Tell me more about that." *(See also Chapter 11 for many more tips!)*
"My vote is private – I don't discuss that with strangers."	*(say calmly, with deference):* I totally respect that. *(slight pause)* Setting aside specific candidates and how you're voting, I'm wondering if you'd be willing to talk about some of the *issues* that are most important to you." *(This may allow you to identify their priorities and perhaps guess at their level of support or opposition.)*
"How do I know you're telling the truth? You could be pretending to be with the campaign – there are so many swindlers and liars out there right now."	*(sometimes I'll sigh, then say with empathy):* "I know, I've gotten some of those calls myself, and it's pretty upsetting. Honestly, I'm just a volunteer – I'm not getting paid to do this, and I'm nervous to be talking with strangers. But there are a lot of hard things going on in the world right now, and I figured I'd better step up and do something to try to make things better. I want to believe that most people are still good folks who want to do the right thing for our community and the country, so that's why I'm reaching out today."

Approaches for Navigating Grumpiness

These approaches aren't always successful in encouraging people to continue the conversation. However, they work a lot better than just barreling on with the canned phone bank or canvassing scripts. There are a few other key elements that increase my success rate:

- **Acknowledge their concerns.** Instead of ignoring or minimizing what they tell you, I say something that explicitly validates their complaint. Phrases like "I hear you!" and "I totally get that" help demonstrate that I'm truly listening to them. Using a slightly apologetic tone is a nonverbal but powerful way to communicate that I know their time is valuable. They don't owe me anything, and they're doing me a favor by talking with me at all rather than hanging up immediately. I'm in their debt, and I try to express my gratitude.
- **Empathize.** When possible, use words and tone of voice that express solidarity with them, rather than setting up a "me-against-them" dynamic. If they talk about how much they hate getting calls like this, you could say how you don't like getting or making calls like this, either. That way you're both in this unpleasant situation together, rather than you somehow taking delight in interrupting their day. By quickly pivoting to the *reason* you're making this call, you invite them to do something concrete to move the country in a better direction.
- **Surprise them with sincerity.** After validating their concerns, you may want to share something that's a little vulnerable about yourself – that you are nervous about making these calls, or are way out of your comfort zone. When people ask if I'm getting paid to make these calls or knock on doors, I've said, "Absolutely not! You couldn't pay

me $100 an hour to do this – it's way too stressful. I'm only doing this because I'm so concerned about the direction our country is headed." Maybe they just feel sorry for me, or perhaps their innate desire to be helpful kicks in, but it's often disarming to say something that a paid employee could never say. I've had initially suspicious voters start off saying their vote is private; by the end of the conversation, they tell me, "You don't got to worry about me. We got this!" I take that to mean they're supporting Democrats, even though *technically* they don't want to tell me who they're voting for.

For other suggestions, please see Appendix B, "Phrase List for Engaging with High-Potential Voters."

What if the Voter is a MAGA Republican?

It's far more likely that you'll encounter someone who says "I don't vote" than someone who is a scary MAGA Republican. However, I wanted to say a few words on this topic because the fear of talking with abusive voters is one of the main reasons our workshop participants cite when we ask them to list reasons *not* to phone bank or canvass.

I want to be clear: if someone is threatening or uses foul language, hang up or leave right away. Your safety and mental health are paramount. You shouldn't ever have to put up with abuse of any kind.

If someone tells me, "Oh, honey – we're all Trumpers in this house," I personally wouldn't spend a lot of time engaging with them. I might say something like, "Thanks so much for letting me know – and thanks for being a voter. Have a great day!" I can come up with *something* to say that's both true and courteous. It allows me to wrap up our very brief conversation feeling good that they will have had one interaction with a Democrat who was respectful. After all, we are brand ambassadors of a sort, and who wants to join a club where people make snarky comments if you disagree with them? (Skylar the Skeptic may say, "But that's what *they* do!" And I'd respond, "I don't let them set the standards for my own behavior.")

But if you're up for it, it could be interesting to ask, in a non-judgmental, friendly tone, "I'd be curious to know what you like most about Trump." Or if you're calling on behalf of a downballot race, such as the U.S. Senate or state legislators, you could try to suss out whether they might be a split ticket voter by saying, "It sounds like you're a pretty big fan of his. I'm curious what, if anything, you think about the candidates for the *other* races in the upcoming election?" I've talked with a number of voters who tell me with pride, "I don't vote a straight party line – I really go by the individual candidates." In those cases, you might be able to earn their vote for other key races, especially if you don't get in a verbal tug-of-war about Trump, and instead pivot gracefully to other topics.

Definitely don't put pressure on yourself to somehow say the magic words to transform a MAGA Republican into voting for your candidate. Those words probably don't exist. However, you *could* find out some interesting viewpoints by exploring a bit more. For example, sometimes people say things like, "I don't like all Trump's drama, but my investments did a lot better when he was in office." That could open a door for further dialogue.

Acting with courtesy and manners when engaging with a Trump supporter feels like a small but important step toward restoring civil discourse in our country. I'd like to believe that it's possible to see people who have different political affiliations as fellow humans, rather than demonizing them. It doesn't take any extra time, and if enough of us do this, perhaps over time it can help subtly change the tone of our national dialogue.

I can't tell you the number of people I've spoken with on the phone or in person who sound almost apologetic when telling me they're voting for Republicans. It's as if they're bracing for a nasty or sarcastic response. They seem slightly surprised when I'm still pleasant and wish them a good day. Just like I don't interact with many Trump supporters in my daily life, I may be one of the few Democrats they ever talk with. I try to behave in a way that reflects the larger values we claim to have as progressives, such as inclusivity, open-mindedness, and care for the community.

Summary

- The first minute of a conversation with a voter can be the most challenging to get through.
- Acknowledge their concerns.
- Channel warmth and empathy with your words and tone of voice.
- Break through the telemarketer mold by surprising them with sincerity, even vulnerability.

Chapter 13

For Grassroots Leaders: How to (Re)Engage Volunteers

(written with Victoria Levi, MD,
and Dara Friedman-Wheeler, PhD)

One of the laments I hear from grassroots leaders is that while there was a huge outpouring of volunteers in 2018 and 2020 in response to the presidency of Donald Trump, once Biden won the 2020 election it was challenging to get many of those volunteers to re-up for the 2022 midterms and beyond. Trump's nomination in 2024 may motivate some people to jump back in the game. However, some former volunteers are burned out, or unwilling or unable to get back into canvassing and phone banking. Others have pivoted to postcarding, which is an important piece of the overall strategy but can never replace one-to-one conversations with voters.

I share those concerns – *and* can also empathize with having given it my all for four or more years, only to be called on yet again to save democracy. Perhaps it's a bit analogous to COVID – while people are still getting sick from the virus and millions are now living with long COVID, the human brain just can't stay at the same alert level indefinitely. Most people have gone back to their pre-pandemic lives, with a few adjustments.

Whatever the reasons, it's a cause for concern. However, I can say from personal experience that the traditional methods of outreach – calling up volunteers and trying to badger, guilt trip or scare them back into phone banking and canvassing – aren't very appealing. In fact, it's quite similar to the dynamic I described in Chapter 11 with high-potential voters: just like voters usually don't respond well to being lectured or bossed around, volunteers don't either!

For example, in 2022 I got a call from an organization that will be left unnamed. The caller said, "I'm reaching out because you've phone banked with us before, and I'm wondering if I can sign you up for an upcoming shift?" I said, "You know, I'm focusing my energy on teaching a lot of voter engagement workshops right now, including a few I've done for your organization to better connect with high-potential voters. I might have more time this fall to do some phone banking myself." The caller said, "Oh, OK. I'll make a note to call you back in September to see if you can phone bank. Have a great day!"

That felt transactional rather than relational. I appreciated that the caller was polite and wouldn't keep pestering me every week, but she didn't express even a whiff of curiosity about the workshops I was teaching to her organization's volunteers, or acknowledge the work I was *already* doing to support the campaign. I felt like I was just a name to check off a list.

If you are a grassroots leader racking your brains about how to recruit new volunteers or bring former volunteers back into the fold, I have a few suggestions. Instead of trying to power through as many calls and nail down as many volunteer signups as possible, I'd humbly suggest a different definition of success. Maybe you have one or two quality conversations an hour with potential volunteers.

Those calls are a success if you can convey gratitude for the person's past service and any current activities, including if they are postcarding. It's a success if you can provide space for the person to be heard, and they feel like their opinions and experiences matter to you and the organization. And it's a success because you've started the process of reengagement. If someone signs up to volunteer, that's fantastic! Helping them reignite that spark of enthusiasm may also have ripple effects – they might invite a friend or two, or share encouraging stories with their networks.

Even if they aren't ready to jump back in, it's a step in the right direction. Similar to high-potential voters, being in dialogue with former volunteers and helping them reengage with this work is often a process rather than an event. We need to play the long game.

I want to give a shout out to Victoria Levi, MD, Susan Labandibar, and Douglas Grant, three volunteers with Boston-based Swing Blue Alliance. After taking our "You and the 34%" workshop, they adapted the material and repurposed it to create a new workshop. It focused on using some of the Motivational Interviewing (MI) approaches mentioned in Chapter 11, "Making 'I Don't Vote' the Start, not the End, of a Conversation," expressly for the purpose of reengaging past volunteers. They even produced a short video modeling their approach.[22]

Vicki and I later collaborated on a similar workshop for San Francisco Bay Area grassroots leaders. She's one of the most amazing volunteers I've met. She has a lively sense of humor and loves taking long-distance road trips to canvass in swing states. She worked for decades as a community psychiatrist in Israel and the U.S., and has deep wisdom about the foibles of human nature. I'm going to turn the microphone (or the pen) over to Vicki for this next section.

Helping Volunteers Overcome Ambivalence

As grassroots leaders, you've been working with campaigns for quite a few years and know a lot. I see you as accomplished activists who have important experience in organizing campaigns and speaking with voters. So is there a difference between the way that you approach voters compared with volunteers?

Actually, there shouldn't be. We know that the obstacle to making changes in our lives – whether it's giving up smoking, getting to the polls, or deciding to volunteer – is ambivalence. People won't change their behaviors just because we ask them to, or because we explain to them that it is *terribly* important that they do. (By the way, that also applies to our family members of all ages!)

You may remember the "Spirit of MI" from Chapter 11, which is illustrated by PACE (Partnership, Autonomy, Compassion and Evoking.) When talking with volunteers, here are some examples of how PACE informs our approach:

- **Partnership**: We are talking to people like us who have been volunteers. We join *with* them to explore or facilitate action; we're not trying to direct them toward action.
- **Autonomy**: We respect the volunteer's right to decide whether or not to phone bank or canvass this cycle.
- **Compassion**: We have empathy for how hard it is to change behavior, and to motivate oneself to do things that can be awkward or unpleasant at times.
- **Evoking**: We want to know about their desires and interests. It's less important what *we* think, and more important what *they* think. Hearing themselves is how we can help them make change.

As Elizabeth mentioned earlier in this book, William Miller, PhD, and Stephen Rollnick, PhD, the founders of MI, recognized that telling people what was good for them was a failed technique. But *asking* them what they thought was the key to exploring their internal conflict and mixed feelings. Perhaps you might relate to some of these inner tensions in other areas of your life:

- "I want to exercise more… oh, but not now. I'm too busy."
- "I want to eat less sweets… but not really."
- "I want to go back to school… but it's too expensive."
- "I want to spend less time on social media… oh, but I can't."

How do we get started? First we need to engage with people, before they hang up. When doing these outreach calls to former volunteers, I introduce myself with my full name and the organization I'm volunteering with. For example, I say, "My name is Victoria Levi. I'm a volunteer with Swing Blue Alliance. I'm calling to thank you for your past volunteer work, and to ask, what is your advice on how we can improve our outreach to volunteers during this important election year?"

Just like with voters, engaging volunteers from the beginning of a conversation starts by asking an Open-ended question. (As you may recall, an Open-ended question can't be answered with a yes or no, and is curious and nonjudgmental. Wait for them to respond – count to 10 in your head if needed.) Some other ideas for Open-ended questions include:

- **"I'm interested in learning more about** what your volunteering experiences were like last cycle?"
- **"We'd love hear your ideas about** – how can we make volunteering more effective?"

By phrasing your greeting in this way, you are making it clear that you are interested in hearing what *they* have to say. You are not selling an idea, and you are not looking for a specific answer.

These adjustments to the way we pose our questions encourage people to share their thoughts and feelings about the purpose of volunteering, their ideas of what works and what doesn't, and how they would like to contribute their time and effort. Of course, we also have to *listen*. People will talk if they sense that someone is actually listening to them.

People who have volunteered in the past, or have expressed an interest in volunteering, have many reasons for staying home this cycle. Our task is to identify those reasons – the pros and cons, their doubts and hopes. Often it is hard to listen to criticism without replying. But don't forget the value of venting – expressing the resentments, hurts, disappointments and paralyzing fears. As the ancient Greeks said, it can be cathartic. We can say:

- "Tell me more."
- "Wow!"
- "That's not easy."
- "That sounds frustrating."

Open-ended questions are important when initiating conversation. But how do you continue to build the connection? Complementing Open-ended questions, Miller and Rollnick described two additional ways to build a connection: Affirmations and Reflections.

Affirmations are different from compliments or giving praise; those contain judgment, as if you were giving them a good grade in school. Instead, with Affirmations we look for and identify strength or effort, based on what they share with us. Try starting the sentence with "You…" For example:

- "**You** worked hard."
- "**You** have a strong sense of justice."
- "**You** have given this a lot of thought."

- "**You** really went beyond your comfort zone in the last election cycle."

Another powerful tool in MI are Reflections, which are statements or observations that show a deeper understanding of what the volunteer has told you. With Reflections, you repeat or interpret what they say. This helps the volunteer hear themselves, and shows that you're really listening. For example:

- "**You** felt frustrated that you didn't reach more voters the last time you phone banked."
- "**You** are worried that too many splinter groups are damaging the cause."
- "**You** are disappointed with Biden's performance and wish there were more inspiring candidates to volunteer for."

Now I'm going to hand the microphone back to Elizabeth.

SAMPLE DIALOGUE: MEETING VOLUNTEERS WHERE THEY ARE

To give you an idea of how some of these concepts might play out in a real conversation with a voter, I worked with another volunteer, Dara Friedman-Wheeler, PhD, to develop a sample dialogue. Dara is a clinical psychologist at Johns Hopkins University who has a wealth of MI experience. She's also an experienced canvasser and phone banker with Allies for Democracy in Baltimore and the co-author of a recent book, *Being the Change: A Guide for Advocates and Activists on Staying Healthy, Inspired, and Driven*. In this example, Dara plays the grassroots leader, and I play the burned-out former volunteer.

Dara: (*Ring, ring*)

Elizabeth: Hello?

Dara: Hi, may I speak with Elizabeth Chur, please?

Elizabeth: Yes, speaking.

Dara: Hi, my name is Dara Friedman-Wheeler, and I'm a volunteer with Allies for Democracy. I'm calling to thank you for all your work in 2020 and to learn more about what that experience was like for you.

Elizabeth: Yeah, I did a lot of phone banking in 2020. It's not really my cup of tea, but I was so desperate to get Trump out of the White House that I was willing to do it.

Dara: You went out of your comfort zone to work for something that was really important to you.

Elizabeth: Yeah, I guess so. But sometimes I felt like I was banging my head against a wall.

Dara: Banging your head against a wall. Tell me more about that.

Elizabeth: Sometimes I'd spend two hours on a phone bank, but we'd waste the first 45 minutes just getting trained on the latest system or script. Then we had to use a manual dialer, and mostly I'd get wrong numbers and voicemails. We weren't even allowed to leave messages, so it felt like a waste of time. The few people who did pick up were either not the people I was trying to reach, or they got angry because I was the third person who'd called them that day. It was so frustrating!

Dara: You really wanted to connect with voters, and felt frustrated that you couldn't talk with more of the people you were trying to reach.

Elizabeth: Yeah, I guess so.

Dara: Yet you kept on phone banking, even with all these obstacles. I'm wondering – what was the best call you had?

Elizabeth: Well, there was this one young woman in Arizona. She'd never voted before, and didn't know where her polling place was. I looked up the address, and she said it was at a church four blocks away. I reminded her to bring her driver's license, and asked when she thought she could vote. She said she'd go to the polls first thing on Election Day, before she went to work. She actually thanked me for calling and said she was glad I'd called. Her parents were out of town and she didn't know who else to ask. That made me feel good.

Dara: That voter was glad you called. You gave her the information she needed to make a plan to vote.

Elizabeth: Yeah, I felt like I was actually doing something useful.

Dara: And Arizona was really close in 2020 – we really needed every vote.

Elizabeth: Yes, we sure did. That was too close for comfort.

Dara: You helped put us over the top. *(pauses)* I'm wondering – what, if anything, are you thinking about doing in this election cycle?

Elizabeth: Oh, I've already written 700 postcards this year! And I *guess* I'll make myself phone bank later on, but I'm waiting until October, when it's most effective.

Dara: Wow, 700 postcards! That's a lot! *(pauses)* I'm wondering – could I tell you a little about what else is going on behind the scenes right now at this stage of the campaign?

Elizabeth: Um, sure – I know we're less than 100 days to the election.

Dara: Yeah, it's definitely all hands on deck. Postcards are great for giving people a nudge. But some people need a little extra help – like that young woman you talked with in Arizona. She needed someone to help her figure out where and how to vote. We're so lucky to have people like you writing postcards. And we *also* have a big need to call voters right now. You might have heard that Arizona has made it a lot harder to vote by mail. For example, if someone hasn't voted early in a recent election, they may be removed from the early voting list. They have to request an absentee ballot all over again, and that has to be done well in advance of the election. So this is a great time to reach out to them. I'm wondering – what do you think about that?

Elizabeth: *(Sighs)* Well, I'll consider it. Honestly, in 2020, I was so motivated to defeat Trump. But Biden has been such a disappointment. He had all these grand plans, but most of it went down in flames.

Dara: I've heard that from some other folks as well. *(pauses)* I'm wondering – what were you hoping that we could accomplish?

Elizabeth: I was excited about free preschool, and real action on climate change.

Dara: I *hear* you. *(brief pause)* I'm curious – on a scale of zero to 10, how likely are you to phone bank this election cycle, with zero being "not at all" and 10 being "very likely"?

Elizabeth: Uh, maybe a three.

Dara: Oh, interesting! Why isn't that number a zero or a one?

Elizabeth: Well, I know that this election is important. And a few years ago we *did* pass the biggest climate bill ever – just barely.

Dara: Yes, that was a big win. I'm wondering – what might help boost your "three" to a four or five?

Elizabeth: Well, maybe if I actually got to talk with more voters during my shift. Sometimes I'd spend a couple of hours calling voters, but only talk with one or two live humans. The rest of the calls were all wrong numbers, voicemail, or disconnected numbers. It's so frustrating to keep dialing and dialing, with almost nothing to show for it. If I'm going to make myself phone bank, I want to feel like my time is being well spent.

Dara: I totally get that. If you'd like, I could text you a link to an upcoming phone bank that I know is using an autodialer. The more people we have on the

	phone bank that day, the more efficient the system will be, since the autodialer needs a critical mass of volunteers to route calls to when a voter answers the phone. What do you think of that idea?
Elizabeth:	Yeah, sure. Go ahead and send me the information, and I'll think about it.
Dara:	Great! I'll do that as soon as we wrap up. I really appreciate the chance to talk with you today, and also want to thank you for all the work you're continuing to do. It's been great talking with you.
Elizabeth:	Oh, thank you for calling.
Dara:	Take care and have a great rest of your day!
Elizabeth:	Bye-bye.

The Power of Listening and Gratitude

Recruiting new volunteers or reengaging past supporters may feel like an uphill climb. However, nagging, guilt-tripping, or emphatically repeating again (and again) how this is the most important election of our lifetime is unlikely to make people jump out of their chairs to join you.

Instead, by using some of the approaches described above, you can transform the quality of the conversations you have with prospective volunteers. Ask Open-ended questions, and listen to their responses with empathy and compassion. Use Affirmations and Reflections to find out more about their experiences. Thank them for their previous work. Demonstrate nonjudgmental curiosity about their past volunteering experience, and invite them to talk about their *best* conversations with voters. Actively solicit their ideas for how you can improve their experience. Gently inquire about what, if anything, they are thinking about doing in this election cycle, and ask what you could do to support them in taking the next step.

Above all, creating a warm environment of appreciation and welcome helps encourage people to give volunteering a try, or to reconnect with the passion that inspired them to volunteer in the past.

SUMMARY

- (Re)engaging with volunteers is very similar to engaging with voters. Be patient and empathetic, and bring your nonjudgmental curiosity to these conversations.
- Thank volunteers for their past work, and ask Open-ended questions to find out more about their previous experience and recommendations for improvement.
- Use Affirmations to underscore their strength and effort, and Reflections to demonstrate you are truly listening to them.

Chapter 14

Spanish for Activists

(written with Mayela Amayrani Galindo Vásquez)

In November 2016, I was doing some last-minute phone banking to Nevada, a critical swing state. Not many people were answering the phone, and some who did only spoke Spanish. Though they were willing to talk with me, I was completely unable to communicate with them. I felt useless, when the stakes were so incredibly high.

After Trump was elected, I promised myself that by the next presidential election I'd be better prepared. I started taking Spanish classes, with the goal of sticking with it for a year. I ended up enjoying Spanish so much that I'm still taking lessons, seven years later. I supplemented classroom learning with listening to Spanish-language podcasts while cooking and cleaning. After a few years I started reading novels in Spanish (side-by-side with their English translations) to help broaden my vocabulary. And while I'll probably never be fluent, less than two years in I was able to have simple conversations with Spanish-speaking voters.

My friend Bren, who has a master's degree in teaching English as a second language, said that for language learning to be most effective the content needs to be both meaningful and relevant. Although I definitely needed to learn the fundamentals of grammar and vocabulary, I found that workbooks and classroom exercises didn't teach me even the basics about real-life applications. For example, I had no idea how to begin a phone conversation with a voter in Spanish. I didn't realize that neither the caller nor the recipient starts off with "Hola." (Keep reading to find out what you can expect to hear instead, and how to reply!)

After taking classes in San Francisco for several years, I went to Oaxaca, Mexico for a couple of weeks to do a homestay and an intensive language course. I booked a private instructor to help me learn some basic "election Spanish" phrases. I recorded our conversations and typed up a phrase list, and had him proofread it.

Back at home, I continued private lessons online with another one of my teachers in Oaxaca, Mayela Galindo, who has since become a dear friend. In addition to continuing to learn about grammar and general conversation, in 2020 we developed an online "Spanish for Phone Banking" workshop together. In 2022 we expanded this to "Spanish for Activists" to include canvassing language.

To date Mayela and I have trained more than 200 volunteers from across the country, and recruited a team of teaching assistants. Our workshops include model role plays to teach vocabulary and demonstrate recommended approaches, as well as several breakout sessions so students can practice the material in pairs. After all, it's one thing to understand a new phrase, but it's another to actually be able to use it in the moment with voters – and practice is the best way to learn.

The rest of this chapter is adapted from our "Spanish for Activists" workshop. The content is specific to Mexican Spanish (the most common form spoken in the swing districts and states where our California volunteers are engaged.) However, some of the context may be interesting even if you don't speak the language but are working in Latino communities with bilingual or English-speaking voters. Also, I try to outline a general approach which is grounded in respect, centers the voter's concerns, and expresses gratitude for their time and help. The spirit of this approach applies to how I aspire to engage with all voters, no matter their language or culture.

If you speak Spanish, you can find a compiled phrase list in Appendix D. Hopefully these suggestions will help you reach more voters. It's always a good idea to practice these phrases at home or with a buddy to help build your skills. Even if you are mainly a canvasser, it might be helpful to do a couple of phone banking shifts in Spanish so you can practice the phrases with the script in front of you before going out to knock doors. You can often search Mobilize for Spanish-language phone banks if you aren't already plugged in to a specific campaign or geographic area.

One note of caution: the material in this chapter is *not* intended to substitute for a working knowledge of Spanish. I don't advise that non-Spanish speakers try to fake their way through a conversation in Spanish. It's not respectful of their time, and can come across as insulting to think you can just wing it if you don't speak the language. It would be better for another volunteer who *does* speak the language to reach out to them another day. In fact, Mayela and I developed another workshop, "Election Spanish for Absolute Beginners," to help novices learn a few phrases to communicate this exact message to voters. If you speak a little Spanish, you can see that suggested script in Appendix E.

Hacer un Clic (Make a Connection)

The most important thing when talking with any voter, but especially a Spanish-speaking voter, is to *hacer un clic* – literally, to "click" or make a connection with them. We try to teach phrases and approaches that demonstrate respect and begin to earn their trust.

In Spanish, there are two words for the verb "to communicate." *Comunicar* means to communicate information, like reminding a voter when Election Day is, or where their polling place is located. This is certainly important for getting across vital details about how and when to vote.

However, the heart of a successful conversation with a voter involves a different verb, embodied by the concept of *comunicarse*, which is a reciprocal verb. This refers to an *intercambio* – an interchange between volunteer and voter. It involves not only talking, but also asking questions, listening intently to what they say, and responding with empathy and compassion. Our Spanish for Activists workshops strive to teach effective phrases and approaches for both types of communication – *comunicar* and *comunicarse*.

We emphasize that it's not critical to speak Spanish perfectly. While basic proficiency is important, I've never had a voter criticize me because I conjugated a verb incorrectly or used the wrong gender for a noun. If their primary language is Spanish, they probably understand the challenges of speaking another language and cut me a lot of slack. Most voters appreciate that I am making an effort to speak to them in words they can understand. "Spanglish" is also useful, and quite common, especially among voters who have lived in the U.S. for a while.

In general, if a voter seems to be older than about 40, we recommend that volunteers use the formal *usted* rather than informal *tú* when addressing the voter. It's better to err on the side of too much politeness rather than not enough, especially with a stranger.

If the voter would prefer that you address them informally, they can always say, *¡Tutéame!* – Use *tú* with me! (It's a bit like meeting somebody famous for the first time and saying, "So nice to meet you, Dr. Fauci," and he says, "Oh, call me Tony." It would be a major faux pas for you to start off saying, "How's it goin', Tony?") The person with higher rank due to age, social standing, or in this case, receiving an unsolicited visit or call, should be the one to determine whether you should use the formal or informal.

(If the voter does say *¡Tutéame!* just remember to shift to the *tú* conjugation of verbs. The rest of this chapter maintains the formal *usted* conjugations because that's likely what you'll be using with most Spanish-speaking voters.)

When introducing ourselves as volunteers with a particular campaign, we recommend using your first and last name. It sounds more professional, rather than me saying, "My name is Elizabeth and I'm a volunteer with the Democratic Party," which leaves them wondering, "Elizabeth who?" As always, use your own judgment based on your personal boundaries and comfort level with disclosing your full name.

Overview

Now for a quick rundown of our suggested flow for these conversations, before diving into the details. I'll explain this flow chart in a moment:

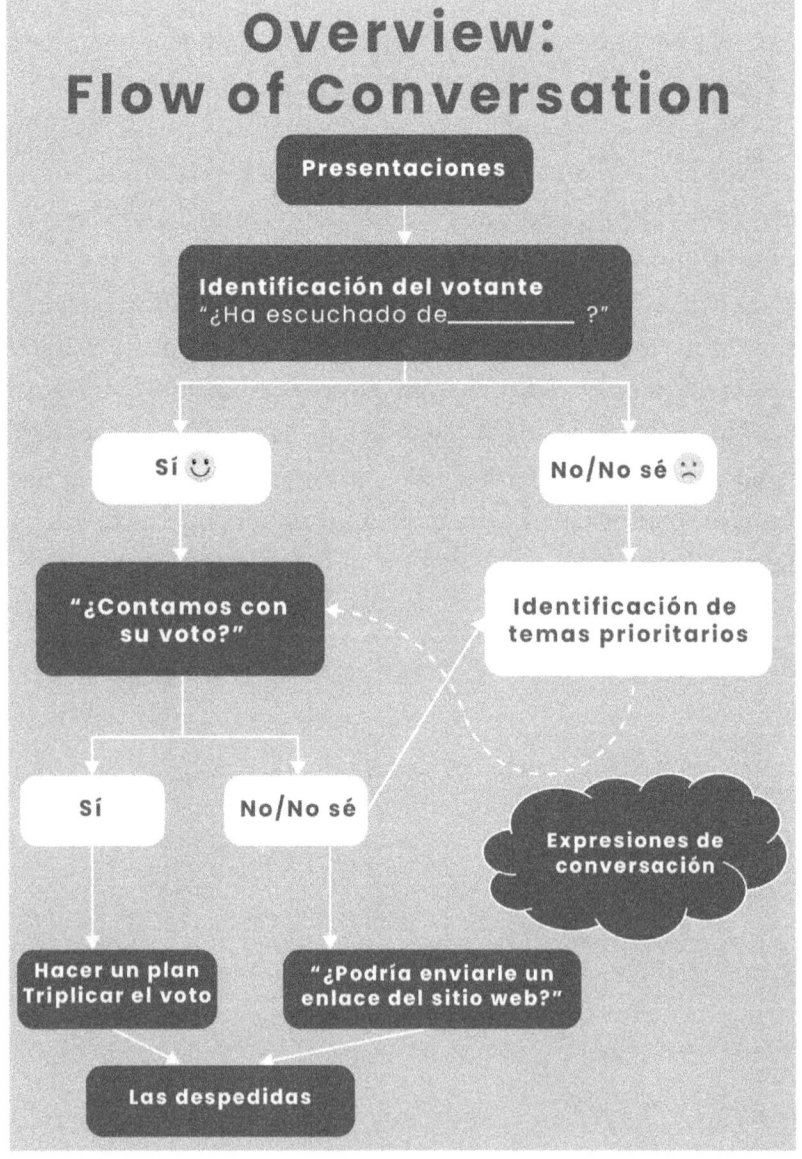

We suggest starting off with *Presentaciones* (Introductions). Because some voters may be initially suspicious or reluctant to talk, this includes some similar content as described in Chapter 12, "Getting Across the Moat: Navigating the First Minute of a Conversation."

Then we describe *Identificación del votante* (Voter identification). This helps us assess the voter's prior knowledge of our candidate, if any, and also what their political leanings might be. If the voter is familiar with our candidate, we can ask, *¿Contamos con su voto?* (Can we count on your vote?) If they say yes, we can help them *Hacer un plan y triplicar el voto* (Make a plan and ask them to encourage three other people to vote) before proceeding to *Las despedidas* (Goodbyes).

However, if they've never heard of our candidate, or they're unsure, we can spend some time on *Identificación de temas prioritarios* (Identifying priority issues) before looping back to *¿Contamos con su voto?* If they're now in support of our candidate, we can proceed as above. If not, or they're still unsure, we can say, *¿Podría enviarle un enlace del sitio web?* (Can I send you a link to the website?) so at least they'll have a little more information to consider. Then we thank them and wrap up the conversation.

Throughout, we can use *Expresiones de conversación* (Conversational expressions), which are polite phrases to let them know we're listening, empathizing, and responding to what they are sharing with us.

Presentaciones (Introductions)

Initiating a conversation in Spanish is a bit more challenging over the phone than in person. Many voters originally from Mexico answer the phone with one of these three phrases:

- *Bueno*
- *Sí, bueno*
- *Dígame*

Instead of responding with a casual *¡Hola!*, it is more appropriate to say:

- *Buenos días/Buenas tardes. ¿Se encuentra el Señor/la Señora ____, por favor?* (Good morning/Good afternoon. May I speak with Mr./Mrs. ____, please?)

The voter or their family member might worry that you are with *la migra* (Immigration and Customs Enforcement, or ICE) or are calling for money.

- If you are phone banking, the voter may say, *¿De parte de quién?* (Who's calling?)
- If you are canvassing, the voter might say, *¿Quién lo/la busca?* (Who's looking for him/her?) or *¿En qué puedo servirle?* (How can I help you?), a polite way of saying, "What do you want?"

Then you can say:

Me llamo ____ y soy voluntario(a) con el Partido Demócrata y:

- **el congresista** Jared Golden. *(male incumbent congressperson)*
- **la congresista** Marie Gluesenkamp Pérez. *(female incumbent congressperson)*
- **el senador** Sherrod Brown. *(male incumbent senator)*
- **la senadora** Jacky Rosen. *(female incumbent senator)*
- Rudy Salas, **el candidato** para el Congreso. *(male candidate for Congress)*
- Stephanie Simacek, **la candidata** para la Cámara de Representantes de Arizona. *(female candidate for the Arizona House of Representatives)*

I am including examples of male and female incumbents and candidates above so you can see the titles and articles for each office, depending on the gender of the candidate.

Then you might want to say:

- *No llamo para pedir dinero, sino para hacer conciencia en la comunidad sobre las elecciones.* (I'm not calling to ask for money, but rather to raise community awareness about the elections.) This lets them know right away that this is not a sales call.

Then you can ask:

- *¿Prefiere hablar en inglés o español?* ("Do you prefer to speak in English or Spanish?")

This is one way you can let the voter guide you about the best language in which to continue the conversation. I've found that this is a respectful, judgment-free way to navigate this issue. I'm not assuming that they *don't* speak English, which could be insulting (since many voters are bilingual). On the other hand, I don't assume they *do* speak English. That could make it hard to communicate if they feel more comfortable speaking Spanish but perhaps wouldn't say so unless you specifically ask.

If they say English is fine, but after a minute of talking it appears that they might participate more fully in the conversation if we spoke in Spanish, I sometimes say:

- *"¿Sería posible practicar mi español con usted?"* ("Would it be possible to practice my Spanish with you?")

This can help voters save face: it frames switching to Spanish as them graciously doing me a favor, rather than me implying that my Spanish is better than their English.

Some voters may appreciate your call, but others may be less thrilled to talk with you. If they're in a hurry or aren't interested in politics, you could use one or more of these phrases:

- *Lo siento. No quiero molestarlo(la), pero estamos escuchando las opiniones de los votantes en la comunidad.* (I'm sorry. I don't want to bother you, but we're listening to the opinions of voters in the community.)
- *Con mucho respeto, solamente tengo unas preguntas.* (Respectfully, I just have a few questions.)
- *Solamente serán algunos minutos.* (It will only take a few minutes.)
- *De antemano, muchas gracias por su paciencia. Mi español no es muy bueno.* (Thanks in advance for your patience. My Spanish isn't very good.)

Expresiones de Conversación (Conversational Expressions)

As I've mentioned throughout this book, earning a voter's trust and forging a genuine connection requires showing empathy and being a good listener. Sometimes voters will talk about difficult things in their lives, or tell you about the extraordinary things they do to make a living and take care of their families. It's important to let them know you're listening and really hearing what they're saying, without taking over the conversation. Here are some handy phrases to demonstrate empathy and nonjudgmental curiosity:

- *¡Bueno!* (Great!)
- *¡Muy bien!* (Very good!)
- *¡Órale!* (Wow!)
- *¿En serio?* (Seriously?)
- *Comprendo.* (I understand.)

- *¡Claro que sí!* (Yes, of course!)
- *¡Por supuesto!* (Of course!)
- *Me alegra mucho escuchar eso.* (I'm really happy to hear that.)
- *Siento mucho escuchar eso.* (I'm really sorry to hear that.)
- *¡Qué lástima!* (What a shame!)
- *Ojalá que todo se mejore.* (I hope things get better.)
- *Cuénteme más sobre eso.* (Tell me more about that.)

I try to use these liberally throughout the conversation, and voters seem to appreciate it. As I mention in Chapter 6, "Empathize, Empathize, Empathize," these phrases are a form of "backchanneling" – using both verbal and nonverbal cues to signal that you are listening and want to hear more.

If you don't understand what a voter is saying or they're talking faster than you can take it in, you can always use one of these phrases:

- *¿Mande?* (Pardon?)
- *Repita, por favor.* (Please repeat that.)
- *¿Podría hablar más despacio, por favor?* (Could you speak more slowly, please?)

Even though it's humbling to ask them to slow down or to repeat something, most voters have been sympathetic and appreciate that I am making an effort. It's better to ask for help rather than pretending that I know what they're saying if I've lost the thread of the conversation.

Identificación del Votante (Voter Identification)

To help guide the rest of the conversation, we want to better understand the voter's prior knowledge of our candidate, if any, and what their level of support might be. If they've heard of our candidate and are supportive, you could use some of these phrases:

- *¡Muy bien! ¿Qué piensa de él/ella?* (Great! What do you think of him/her?)
- *¡Excelente! ¿Contamos con su voto para _____?* (Excellent! Can we count on your vote for _____?)
- *¡Muchísimas gracias! ¿Y también contamos con su voto para todos los demócratas, incluyendo los candidatos municipales, estatales y federales?* (Thank you so much! Can we count on your vote for all the Democrats, including the city, state and federal candidates?)
- *¡Perfecto! ¿Quisiera ayudar a la campaña de _____?* (Perfect! Would you like to help the campaign of _____?)
- *¡Mil gracias! Por favor, ¿podría darme su número de teléfono? Mi compañero va a llamarle.* (Thanks so much! Could you please give me your telephone number? My colleague will call you.)

Identificación de Temas Prioritarios (Identifying Priority Issues)

On the other hand, if the voter has never heard of our candidate, is undecided, or tells you they don't vote, it's important to take some time to better understand their most important issues. That way you can tailor what you share with them to their interests. (As you might remember from Chapter 11, "Making 'I Don't Vote' the Start, not the End, of a Conversation," this is a *really* important part of engaging with voters, especially high-potential voters.) You could start out by saying:

- *Tengo interés en sus prioridades.* (I'm interested in your priorities.)
- *Por favor, me podría decir, si usted pudiera cambiar dos o tres cosas sobre el país, ¿qué cambiaría?* (Please tell me – if you could change two or three things about the country, what would you change?)

Depending on what they share with you, you could tell them how the candidate stands on what's most important to them. These are general Democratic talking points, but probably hold true for most Democratic candidates:

[Name of candidate] está luchando para: ([Name of candidate] is fighting to):

- *defender y expandir Obamacare, y limitar los precios de los medicamentos, incluyendo la insulina.* (defend and expand Obamacare, and limit the prices of medications, including insulin.)
- *crear más viviendas a precios accesibles.* (create more affordable housing.)
- *crear trabajos buenos que paguen más que el salario mínimo.* (create good jobs that pay more than the minimum wage.)
- *proteger el Seguro Social.* (protect Social Security.)
- *invertir en la educación pública.* (invest in public education.)
- *proteger a los inmigrantes y crear un sendero hasta la ciudadanía para los Dreamers y campesinos.* (protect immigrants and create a path to citizenship for the Dreamers and farmworkers.)

If the voter expresses support for our candidate after hearing more about them, you can loop back up to some of the phrases under *Identificación del Votante* (Voter Identification), above, then continue on below with the rest of the conversation.

If the voter still is uncertain or needs more information, you can say:

- *¿Podría enviarle un enlace del sitio web con más información?* (Can I send you a link to the website?)
- *¿Podría enviárselo a este número?* (Can I send it to this phone number?)

After the call, you can text them a link to the candidate's website.

Votación: Hacer un Plan (Voting: Making a Plan)

This next section is *very* dependent on where in the election cycle we are, and the particular rules of the county and state. Check with your canvass or phone bank captain about the most accurate information to share with voters. To increase turnout, some campaigns encourage people to vote as early as possible and to vote by mail when these options are available. The following is just sample language that you might use as a starting point.

You may ask the voter:

- *¿Cómo va a votar: en persona o por correo?* (How will you vote: in person or by mail?)

If they tell you they'll be voting by mail, you can say:

- *¡Excelente! ¿Ya recibió su boleta por correo?* (Excellent! Have you received your ballot in the mail yet?)

Voters may say, *Sí, ya la envié* (Yes, I've already sent it), in which case you can thank them for being a voter and move on to the closing. If a voter says, *No, todavía no* (No, not yet) – in other words, they haven't yet received their ballot – check with your canvass or phone bank captain for how to respond.

Other voters may say, *Sí, ya la recibí* (Yes, I've already received it), but they haven't yet sent it in. Depending on the rules of that county and state, you could say something along the lines of:

- *Yo le recomiendo que llene su boleta y la envíe lo más pronto posible.* (I recommend that you fill out your ballot and mail it as soon as possible.)
- *También puede llevarla al centro de votación temprana o en un buzón electoral, o en el Día de las Elecciones.* (You can also bring it in person to an early voting center or a ballot drop box, or on Election Day.)
- *Por favor, asegúrese de firmar y ponerle la fecha al sobre, y también de que su firma sea la misma que la de su ID/su licencia de manejar.* (Please make sure to sign and date the envelope, and make sure your signature is the same as it is on your ID/driver's license.)

Again, *please* check with your canvass or phone bank captain to make sure you are sharing correct information. The above language is just a suggestion, and is tailored to the voting procedure in California, which has one of the most progressive voter systems in the country.

I have included language about encouraging voters to sign and date their vote-by-mail ballot with care. I have spent many days curing ballots for voters who forgot to sign their ballot or did it in a hurry. In these situations, we needed to make sure they signed an affidavit to fix or "cure" their ballot in order for it to be counted. Therefore, it's helpful to remind voters to take their time with this part. Every properly signed ballot is one less that the campaign (and you) will need to cure later on!

If the voter wants to vote in person, or if vote-by-mail access is limited, you can encourage them to vote early, if that is available in their particular county. (Again, please check with your canvass or phone bank captain about the best message to share with the community):

- *Le recomiendo que vote antes del Día de las Elecciones en un centro de votación temprana si fuera posible.* (I recommend that you vote before Election Day at an early voting center if you can.)

Triplicar el Voto y 'Cerrar el Trato' (Vote Tripling and 'Closing the Deal')

It's always good to reaffirm the importance of voting, and emphasize that their vote could make all the difference. If a voter is an enthusiastic supporter of the Democrats, we can ask them to "vote triple" by making sure that three people they know also cast their ballot. (Please note that we are *not* asking them to vote three times, but rather inviting them to reach out to like-minded family and friends to make sure they also vote.) Some useful phrases for "closing the deal":

- *Los resultados para las elecciones casi podrían ser un empate.* (The results of these elections could almost be a tie.)
- *¡Es posible que un solo voto decida las elecciones!* (It's possible that a single vote could decide the elections!)
- *¡Cada voto cuenta!* (Every vote counts!)
- *Por favor, no olvide votar lo más pronto posible, y corra la voz con sus familiares, amigos y vecinos.* (Please don't forget to vote as soon as possible, and spread the word to your family, friends and neighbors.)
- *¿Contamos con su apoyo para que hable con tres conocidos y se asegure de que voten?¿Podría nombrarme a esas tres personas?* (Can we count on you to talk with three people you

know and make sure they vote? Could you tell me their first names?

Las Despedidas (Goodbyes)

It's always a good idea to end with gratitude, no matter how the conversation went. Here are some courteous phrases for saying goodbye:

- *Fue un placer hablar con usted.* (It was a pleasure talking with you.)
- *Muchas gracias por su tiempo y por ser un(a) votante.* (Thank you very much for your time and for being a voter.)
- *Le agradezco su apoyo. Cuídese mucho.* (I appreciate your support. Take very good care.)
- *Que tenga un buen día/una buena tarde/una buena noche.* (Have a good day/evening/night.)

Found in Translation: Other Language Tips

Even if you speak Spanish, there are probably other languages you don't speak. I remember spending a canvassing shift in Modesto and being sent out to a neighborhood that was primarily Assyrian. I was completely unable to communicate with most of the voters who answered the door. I was kicking myself, thinking, "Darn, I forgot to learn Assyrian!" When I got back to the campaign headquarters, I did meet a volunteer who was from the Assyrian community and asked for his phone number so I would be better prepared in the future.

I have also reached out to my friend network and past workshop participants to ask if any of them would be willing to help communicate with voters who speak other languages I don't know. Some people who may not have time to canvass or phone bank themselves said they'd be willing to receive a text or phone call from me if I'm at a voter's door, and could help me with interpreting over the phone. I program their numbers into my phone, and include the language they speak in the "Last Name" field. That way, if I'm flustered and can't remember their name, I can type in the language I'm seeking and their contact information will pop up.

It's great to build your personal team of people with language superpowers – you never know when you might need to tap that talent when you're in the field. (By the way, looping in a bilingual friend to help interpret could also work for phone banking: please see the section in Chapter 15 for details about how to initiate a three-way call.)

During the 2018 midterms, there was a huge "Red to Blue" phone bank headquarters in San Francisco in a building that used to house a Pottery Barn. I remember reaching a voter who only spoke Portuguese. I knew that Rodrigo, one of the phone bank captains, was Brazilian, so I tracked him down in the noisy building and handed him my phone. He was able to talk with the voter directly, which felt like a victory. (I also have Rodrigo's phone number saved in my contacts, just in case that situation arises again.)

As I mentioned in Chapter 10, "Embrace Your Inner Detective," you can also ask friendly voters to help you cross the language barrier. Often they are rightfully proud of their ability to speak multiple languages, and happy to help others in their community exercise their right to vote by helping me communicate.

I haven't tried using Google Translate at the door to bridge a language gap, but I'd be willing to try it out if it was a choice between that and not being able to communicate at all in a language not spoken by campaign staff or other volunteers. (Since voters' literacy levels may vary, if they have trouble reading the translated text on the screen you could try playing the audio version for them instead.)

Sometimes you just do the best you can in unexpected situations. In 2019, I was canvassing in the suburbs of Virginia for the House of Delegates candidate when I saw a young man in his 20s standing in front of his house. I called out, "Hi, are you Eric?" He ignored me and kept looking at his phone. I thought, "Wow, young people are so rude these days! They can't even look away from their phone to respond to a greeting." I walked up his driveway and repeated my inquiry, and he looked at me and made an agitated gesture. I couldn't understand why he was so annoyed at me, or why he wasn't saying anything – until I asked myself, "I wonder if he's deaf?"

I had learned to sign the alphabet in grade school, so I spelled out, "Are you Eric?" He nodded, and when I said I was a volunteer with the Democrats and showed him the door hanger for Sheila Bynum-Coleman, my candidate, he smiled and gave me a big thumbs-up. Then he gestured for me to wait. He dug around in his pocket until he fished out an "I Voted" sticker, which he proudly held out for me to see. We both laughed and gave each other a high five.

If I were in that situation again, I might ask for his cell phone number so we could communicate by text, even if we were standing a few feet apart. That would probably be more effective than my very limited signing abilities. Even so, between the two of us, we were able to have a very basic communication.

Finally, if you are a volunteer organizer, you might consider doing direct outreach to friends, colleagues and others who are fluent in Spanish or other languages commonly spoken by voters in your target races. Of the 200 volunteers we trained in our Spanish for Activists workshop, a sizeable number had never canvassed or phone banked before. They were motivated to step up for phone banking because they knew their language superpowers would allow them to communicate with a population that is often overlooked or underserved. We need all hands on deck, and the Spanish-speaking community in particular could decide the outcome of some close races in the upcoming elections.

Summary

- The most important thing when talking with any voter, but especially a Spanish-speaking voter, is to *hacer un clic* – to make a connection.
- You can increase your chances of doing this by showing respect, working to earn their trust, and demonstrating interest in what they have to say.
- If you can, find a buddy to practice some of the phrases listed in this chapter to increase your comfort level. You can see a complete list in Appendix D.

Chapter 15
Gear: Tools of the Trade

I'll admit it: I tend to be overprepared for most situations. My friends make fun of how big my backpack is, and my tax preparer tells me I'm her most organized client. But for canvassing and phone banking, this tendency can be an asset. When I've taken time off work, traveled hundreds of miles to a swing district, and am worn out from a long election cycle, having the right gear and functional systems helps me maximize my productivity. That can make all the difference when the outcome might come down to a handful of votes. At the end of this chapter, I also list a few helpful items and tech tools to enhance your phone banking experience.

It can be helpful to spend a little time beforehand thinking about what tools and systems will help *you* to do your best work. That looks different for each person. My dad had over a dozen keys on his keychain to all the places in his life: home, various job sites, three cars, tool shop, his boat, and more. Always the engineer, he carried two complete sets of keys – one in his right pocket, the other in his left. He once told me, "That way, if I lose one of them, I'll always have a backup." (On the other hand, my mom spent so much time looking for things she'd misplaced that it became a running joke for her to say, "I can't find it – I must have put it in a *safe place*!") Like everything else in this book, your essential gear comes down to personal preference and budget, as well as the environment and weather if you're canvassing.

From my experience canvassing in urban, suburban and rural areas, here are my essential and nice-to-have bonus items.

My Essential Items for Canvassing

- **Sun protection:** The sun can be relentless in the Central Valley. I always wear a broad-brimmed hat with a neck cape. I remove it at the door as a sign of courtesy, unless it's really hot. If you wear sunglasses, it's also recommended that you remove them so you can make better eye contact with voters, which can help you establish rapport. I also wear a long-sleeved white shirt for sun protection; shirts with front pockets are very handy for easy access to my phone. Sunscreen is essential if you burn easily.
- **Layered clothing:** Temperatures can vary by 30 degrees or more during a single day. Wearing (or bringing) several different layers helps me stay comfortable.
- **Sturdy shoes:** Depending on the weather, I wear tennis shoes or hiking boots. I definitely wear close-toed shoes, given the uneven terrain, broken glass, and the free-range dogs I encounter in the Central Valley.
- **Cargo pants:** I love having lots of pockets to hold my phone, palm cards (those postcard-sized pieces of literature) and other items without having to dig through my bag at

each door. Other people use a fanny pack or small shoulder bag to easily access small items.

- **Small backpack:** I use this to carry water, snacks, an extra layer or two, and other items so my hands are free.
- **Clipboard or folder:** Depending on what campaign literature or forms I'm carrying, it can be helpful to have a hard surface to write on, or a folder with pockets to organize multiple pieces of literature. I keep about 10 pieces of literature at the ready, and stash more in my bag so I don't have to keep going back to my car to restock. Call me OCD, but I bring my own clipboard, which has a really strong metal clip that holds flyers or papers snugly against the board. I've found that campaigns often buy the cheapest clipboards with weak clips, and I spend too much time picking up scattered literature off the ground.
- **Hydration bladder:** I really appreciate staying well hydrated without having to stop to pull a water bottle out of my bag. Using a hydration bladder made by CamelBak or HydraPak (my current favorite) lets me sip as I'm walking between houses. On hot days, I keep a separate water bottle in my car and dissolve an electrolyte tablet in it to help me replenish minerals that I lose when I'm sweating a lot.
- **Cell phone:** A smartphone is essential for canvassing, since you access your turf, navigate between houses, and record voter data through the app. I also bring a small power bank or two with charging cable so I never run out of juice. (Even if I don't need to charge my phone, I've canvassed with other people who ran out of charge. Loaning them one of my power banks is an easy way to keep a fellow volunteer up and running, doubling my impact.)
- **Post-it notes:** I keep a pad of 3"x3" yellow Post-it notes in my pocket, and try to pre-write about 10 or 20 pages

with a short, friendly message. (I find it easier to write a bunch at home or in the car, when I can write faster and more neatly than when standing at the door.) If the voter isn't home, I write their name at the top of the mostly pre-written note and attach it to the leave-behind literature. I hope that a voter seeing their name and a handwritten note might slightly increase the chance that they'll actually glance at the literature instead of throwing it straight into the trash. I might even add a postscript complimenting them on their door decorations or beautiful rose bush, or thank them for posting a campaign sign in support of my candidate. Depending on the day's ask, my note might say:

Dear Mr. Salazar,
Sorry I missed you.
I hope Candidate X can earn your vote!
Respectfully, Elizabeth

Again, I bring my own Post-it notes, since I find that campaigns get cheap off-brand ones that aren't very sticky. These easily fall off campaign literature and become trash in the voter's yard – not a good look!

- **Small notebook:** I carry a pen and a 3" x 5" spiral notebook in my pocket, and jot down a few reminders and notes to myself, along with the date. For example, if someone says yes to a yard sign, needs a ride to the polls, or has a question I can't answer, I write down their name, address, phone number, best time to reach them, and any other notes that will help me follow up on tasks. I put a little box next to their name, and then put an "X" in the box when I've completed the task.

On the last pages of the notebook I keep a running log of my turf numbers and login passwords, as well as my daily totals of doors knocked and voter contacts. I can write important information on the inside cover of the notebook that I might need to refer to frequently, like the location and address of the nearest drop box and polling place.

You may be able to do all this on your phone. I'm old school and like to be able to flip through my notes in case I need to dig up a contact from a few days prior, or want to double-check that I completed all pending tasks at the end of the day.

If you are canvassing in cold temperatures, it can be useful to have a pencil instead of a pen, since it still works even if the temperature drops below freezing.

- **Lunch and snacks:** I like to have plenty of high-quality food available to keep me going. I crave protein when I'm really hungry, as well as salt if I've been sweating a lot. I started keeping a block of tofu slathered with miso in my cooler to eat as a snack before driving home; it doesn't spoil even in hot weather, and gives me more energy than sugary carbs.
- **First aid kit:** I bring a small Ziploc bag with Band-Aids, alcohol wipes, blister pads, painkillers, and a mini Swiss Army knife.
- **Toiletries:** In addition to hand sanitizer, I always bring a one-ounce bottle of liquid soap to wash my hands before eating. It's less likely to dry out my skin, especially if the climate is particularly hot, cold or arid. I also carry lip balm, tissues, and a few feet of toilet paper for less-than-luxurious bathrooms.

On that note, after saying yes to all those bottles of water, I take advantage of restrooms in gas stations, fast food restaurants, parks, public libraries, supermarkets and hospitals. Big box stores like Target often have bathrooms right at the front of the store.

Bonus Items for Canvassing

These items may seem over the top, and some might not be possible if you're tight on space or money, but most of these have come in handy more than once:

- **Dog treats:** I'm not a dog person, and am often more scared of the dogs than their humans. I've been able to bribe many dogs into letting me access the front door of a house by throwing a treat in their direction. If the owner is present, I may ask if I can give their dog a treat; sometimes I can soften up the owner if their dog seems to like me (or at least my treats).
- **Headlamp:** If it's getting dark, having a headlamp helps prevent draining the battery on my phone if I need to use the flashlight feature. It also can help prevent me from twisting my ankle when walking across uneven ground, helps me see house numbers, and keeps my hands free.
- **Reflective jacket or tape:** If it's dark out, I like to wear some sort of reflective clothing, especially if I'm walking on a busy road or it's raining.
- **Backup phone:** I know, this seems extravagant – but without a smartphone with internet connection, I am pretty much useless in the field. If I drop my main phone in the toilet or lose it somewhere, the last thing I want to do is to spend several hours during GOTV weekend trying to replace it. I bought a cheap smartphone, keep bare-bones service on it, and normally keep it in my go bag at home. I

bring it along on canvassing trips, and one time did need to use it when my main phone stopped working. Also, sometimes phones temporarily conk out if they get overheated, which is not uncommon if the temperature is in the 90s or higher. Having a spare phone allows me to continue canvassing; I can try to cool one phone off while using the other to keep knocking doors.

- **Cooler:** Speaking of keeping things cool, I bring a little cooler so my lunch doesn't spoil on hot days. My friend Rochelle also gifted me a padded, collapsible cooler that I can take on an airplane. It doesn't keep things quite as cold, but if you have to fly to your canvassing site, it can be better than nothing.
- **Electric generator:** This is part of my emergency preparedness kit at home, and I toss it in my trunk when I'm canvassing. It's basically a big rechargeable battery with USB and 110 volt outlets, which stores a lot more electricity than a small power bank. Obviously I can't carry a generator around with me while canvassing, but if there's a power outage or I just need to recharge my phone during lunch, I like knowing I'll always have access to electricity. I have a Jackery Explorer 300 generator, which weighs about seven pounds and can recharge a phone about 15 times.
- **Portable printer:** I originally bought this for work, but it's been amazingly handy out in the field. I have a small color inkjet printer that's about the size of a thick three-ring binder. Some portable printers come with a rechargeable battery; I plug mine into my electric generator. After registering someone to vote online, I've been able to print out the registration affidavit from the trunk of my car and give it to the voter on the spot. This is especially helpful because most people I've registered are elders who don't have email,

a computer, or a printer. (With their permission, I have the affidavit sent to my email address and print it out for them.)

This also came in handy when I was sent to cure a ballot from a voter just over the county line. The campaign only gave me ballot cure forms for one county; it would have taken me another 90 minutes to drive back to the campaign office and return to the voter's house with the correct form. Instead, the campaign emailed it to me, and I was able to print it out from my phone and hand it to the voter to sign.

I also keep an extra set of ink cartridges in my car so I won't run out at a crucial moment, as well as a stash of printer paper.

Figuring out how to print wirelessly from my phone took some practice. I did some test runs at home, typed up basic instructions to myself, and taped these to the printer itself to remind myself how to do this when I'm out in the field.

- **Rain gear:** I bring a wind-resistant, bright yellow umbrella that's less likely to be blown inside-out. I'm an avid bicyclist, so I bring my waterproof jacket, rain pants and waterproof biking socks, as well as a pack cover to keep my backpack dry. These have the added advantage of having reflective tape that makes me more visible to cars. I wear a waterproof, large-brimmed rain hat for hiking that sheds water. I have waterproof Hunter boots, and keep a spare pair of shoes and clothes in the car if I need to do a costume change midday. I also bring a plastic folder with pockets or a small plastic accordion folder; this keeps campaign literature dry and organized even if it's raining.
- **Spare glasses:** Everything looks like a Monet painting without my glasses. I keep an old pair in my car just in case I break the ones I'm wearing, so I can still drive myself home safely.

My Essential Items for Phone Banking

For phone banking, I need a smartphone, tablet or laptop, and headset. I always keep a pen and spiral notebook at the ready to jot down a few notes. Similar to canvassing, if I have a conversation that gets beyond the first minute, I write down the date, the voter's name and phone number, if it's listed, as well as their main concerns. It's actually easier to take more detailed notes when I'm phone banking, because I have a surface to write on and I don't have to maintain eye contact. If we get disconnected, I'm able to call the voter back and continue the conversation.

If they agree to have me text them some follow-up information like the candidate's website or information about their early voting center or polling place, I make a note, then check it off after I've completed it. If our conversation has been friendly, I often ask, "Would it be all right for me to reach out closer to Election Day to see if you had any other questions?" Most people have given me permission, so I do call them back and confirm whether they voted yet or need any help. Because I've taken some notes, I can also reference things they mentioned the first time we talked, which helps to personalize our conversation. It's incredibly gratifying when I loop back and find out people actually voted. It's an encouraging reminder that the work all of us phone bankers and canvassers are doing really does have an effect.

Bonus Tools for Phone Banking

- **Alternate phone number**: As I noted in Chapter 3, "Safety First," you can also get an alternate phone number for free through Google Voice. If a phone bank requires you to use your own phone to dial directly (rather than calling in to a toll-free number that shields your phone number), this can be a way to protect your privacy. You can call, text and receive voicemails at this number just like you normally would. You can even set up a separate voicemail box with a customized outgoing message. The only difference from using your own phone number is that the voter sees your temporary number on their Caller ID.

One limitation with Google Voice is that you only get one alternate phone number. If you're calling to multiple states or districts, you can't customize a phone number so the area codes match where you are calling. If that's a feature you want, you can also "rent" one or more temporary phone numbers for a few dollars a month using apps like Burner. Just like Google Voice, you keep your regular phone number, but the Burner app allows you to add as many alternate phone numbers as you want; these are all linked to your phone. Because you get to choose the area code of your temporary phone number, it may slightly increase your odds that voters pick up your call, since it looks like a local number to them.

At the end of the 2020 election cycle when I was doing a lot of phone banking (and canvassing was off the table because of the pandemic), I had about six different temporary Burner numbers on my phone – one for each state I was calling. Once you're done using them, you can cancel the numbers (which also deletes any associated texts or voicemails) and stop paying the monthly fee.

You can also set up an alternate phone number using Google Voice or Burner if you are canvassing and want a more private way to make follow-up calls and send texts to voters you meet.

- **Three-way calling:** As I've described elsewhere in this book, this feature (which is included in almost every cell phone and landline calling plan) can be very handy for helping voters navigate bureaucracy. For example, instead of just giving a first-time voter a number to call for more information, you can keep them on the line and place a three-way call to the voter hotline or an organization that provides rides to the polls. This way, both you and the voter are on the line together. (When the third party picks up, just explain to the third party that you have a voter on the line with you.) If the voter is shy, doesn't know the specific questions to ask, or doesn't speak fluent English, you can help advocate for them on the call, and cut through any red tape or obstacles that might arise.

  You can Google for detailed instructions, but here are quick-and-dirty tips for making a three-way call:

  - **iPhone:** With the voter on the line, tap "Add Call" and dial the third party's number. Once they pick up, tap "Merge Calls." The three of you should now all be on the call.
  - **Android:** With the voter on the line, tap "Add Call" or "Merge" icon (depending on your operating system version) and dial the third party's number. Once they pick up, tap "Merge Calls." The three of you should now all be on the call.
  - **Landline:** With the voter on the line, quickly press and release the "Flash" button on your phone and dial the third party's number. Once they pick up, quickly press and release the "Flash" button again. The three of you should now all be on the call.

Just in case, confirm the voter's phone number and write it down before you try patching in the third party, in case you get disconnected. That way you can always call them back and you won't lose all the time you've already invested. Please note since you initiated the three-way call, if you hang up it will likely terminate the entire call. Unfortunately, you can't hang up and let the voter and a third party continue chatting on their own. So if you initiate a three-way call, be prepared to stay on the line until the call is finished.

If you've never used three-way calling before, it may be helpful to practice first with a couple of friends. It may feel clumsy at first, but after a few tries it will probably be smooth sailing.

- **Customizing text messages:** Whether I'm canvassing or phone banking, I often ask voters if I can follow up by sending them information such as the candidate's website, a link to reregister to vote, or information about ways to vote early. (Please note that I *only* text a voter with their permission – sending them an unsolicited text feels like spam.)

  I usually write up a template, then copy, paste, and customize the text so it includes their name and perhaps references something specific we talked about. For efficiency, I may draft a text and send it to myself, and use this as my template. That way I can easily find it. These instructions may be obsolete by the time you read them, so Google this if you need more up-to-date instructions:

  - **iPhone:** Touch a conversation in your message list, then touch and hold the chat bubble you'd like to copy. Choose "Copy" from the popup menu at the bottom.

Type in the number of the voter you're trying to reach, then select "Paste." Customize the message as you wish.

- **Android:** Open to the text you want to copy. Touch the message and hold your finger on the screen for several seconds until it changes color, indicating it is selected. At the top of your screen, next to the Trash Can icon, there is probably a "Copy text" icon that looks like two pieces of paper, one on top of another.

Tap that icon. The text of your template message is now copied to your clipboard. Go back to the home screen for your messaging app and tap on "Start chat." Type in the cell number of the voter. In the space where you would normally start typing a message to them, touch and hold your finger there for a few seconds. A dialog box should pop up with the option to "Paste." Tap on it, and the words of the template message should appear in the text message area.

Alternately, there may also be an image of a clipboard above the typewriter section of your screen with the first words of the template message. If you tap on the clipboard, the template message will appear in your new text message. Customize the message as you wish.

This may seem like a lot of work at first, but it is a nice extra tool in the toolbox for providing concierge service to voters, and can eventually save you time compared with writing messages to each voter from scratch.

Summary

- Ensuring you are adequately fueled and hydrated, protected from the elements, and have easy access to communication tools and campaign literature can help you make the most of your time in the field.
- Spend some time beforehand thinking about what tools and systems will help you do your best work. The goal is to be as comfortable and organized as possible, so you can maximize each encounter with a voter.
- For phone banking, jotting a few notes from substantive conversations with voters can help you get the most out of each conversation. Consider learning how to make three-way calls, and how to copy and paste follow-up text messages if voters agree to receive them.

Chapter 16

Preventing Burnout: Self-Care for the Long Haul

Talking with voters and trying to listen with my whole heart and mind can be very rewarding. A good conversation can uplift me for days. Writing this book has allowed me to remember the satisfaction of helping voters overcome obstacles to casting their ballot. It's a thrill like no other to watch someone move from "I'm not voting" to "I'll consider it" or even "I'll vote, and make sure my whole family does, too!"

For every story with a positive outcome I've recounted here, there are many more where my efforts fell flat, or where I'll never know the outcome. But if I've learned anything since 2016, it's that working to shore up our democracy is going to be a perpetual work in progress. There is no one election or candidate that will save us, once and for all.

How do I keep going, knowing this work will never end? And what can I do to show up as the best version of myself for sometimes challenging conversations with voters? I've learned the hard way that self-care is not a luxury; it's an essential part of engaging in a sustainable way. I hope to still be phone banking (if not canvassing) into my 90s, if I'm lucky enough to live that long and still have my wits about me. I aspire to still be animated by a spirit of joy and discovery. There are few things less appealing for a voter than to be contacted by a stressed out, grouchy and judgmental volunteer. I try hard not to *be* that person.

Through trial and error, I've found several things that help me do my best work in the field. Everyone has their own list, but I'd like to share mine with you.

- **Remember the big picture.** I'd be lying if I said I didn't care about the election results. I'm not Zen enough to have complete non-attachment to electoral outcomes. I'm elated and relieved when we eke out a win, and heartbroken and deeply disappointed when we lose. However, I try to toggle back and forth between this particular election and my larger goals. I work my heart out for each election. Because I choose to canvass and phone bank where it has the potential to do the most good – in close races where Democrats are the slight underdog – my candidate often ends up losing by a few hundred or a few thousand votes. If I invest my entire sense of purpose in winning elections that my team loses, I'm either a glutton for punishment or setting myself up for flaming out.

  I definitely give myself time to rest and lick my wounds after losing an election. However, I find even more comfort in refocusing on my personal goals, both during the campaign and after it ends. In addition to my desire to help my candidate win, I try to bring a learning mindset to each day I spend talking with voters. At the end of each shift, I ask myself questions like, "What did I learn today? How might I handle that difficult situation another way? What's the best conversation I had today, and why?"

That way, win or lose, I know I'm always making progress toward my personal goals of becoming a better canvasser and phone banker, and adding to my repertoire of skills. Election outcomes are the collective result of hard work by countless people. I'm just one worker bee among many. Still, I can take the lead on getting better at what I do and how I do it. That provides lasting satisfaction.

Incidentally, if you ever have the chance to teach others what you know about canvassing or phone banking, I highly encourage it. Whether that's buddying up with a newer volunteer to show them the ropes, serving as a phone bank or canvass captain, or teaching a workshop on how to be more effective in the field, go for it! My own experience of teaching workshops to thousands of volunteers from across the country – including from many swing districts and states – helped me realize that teaching is the ultimate hedge. Elections come and go, but teaching multiplies my impact far beyond what I could ever do alone. It confers a small measure of immortality to my own limited efforts.

- **Know your strengths and limitations.** Everyone has their superpowers, and optimal conditions that support them in making their greatest contribution. Try to leverage these, while knowing your weaknesses and troubleshooting or working around them. For example, I generally prefer to canvass on my own. I like to take my time with voter conversations, and most other volunteers move at a faster pace.

    Also, I'm not a morning person. My body can get to the launch site, but my brain is a few hours behind. When possible, I try to schedule my canvassing for late morning through the evening. I don't need to do it all – I can let the early birds shine during their best hours. When they are cashing it in around 4 p.m., I'm just hitting my stride, and can connect with voters who are coming home from work. I need to remember that I'm part of a huge team, and we all have our part to play.

Similarly, I tend to do better with longer chunks of time rather than smaller bites. I'd much prefer to spend a long weekend (or an entire month!) canvassing, rather than spending two hours each way driving to the Central Valley for a four-hour shift. Other people thrive on those daylong experiences, or find it's a better fit for their work, family care schedule or budget. Neither option is better than the other. It's all about what works best for *you*, given your personal style and the constraints you're working within.

Don't compare yourself to others. Instead, accept who you are and how you roll. Figure out what you need to be as effective as possible, and do what you can to honor your needs. Remember, whatever you do is light years ahead of doing nothing!

- **Eat well.** I need to fuel myself with healthy food to have the energy to canvass or phone bank. Even though it takes more time and planning than eating free muffins at the campaign headquarters (if there's even that), I do better when I bring my own food. I generally also pack my own bag lunch and keep it in a cooler in my car. Some of the places where I canvass are food deserts, or I don't know where to get healthy food on the go. I don't want to spend a lot of time trying to find something to eat, especially when I'm really hungry. I also bring lots of snacks, such as nuts, dried fruit, crackers and cheese, and beef jerky.

If you're carpooling or canvassing with a buddy or small group, coming well-provisioned with nutritious food and a thermos of coffee, tea or whatever fuels you best also saves time for the whole group. That helps reduce tensions that can arise if each person needs to make frequent additional stops for meals and beverages.

In hot weather, I drink a dissolvable electrolyte tablet before heading out to the field, and sometimes another one at lunch to make sure I don't get dehydrated. I also try to drink plenty of water during the day, and use a hiking hydration bladders (like CamelBak or HydraPak) so I can easily sip in between houses.

I try to find a relaxing place to eat lunch, such as a grassy public park (ideally with a bathroom). If that's not possible, I'll park in a shady spot and eat in the backseat of my car, rolling down the windows if it's hot. I try to really take a break at meals, whether it's laughing with my canvassing buddies, reading a juicy novel, calling a good friend from home, or meditating for a few minutes after I finish eating.

Everyone's eating needs and habits are different. Just figure out what works best for you, and invest the time to make sure you're well-nourished and hydrated for the hard work you're stepping up to do.

- **Take a day off.** I know, it can be really hard to carve out time to rest and recuperate, especially if you have a day job, limited vacation time, and family responsibilities. I recognize the privilege this entails, and that it's not realistic for everyone. Nevertheless, if at all possible, schedule in time to catch your breath. When I canvass for a long weekend or GOTV week, I try to block out the day after I return home to rest and do chores. Canvassing takes a lot out of me; even though I have lots of work to catch up on, I shoot myself in the foot if I push myself to jump back into normal life as if I've just returned from a relaxing vacation. If I can't take a whole day off, even blocking out a few hours, or at least not scheduling anything really taxing that first day back, helps me get my mojo back faster.

When I went to the Central Valley for a month in 2022, I was lucky enough to be able to rent an AirBnB with a kitchen. I took off every Monday (except the day before the election). Even though I wanted to maximize my time in the field, it really helped to have a day to sleep in, go grocery shopping and do laundry. I also cooked a big pot of food for the week so I'd have dinner ready to eat when I got home each night from canvassing, ravenous and exhausted.

- **Exercise if possible.** Yes, I got some steps in while canvassing, but given how long I spent talking with voters and how much time I spent driving out to my rural turfs, I didn't actually get much of a cardio workout. I love to swim, and in Bakersfield I found a gorgeous public pool 10 minutes from my lodging. I was able to swim two or three times a week, which helped me manage my stress and gave me more energy. I also have had some back problems, so I took time to do physical therapy and core strengthening exercises most mornings to keep me healthy and in shape for canvassing.
- **Meditate.** Canvassing and phone banking are physically, intellectually and emotionally demanding. I really need to be on my game to talk with voters. When I'm digging deep to empathize with someone I disagree with, or am trying to draw out the inner motivations of a high-potential voter,

it can be easy to let impatience and irritability get the best of me. Having a consistent meditation practice helps me connect with that inner calm that allows me to ride it out. I try to sit quietly for 10 minutes each morning. Other people listen to guided meditations, have a yoga practice, or find some other way to get grounded. Whatever your mindfulness groove, make time for it, even if it's two minutes of deep breathing in your car before heading out to knock on doors.

- **Get enough sleep**. This is one of the hardest challenges for me, but being well-rested makes all the difference in my day. I'm often tired but wired after canvassing, and sometimes have a difficult time unwinding. Swapping stories with other volunteers over dinner, calling people back home to share the victories and challenges of the day, or writing in my journal helps me process the intensity of my experiences and settle down. Prioritizing my zzzzs makes everything a little easier, and I'm ultimately more effective the next day.
- **Let it be enough**. There will always be more doors to knock and more voters to call. I'm often haunted by the prospect of losing an election by one vote, and wonder if we might have prevailed if I had tried just a little harder. But we all have our limits, and I ignore mine at my peril. If winning the election depends on me repeatedly pushing myself beyond the brink, maybe what we really need to focus on is recruiting more volunteers, and supporting both them and campaign staff in doing their best work.

On the positive side, I try to remember that it's not all on me. I'm part of a huge team, not just on this particular campaign, but across the country. I'm far more engaged that I ever was before 2016, and there are thousands of others who have stepped up as well. As much as I want to win this year's election, and for all the pressure of perpetually facing "the most important election of our lifetime," ultimately I'm just a tiny part of a grand effort whose contours I can't even begin to comprehend. Win or lose, I'm building skills and learning new approaches that will serve me in all my future work. That's a victory, no matter what the outcome of this particular election. I can feel good about whatever I contribute, and trust that together with everyone else, we *are* making a difference.

Finally, I take inspiration from this excerpt of the Romero Prayer,[23] written by Bishop Kenneth Untener and inspired by the life of St. Oscar Romero, the martyred Archbishop of San Salvador:

We cannot do everything, and there is a sense of liberation in realizing that.

This enables us to do something and to do it well....

We are workers, not master builders;

Ministers, not messiahs.

We are prophets of a future not our own.

Summary

- Strengthening democracy is a lifelong endeavor. Tending to your physical and emotional well-being can help prevent burnout and allow you to engage in a sustainable way.
- Play to your strengths and honor your limitations. No need to compare yourself with others.
- It all counts! Whatever you can contribute helps. You are part of an enormous community of fellow Americans who are each doing our part. Thank you for all you do.

Conclusion

When I spent a month in the Central Valley canvassing and ballot curing for the 2022 midterms, I stayed in an AirBnB run by a Japanese couple. Along with the house rules and listings of local attractions, their guestbook included the saying *"Ichi-go ichi-e."* It roughly translates to "One lifetime, one meeting," and is associated with the Japanese tea ceremony. It reminds us that we may only meet once in this lifetime, so let us be fully present to this encounter, with our whole heart and mind.

As I was packing up my car to leave Bakersfield and drive home, I met my AirBnB hostess, Nobuko. I asked her to tell me more about the context of *"Ichi-go ichi-e."* She paused, trying to find the right words. It's a profound concept, not easily translated across language or culture. She told me, "A once-in-a-lifetime meeting is really important, so we should do our best. Right now we have little experience, but maybe in 20 or 30 years, we will remember what someone said, and understand the meaning more fully."

That perfectly encapsulated my monthlong immersion in voter engagement, as well as the many other conversations I've had since starting this work in 2016. Most of the people I've met I will probably never see again. Yet these fortuitous "one lifetime, one meeting" connections have indelibly shaped me, surprised me, given human form to abstract ideas. I know the deeper meaning of these conversations will continue to unfold over time, in ways I cannot yet fully understand. My life is undeniably richer for their generous gifts of time, trust, story, and the bounty of their labor. Those experiences are seeds planted in my heart, which will someday come to fruition in their own mysterious rhythms and seasons.

Coming Full Circle

As I mentioned at the beginning of this book, in the early 1990s I was a college senior applying for research fellowships for the year following graduation. At the time I was interested in journalism, and I daydreamed about becoming a foreign correspondent. In those heady early years after the fall of the Berlin Wall, I proposed a project to study development of free press in Eastern Europe.

In that pre-internet era, I reached out to potential contacts in Berlin, Leipzig, Prague and Budapest using the career development office's phone and fax machine. I looked up background material about Eastern Europe on the library's LexisNexis account. I also talked with many of my college's professors, and was especially excited to meet with one who was an expert in Eastern European government. I was stunned when he told me, "You'd do better to just stay home and read about Eastern Europe in academic journals. You won't find out much by going there yourself." I don't remember the reasons he gave for his opinion. I nodded, politely thanked him for his time – and then ignored his advice and went right ahead with applying for my fellowship.

I was incredibly fortunate to receive a Thomas J. Watson Fellowship, which lets graduating college seniors pursue a yearlong self-designed project anywhere in the world except the U.S. I spent 14 months in Eastern Europe interviewing journalists of all stripes. Those included former Communist Party loyalists at state-run papers, editors of a satirical magazine in East Berlin, and clean-cut young Germans at a far-right monthly paper. I also interviewed a Czech writer who had contributed to an underground feminist paper, only to end up translating Harlequin romance novels after the fall of communism to make a living. I could write a whole other book about that fantastical odyssey.

Even in my most feverish imaginings, I could never have invented the cast of characters I met that year. I would never have dreamed up the rich details, ironies, moral conflicts, and specific dilemmas each of my interviewees faced under communism. I developed a much fuller picture of how authoritarian governments crush every facet of civic life, how the erasure of truth poisons the capacity to trust, and how very fragile democracy is. I would never have gained those complex, nuanced perspectives if I'd taken the advice of that college professor and just stayed home to read about the changes in Eastern Europe.

I've never seen any of those journalists again, but their stories have stayed with me. One lifetime, one meeting. And with the rise of authoritative regimes in recent years – not just in the U.S., but in many other parts of the world – I think back to those first-hand reports as a cautionary tale for where we may be headed. I can't just assume that others will do the difficult work of defending democracy, that somehow everything will just work out, or that it won't be that bad. Thirty years ago, I never could have imagined that the U.S. – our beloved country, this beacon of democracy – would be at such a perilous historical moment. It's been three decades since I returned home, but I see those stories in a new light. As Nobuko told me, "Maybe in 20 or 30 years, we will remember what someone said, and understand the meaning more fully."

Three Journeys

I've heard that when we travel, we actually take three journeys: the one we plan, the one we actually take, and the one we remember. My year in Eastern Europe was one of those experiences – from faxing and calling journalists in Eastern European capitals and cobbling together a grant proposal, to actually meeting them face-to-face, and now remembering and interpreting their stories in the light of our own political challenges here in the U.S.

My journey of voter engagement seems to be following a similar trajectory. When I first started in earnest in 2017, I was fueled by a desperate need to do *something*, anything, to bring about regime change in our country. As I have gotten deeper into this work, I realized that these conversations with my fellow citizens have the potential to surprise me, educate me, and ultimately inspire hope in times where hope can feel scarce, even foolhardy. Where that hope leads is something that will only emerge in the journey I remember.

That outcome depends not only on my journey, but the choices each of my fellow Americans make in this election.

I began phone banking and canvassing with the burning need to win elections and reclaim our country from autocracy and hateful division. What has been a slow reveal is that if I am receptive, talking with voters actually has the power to transform *me*. Entering into dialogue with another human about their fears and struggles, hidden hopes and buried yearnings, has given me a privileged window into the lives of people I would never have met. At their best, these connections can be a sacred encounter with another human being which can enrich us both.

Today, so much of our information is filtered, mediated, and framed by structures designed to maximize profit and outrage. A return to the oldest form of human communication is deceptively radical, perhaps even revolutionary. It is an antidote to the forces which would pit us against one another, too afraid or angry to talk with each other and hear each other's truths. Creating respectful person-to-person connections, rooted in nonjudgmental curiosity, truly is democracy at its finest. It's a step along the way to repairing the torn fabric of our civil society.

I hope this book will support your vital conversations at the doorstep and on the phone with our fellow Americans. I am honored to be in community with so many brave, beautiful souls – voters and volunteers alike – all across the country. May our "one lifetime, one meeting" conversations sustain us, inspire us, and help transform our world into a community of justice, peace and joy.

Acknowledgments

One of the greatest joys of talking politics with strangers is the opportunity to meet incredible people along the way. Many of the other volunteers engaged in this work have become friends who have enriched my life immeasurably. I am grateful for the many individuals who have so generously shared their time, expertise and resources to help me write this book. As someone who found it challenging to accept a bottle of water not so long ago, you can imagine how humbled I am to receive such abundant support. For those I inadvertently missed below, please accept my sincere apologies and appreciation.

First, I owe a debt of gratitude to my dear friends and fellow activists Charlie Varon and Myra Levy. Thank you for suggesting I write a book about my experiences and believing these stories could help inspire other volunteers. Charlie, I'm so glad our paths crossed on public transportation after I saw you reenact your canvassing experiences as part of your solo performance monologue in "The Great American Sh*t Show." Thank you for encouraging me to pursue my vision of teaching other volunteers, and for giving perceptive feedback at important junctures. Myra, it has been a joy to develop and teach so many workshops together, in partnership with our other comrades-in-activism. I appreciate laughing together, especially at situations that make us want to say, "Tell me *less* about that." Let's make sure we get a bed and a light written into all our future contracts.

To Heidi Cartan and Philippe, Noah and Matthew Habib, thank you for welcoming me to your beautiful home, making me delicious dinners, and giving me space and time to embark on this daunting project. It was a gift to have both solitude and community in the initial phases of writing. I am so blessed that the friendship that began more than 65 years ago between our families in Germany continues to flourish today. I know that Tante Effi, Tante Marion, Onkel Bob, and my parents would be so pleased that we remain connected.

I have been lucky to collaborate with many wonderful activists in developing voter engagement workshops. To my fellow introverts, Myra Levy and Debbie Benrubi, thank you for leading the way in turning lemons into lemonade when our March 2020 "Canvassing for Introverts" training had to shape-shift in a hurry, under the twin pressures of shelter-in-place and the looming elections. I'm so proud of the work we did together with our "Phone Bank Training for Introverts (& Friends)" workshops.

Jackie Tulsky, it must have been kismet that I was assigned to interview you for work. Thank you for being willing to continue the conversation about Motivational Interviewing, and to become my co-teacher for "You and the 34%: How to Have Meaningful Conversations with High-Potential Voters." I've learned so much from our many talks and midnight rehearsals, and try to channel your warmth and gentle wisdom when I talk with voters. Even though it's only been a few years, I feel like I've known you for a lifetime!

To Mayela Galindo, my fantastic Spanish teacher: you have the patience of Job, and make even the endless mysteries of the subjunctive fun. Thank you for developing and teaching the "Spanish for Activists" and "Election Spanish for Absolute Beginners" workshops with me. You infuse the learning process with such a spirit of joy. ¡Muchísimas gracias por todo, amiga!

So much work goes on behind the scenes for each workshop. I'm deeply grateful to work with our outstanding team of teaching assistants and tech crew, including Genna Beier, Sam Chavez, Lynda Cornejo, Liz Escobar, Sally Faison, Cheryl Fippen, Dara Friedman-Wheeler, Marc Jacobson, Martha Knutzen, August Larsen, Vicki Levi, Myra Levy, Amanda Newstetter, Berta Segall McDonnell and Charlie Varon. Thank you for so generously sharing your time and talent to make these trainings a high-quality, interactive experience. I also appreciate the more than 2,500 workshop attendees who have participated with such enthusiasm, and whose feedback has helped us continue to improve our trainings.

Special thanks to Jackie Tulsky, Vicki Levi, Dara Friedman-Wheeler and Mayela Galindo for co-authoring some of the chapters in this book, based on workshop material we developed together.

As a lifelong aspiring teacher, I've always taken mental notes on the teaching styles of the many incredible educators and mentors who have guided me. There are far too many to name here, but I do want to especially acknowledge my first piano teacher, Jennie Lois Windle; my high school English teacher Heather Matheson; my Oakland Urban Journalism Workshop teachers Denise Bridges, Ira Hadnot, Steve O'Donoghue and Wanda Ravernell; my Oberlin professors Randy Coleman, Jan Cooper, Nick Jones, Susan Hradil, Steve Huff, Steve Plank and John Olmsted; my documentary radio teachers and editors Jay Allison, Rob Rosenthal and Sandy Tolan; and my first Spanish teachers, Rocío Rødtjer and Ricardo Romero.

Speaking of learning, writing my first book has involved a steep learning curve. Of course, I take complete responsibility for any errors or inaccuracies in this book. I am hugely grateful to my editor, Mary Ladd, who sharpened my writing and shared invaluable guidance on self-publishing. I also deeply appreciate encouragement and expert advice from David Brightman, Chloe Maxmin, Sonia Shah, Elise Riley and Meredith Walters. Many thanks to Lori Lawton for transcribing my interviews with voters.

I was humbled that so many people took the time to read my manuscript and provide thoughtful suggestions, including Mary Boergers, David Brightman, Elisabeth Fall, Cheryl Fippen, Susan Labandibar, Vicki Levi, Tricia McInroy, Martha Merson, Ruth Schoenbach, Jackie Tulsky, Charlie Varon and Meredith Walters. I am particularly grateful to Hortencia Cabral, Norberto Gonzalez and Alicia Martinez for providing nuanced cultural and linguistic insights.

I have met so many passionate, inspiring activists through this work. Their generosity of spirit gives me hope for the future of our country. In particular, I want to thank Judith Bolker, Susan Bolle, Shannon Edwards, Susan Labandibar, Holly Scheider and Pam Tellew for inviting me to present at various events, and for connecting me with many others at key times. Mary Boergers is my fairy godmother of canvassing. She initially encouraged me to travel further south to the Hanford-Bakersfield area, and patiently addressed all my concerns when I considered throwing in the towel. She's always provided such sage guidance, along with her wry and raucous sense of humor. Gordon Lake spontaneously offered to be my canvassing buddy my very first time knocking doors in the Central Valley, and has become a close friend over the years.

Some of the other activists who have been an important part of my journey include Bill Bagnall, Natalie Burdick, Bonnie Dobson, Jenny Eis, Cheryl Fippen, Kristina Fullerton Rico, Nancy Goodban, Emiliana Guereca, Denise Hunt, María Jiménez, Martha Knutzen, Michelle Maine, Colleen McCarthy, Ann Merrill, Andrea Miller, Cecilia Minalga, Finale Norton, Caitlin Patterson, Mary Rarick, Jim Roberts, Cathee Romley, Sylvia Russell, Susan Shain, Ogie Strogatz, Joan Sturm, Beatrice von Schulthess, Robbin Warner and Sheila Yeh.

ACKNOWLEDGMENTS

A huge thanks to the many partner organizations we've collaborated with, including Activate America (formerly Flip the West), Arizona Democratic Party, Bay Area Coalition, California Democratic Party, Call 4 Change, Central Valley Empowerment Alliance, Central Valley Workers Center, Common Power, Democracy Action Marin, Democracy Action San Francisco, Democratic Party of Wisconsin, Democratic Women of Kern, Joan's Democracy Café, Larry Itliong Resource Center, Network NOVA, Northeast Arizona Native Democrats, Reclaim our Vote and the Center for Common Ground, Sanity Group, Swing Blue Alliance, Swing Left, Swing Left San Francisco, Together We Will Albany-Berkeley, Together We Will Los Gatos, Training to Win Summit, and the Women's March Foundation.

I also appreciate all the hardworking, dedicated campaign staff I've met. Thank you for providing encouragement and local context, taking stressed-out calls from the field, and partnering with volunteer groups. A special shout-out to Eric Arias, Tearanie Chinn, Kyle Costello, Kate Foxworthy, Armando Garcia, Norberto Gonzalez, Abby Olmstead, Carla Rivas-D'Amico, Priscilla Sanchez-Olivares, Aaron Smith, Esperanza Tyson and Kerri West.

I gratefully acknowledge fundamental insights from the many strategists whose work has helped shape my thinking, including Donnie Fowler, Jane McAlevey, Michael Podhorzer and Anat Shenker-Osorio. Thank you, also, to some of the key people helping to spread the word about this book, including Matt Caffrey, Jessica Craven, Ricky Gonzalez, Lee Goodall, Nick Hutchins, Dan Kalik, Yasmin Radjy, Deborah Richardson, Andi Riveron and Susan Schaeffer.

This book has been a labor of love. It's been humbling to receive such an outpouring of encouragement and financial support from people who believe in it, including Anonymous, Ellen Bender, Susan Bolle, Shannon Edwards, Davis Everett, Sally Faison, Elisabeth Fall,

Cheryl Fippen, Carole Flores, Dara Friedman-Wheeler, Nadine Halusic, Ajila Hart, Meg Holmberg, Cindy Holstrom, Anna Honda, Susanne Huttner, Colleen Irwin, Nick and Sue Jones, Beth Krackov, Susan Labandibar, Gordon and Sally Lake, August Larsen, Vicki Levi, Ramey Littell, Margaret Lord, Jenny Love, Anna Lynch, Jane McClure, Tricia McInroy, Susan Morgan, Jan O'Brien, Margaret Partlow, Susan Pfeifer, Vera Sandronsky, Berta Segall McDonnell, Tom Shaw, Pam Tellew, Cristina Thorson, Leigh Ann Townsend, Jackie Tulsky, April Vargas, Meredith Walters, the Weitl Family, Rochelle Wheeler, Laurel Wigham, Kathleen Wolf, Raymond Yee, Sheila Yeh and Kathryn Zeidenstein.

I am grateful to all the doctors, scientists, trainees, staff and patients I've interviewed over the past 18 years as a medical writer. I have learned so much about medicine, science, health care systems, health equity and the human condition from you. A particular thanks to all my clients who have graciously rearranged project schedules so I could carve out time during election seasons for my volunteer work.

I am forever grateful to the Thomas J. Watson Foundation for giving me the opportunity to spend a full year after college studying development of free press in Eastern Europe. That fellowship was truly life-changing, and those experiences continue to shape my life today.

There's a wonderful saying in German: *Zeig mir deine Freunde, und ich sage dir, wer du bist* – show me your friends, and I'll tell you who you are. I am blessed beyond measure by the many friends who have supported me throughout the writing of this book, including Bren Ahearn and Doug Brown, Maude Ballinger, Alton Byrd, Elizabeth Donoghue, Sally Faison and Sarah Pollak, Elisabeth Fall, Cheryl Fippen, Ajila Hart, Fr. Dan Lackie, Gordon and Sally Lake, Anna Lynch, Tom Metz and David Brightman, Erich Miller, Marie O'Connor, Grete Stenersen, Meredith Walters, Peter, Jenni, Lucca, Leopold, Lancelot and Laraby Weitl, and Helen Wood. Thanks for your patient listening, your encouragement, and all the belly laughs.

ACKNOWLEDGMENTS

Deep gratitude to Aunty Diane for your steadfast interest in this project and all my endeavors. Thank you for being the keeper of family stories, and for showing me how to live with such zest, like buying a red Karmann Ghia straight from the factory and driving it all over Europe back in the early 1960s. If I'm lucky enough to reach your age one day, I hope to stay as sharp and have at least half your spunk.

I wish my parents were still in this earthly realm to see this book, but I know they are proud of me from the great beyond. Thank you to my dad, Gaylord, for always encouraging my curiosity and pursuit of eclectic hobbies. I try to emulate your organizational skills and ultra-preparedness, and appreciate your unwavering confidence in me. Thank you to my mom, Lillian, for cultivating my love of reading and for your daily acts of kindness. You embodied the importance of service, friendships and community. As you wished, I think of you when I laugh, and I know you will love me forever.

Heartfelt gratitude to my travel buddy, East Bay sage, and dearest friend, Rochelle Wheeler. I so appreciate your many hours of patient listening about this book, as well as your practical suggestions and encouragement. Thank you for always being there through life's ups and downs. It's a great joy to spend time together, whether we're telling the long version of stories on the trail, lingering over delicious meals, or going on more than 100 travel adventures together over the last 30 years. When we get old, we can finally caption all our photos together, but in the meantime, let's take more trips!

Finally, my deepest gratitude to all the voters who so generously shared your time and stories with me. Your struggles touch my heart. Your efforts inspire me. And your unexpected kindness rekindles my hope in the future of our imperfect, beautiful democracy.

Glossary

Ballot curing
The process of resolving issues with vote-by-mail ballots, such as a missing signature or a signature that does not match the one in a voter's record, to ensure that they are counted. Not all states offer ballot curing, and procedures vary by state. Some states require that voters appear in person at the registrar's office, while others allow voters to sign and return an affidavit with a signature verification statement.

Ballot drop box
A ballot drop box is a safe, secure, designated location where voters can deposit their completed vote-by-mail ballots without using the U.S. Postal Service. These drop boxes are typically placed in accessible public areas, such as within or in front of government buildings or public libraries. Using a ballot drop box provides voters with an alternative method for returning their ballots that does not require postage and is convenient, especially in elections where vote-by-mail voting is prevalent.

Blue wave
A surge of Democratic or progressive victories in elections, this metaphorical term suggests strong and widespread support for Democratic candidates or policies.

Canvassing
Going door-to-door or approaching people directly to discuss political issues, promote a candidate, or encourage voter turnout.

Canvassing or phone banking script

A set of questions and talking points prepared by the campaign, used by volunteers when canvassing or phone banking. The scripts are designed to elicit responses to specific questions, such as the voter's familiarity with the candidate, their most important issues as a voter, and their level of support for him or her.

Cure form
A form to correct discrepancies in the voter's signature on a vote-by-mail ballot to ensure it will be counted. (See Ballot curing, above.)

Early voting
The option for voters to cast their ballots before Election Day at designated polling places, often used to increase voter turnout and flexibility.

GOTV
An acronym for "Get Out the Vote," a campaign strategy that encourages supporters to vote at the polls or turn in their vote-by-mail ballots.

High-potential voter
This term, coined by Democratic messaging expert Anat Shenker-Osorio, is a reframing of "low-propensity voters." It refers to eligible voters who rarely or never vote. ("Eligible voters" refers to U.S. citizens 18 years or older who are not barred from voting because of a past felony conviction, depending on the laws in their state.)

Motivational Interviewing (MI)
An evidence-based method for talking with people about change and growth. Developed by clinical psychologists William Miller, PhD, and Stephen Rollnick, PhD, Motivational Interviewing (MI) originated in the field of addiction treatment. It encourages individuals to explore their own reasons for change, and helps them identify and overcome barriers to achieving their goals. MI has been widely applied across various fields, including health care and education, to facilitate positive behavioral changes. Its tools can help volunteers engage productively with voters, especially high-potential voters. Miller and Rollnick's book, *Motivational Interviewing: Helping People Change and Grow*,[21] provides a useful overview.

Phone banking
A method of contacting voters via telephone to discuss political issues, share information about a candidate, or remind voters about upcoming elections.

Swing district
The most competitive Congressional races, in which either party has a good chance of winning that district's House seat.

Swing state
A state targeted by presidential campaigns because it is believed to be a close race in which either candidate could win that state's Electoral College votes. Also known as "purple" or "battleground" states.

Swing voter
A voter who is not firmly aligned with a political party or candidate and whose vote could potentially swing an election.

Turf
The specific neighborhood volunteers are assigned to visit. Most voter contact apps list basic information available through public records for target voters within that turf, such as name, address, age, gender, party affiliation if available, and how many times that person has cast a ballot during the five most recent elections.

Voter suppression
Any strategy, policy or action designed to prevent or discourage specific groups of people from voting. Some examples include restrictive voter ID laws, purging voter rolls, limiting early voting opportunities, making polling places difficult to access without a car, misinformation campaigns, and intimidation tactics. The goal of voter suppression is often to influence election outcomes by making it more difficult for targeted groups, such as people of color or low-income people, to exercise their right to vote.

Voter targeting
The process of identifying specific groups of voters based on demographics, voting history, or other criteria to tailor campaign messages and outreach efforts.

Vote tripling
A strategy in which volunteers encourage supportive voters to remind three like-minded friends or family members to vote. This approach can multiply the impact of voter turnout efforts.

Appendix A:
Activities to Build Your Listening Skills

Sometimes people tell me, "You're just a natural when it comes to talking with voters – but I could never do that." I appreciate the compliment, but humbly disagree that this is a talent that people either have or they don't. Like most things, listening and responding thoughtfully are skills you can practice and improve. Personally, I hope to keep getting better at this for the rest of my life.

The foundation of having good conversations is to start by being a good listener. Here are some ideas for building those skills:

- In the next week, practice asking open-ended questions and listening more than you talk. Try this out in your conversations with people you already know, such as family members, friends or co-workers. See if you notice any change in the quality or feel of these interactions.
- If you don't know where to start, try using these phrases – then count to 10 and wait for their response.

- "That sounds really _____." *(Fill in the blank with "hard," "interesting," "scary," or other word that reflects back the vibe of what they just shared with you.)*
- "Tell me more about that."
- "If you could change two or three things about *(fill in the name of difficult situation)*, what would they be?" *(Listen to their response, and refrain from jumping in to give opinions or your advice.)*

• Ask someone you know if you can use your phone to record audio of a conversation with them. Ask them to tell you about something exciting or challenging that happened in the past week. Dig for details about their experience. Later on, when you have some quiet time, listen back to the recording.

- How much did your conversation partner talk, compared with how much you talked?
- Did you let them finish their sentences, or did you interrupt them?
- Write down any open-ended questions you asked.
- If they were reluctant to open up, what other questions could you have asked to invite them to say more? If you're stumped, consider asking your conversation partner, "What, if anything, could I have done differently that would have made you want to open up more in that conversation?"

Many of our workshop participants say that the skills they learn in our trainings help them have better conversations not only with voters, but with everyone. I invite you to practice your listening and conversational skills in all areas of your life. See if this starts to change the quality of your connections with others.

Appendix B:
Engaging with High-Potential Voters: Phrase List

Developed by Elizabeth Chur and Jacqueline Tulsky, MD

Handy all-purpose phrases (silently count to 10 after using these, and listen carefully to the response!)
• Tell me more about that. • I'd really like to know more about … • That sounds really hard. • It sounds like … (*try to summarize what you heard them say.*) • I'm curious – if you were in charge of the country, what 2 or 3 things would you change? • *(To gently redirect the conversation):* I *hear* you. *(Brief pause.)* What I'd really like to know more about is … • Make up your own! (Suggestion: create phrases that are curious, non-judgmental, and can't be answered with yes/no.)

THE JOY OF TALKING POLITICS WITH STRANGERS

Navigating the start of the conversation	
If the voter says…	**You could say…**
Who's calling? What is this about?	• Thanks so much for taking my call! • My name is _____, and I'm a volunteer with _____. I'm *not* calling to ask for money. I just had a couple quick questions about the upcoming election. I'm wondering – what, if anything, have you heard about the candidates in this race?
	(or) • I'm a volunteer with Senator Jacky Rosen, the Democratic candidate for US Senate, and I'm calling because her campaign has asked us to reach out to every voter in Nevada to ask – what 2-3 issues are most important to you?
I'm busy right now.	• It sounds like you've got a lot going on. I'll make this quick – it should just take a couple minutes. • *(If they still can't talk):* I'm so sorry to catch you at a bad time. Could I text you information about why I'm calling?
I hate getting these calls.	• I hear you! I actually hate making these calls, too. But this issue is so important to me that I'm going outside my comfort zone. • I'm really concerned about the future of our country, and I'm trying to step up by talking with people in the community. • I'm wondering if you had just two minutes to talk?
Somebody just called about this yesterday.	• Oh, sorry to bother you again! But *I* didn't get to hear your response, and I'd really like to hear what you think about _____.
Eliciting change talk	
If the voter says…	**You could say…**
All politicians are crooks.	• It sounds like it's important for you to support candidates who have integrity. • I'm wondering – if a candidate who *really* listened to you got elected, what would be different in a year?

APPENDIX B: ENGAGING WITH HIGH-POTENTIAL VOTERS

My vote doesn't matter.	• Could you tell me more about that? • I'm wondering, if you could change 2-3 things about Nevada, what would they be? • Many states are making it harder for people to vote. If one vote doesn't matter, why do you think they're trying so hard to keep people from voting? *(You can mention examples that might be compelling to that voter: excluding college IDs as valid voter IDs, removing people from the voter rolls if they've missed a few elections, reducing early voting opportunities, etc.)*
Voting isn't going to fix everything.	• I agree. Voting doesn't fix everything, but it's an important first step. It's like the down payment on a car – you need it to buy a car, but you've still got to work hard to pay it off. What do you think about that?
I don't have time to research the issues/candidates.	• You want to make sure your vote reflects your values. • I'm curious – if you were in an elevator with Jacky Rosen for two minutes, what would you ask her to change, and why?
Politicians make lots of promises, but nothing ever changes.	• It sounds like you have some ideas about how Nevada could improve. Tell me more about that!
I haven't voted in decades.	• What inspired you to vote the last time you did?
I'm not interested in voting.	• Is there *anything* that might motivate you to vote?
My vote is private.	• I totally respect that! Thank you for being a voter. Could I tell you a bit about why people are supporting Jacky Rosen? • *(alternatively):* Of course. *(brief pause)* We're really interested to know what *issues* are most important to the community.
(If voter's top issues align with Democratic priorities)	• Jacky Rosen agrees with you on that. She'll be your voice in Congress.

Wrapping up the conversation	
Assessing support	- On a scale of 0-10, how likely is it that you'll vote in the upcoming election, with 0 being very unlikely and 10 being very likely? - What might make your [number] increase to a [slightly higher number]?
Sharing information	- Could I send you information about Jacky Rosen and the upcoming election? - Is this a good number to text you information, or would you prefer email?
Making a plan	- When do you think you'd be able to vote?
Vote tripling	- Would you be able to tell three friends or family members about the upcoming election, and encourage them to support Jacky Rosen and Democrats in all the races? - If I texted you information, would you be willing to share this on social media or by email to people you know?
Permission to follow up	- Would it be OK to call or text you in a few weeks to see if you have any questions? *(If they say yes, write down their contact information and make a note to check in with them closer to the election.)*
Expressing gratitude	- I really appreciate your time. - Thanks so much for talking with me.

Appendix C:
(Re)Engaging with Volunteers: Phrase List

As described in Chapter 13, if you are a grassroots leader who wants to recruit new volunteers or reengage former volunteers, you can use some tools of Motivational Interviewing (MI) to help you have more effective conversations with prospective volunteers. (This also works if you are just trying to encourage your friends and family to join the effort!) In combination with the MI tools described earlier, here are a few suggestions for responses to common hesitations.

Volunteer	Caller
I'm writing postcards this year.	• I've heard that from several other people. *(brief pause)* • I'm curious to know your thoughts about getting involved in other kinds of volunteer opportunities this election cycle.
I'm waiting until October to phone bank.	• Tell me more about that. • I'd really like to know what you think about helping voters sign up to get an absentee ballot.

I'm so disappointed in the Democratic Party.	• What were you hoping could be accomplished? • If you in charge of the Democratic Party, what would you change? • If we were able to flip the House, win more Senate seats, and keep the White House, what do you think might be possible?
I'm too anxious to phone bank.	• It's been a really hard few years. *(pause and listen)* • What kinds of activities do you think would help address that? • How might you imagine channeling your energy to improve things?
I've got a lot going on right now.	• Sounds like you've got a lot on your plate, and you're always looking to make the most of the time you have. *(pause and listen)* • What, if anything, would feel doable in this election cycle?

Let the conversation unfold. As you are wrapping up, you could try some of these approaches.

Assessing support	• On a scale of 0-10, how likely are you to phone bank or canvass this cycle, with 0 being very unlikely and 10 being very likely? • What might make your [number] increase to a [higher number]?
Sharing information	• Could I send you information about upcoming volunteer opportunities?
Expressing gratitude	• I really appreciate your time. Thanks so much for talking with me.

Appendix D:
Spanish for Activists: Phrase List

Developed by Elizabeth Chur and Mayela Amayrani Galindo Vásquez

THE JOY OF TALKING POLITICS WITH STRANGERS

(gray = voter; white = volunteer)

Presentaciones	Introductions
Votante: *(Por teléfono):* ¿Bueno? / Dígame. *(En persona):* Buenos días / Buenas tardes. ¿Qué se le ofrece?	*Voter:* *(By phone):* Hello? *(In person):* Good morning / Good afternoon. What can I do for you?
Voluntario(a): Buenos días / Buenas tardes. ¿Se encuentra el Señor / la Señora ____, por favor?	*Volunteer:* Good morning / Good afternoon. Is Mr. / Mrs. ____ available, please?
Votante: *(Por teléfono):* Sí, él / ella habla. ¿De parte de quién? *(En persona):* Sí, soy yo. ¿Quién lo / la busca? ¿En qué puedo servirle?	*Voter:* *(By phone):* Yes, that's me. Who's calling? *(In person):* Yes, that's me. Who's looking for him / her? What can I do for you?
Voluntario(a): Me llamo ____ y soy voluntario(a) con el Partido Demócrata y: • el congresista Jared Golden / la congresista Marie Gluesenkamp Pérez. • el senador Sherrod Brown / la senadora Jacky Rosen. • Rudy Salas, el candidato para el Congreso / Stephanie Simacek, la candidata para la Cámara de Representantes de Arizona. No llamo para pedir dinero, sino para hacer conciencia en la comunidad sobre las elecciones. ¿Prefiere hablar en inglés o español?	*Volunteer:* My name is ____ and I'm a volunteer with the Democratic Party and: • Congressman Jared Golden / Congresswoman Marie Gluesenkamp Pérez. • Senator Sherrod Brown / Senator Jacky Rosen. • Rudy Salas, the candidate for Congress / Stephanie Simacek, the candidate for the Arizona State House. I'm not calling to ask for money, but rather to raise community awareness about the elections. Do you prefer to speak in English or Spanish?

APPENDIX D: SPANISH FOR ACTIVISTS

Presentaciones	Introductions
Voluntario(a) (si el votante suena dudoso/sospechoso): • Lo siento. No quiero molestarlo(la), pero estamos escuchando las opiniones de los votantes en la comunidad. • Con mucho respeto, solamente tengo unas preguntas. • Solamente serán algunos minutos. • De antemano, muchas gracias por su paciencia. (Mi español no es muy bueno.)	*Volunteer (if the voter sounds hesitant/ suspicious):* • I'm sorry. I don't want to bother you, but we're listening to the opinions of voters in the community. • Respectfully, I just have a few questions. • It will only take a few minutes. • Thanks in advance for your patience. (My Spanish isn't very good.)
Expresiones de conversación	**Conversational expressions**
Voluntario(a): • ¿Mande? Repita, por favor. ¿Podría hablar más despacio, por favor? • ¡Bueno! ¡Muy bien! ¡Órale! ¿En serio? • Comprendo. ¡Claro que sí! ¡Por supuesto! • Me alegra (mucho) escuchar eso / Siento (mucho) escuchar eso. • ¡Qué lástima! Ojalá que todo se mejore. • Cuénteme más sobre eso.	*Volunteer:* • Pardon? Please repeat that. Could you speak more slowly, please? • Great! Very good! Wow! Seriously? • I understand. Yes, of course! Of course! • I'm (really) happy to hear that / I'm (really) sorry to hear that. • What a shame! I hope things get better. • Tell me more about that.
Identificación del votante	**Voter identification**
Voluntario(a): ¿Ha escuchado de _____?	*Volunteer:* Have you heard of _____?

(Votante está accesible) ☺	(Voter is supportive) ☺
Voluntario(a): • (Si "Sí"): ¡Muy bien! ¿Qué piensa de él / ella? *(escuche)* • (Si el votante está a favor del candidato): ¡Excelente! ¿Contamos con su voto para ____? • (Si "Sí"): ¡Muchísimas gracias! ¿Y también contamos con su voto para todos los demócratas, incluyendo los candidatos municipales, estatales y federales? • (Si "Sí"): ¡Perfecto! ¿Quisiera ayudar a la campaña de ____? • (Si "Sí"): ¡Mil gracias! Por favor, ¿podría darme su número de teléfono? Mi compañero va a llamarle.	Volunteer: • (If "Yes"): Great! What do you think of him / her? *(listen)* • (If the voter is in favor of the candidate): Excellent! Can we count on your vote for ____? • (If "Yes"): Thank you so much! Can we count on your vote for all the Democrats, including the city, state and federal candidates? • (If "Yes"): Perfect! Would you like to help the campaign of __? • (If "Yes"): Thanks so much! Could you give me your telephone number, please? My colleague will call you.
(Votante está dudoso/indeciso) 😐	(Voter is doubtful/undecided) 😐
Voluntario(a): • (Si el votante nunca ha escuchado de ____): Está bien. ____ apoya a invertir en viviendas a precios accesibles, seguro médico, y trabajos buenos. • (Si el votante está indeciso o no apoya a ____): Cuénteme más sobre eso. • (Si el votante todavía está indeciso): ¿Podría enviarle un enlace del sitio web de ____ con más información? (Si "sí"): ¿Podría enviárselo a este número?	Volunteer: • (If the voter has never heard of ____): OK. ____ supports investing in affordable housing, health care, and good jobs. • (If the voter is undecided or does not support ____): Tell me more about that. • (If voter is still undecided): Could I send you a link to ____'s website with more information? *(If "yes")*: Could I send [text] it to this number?

APPENDIX D: SPANISH FOR ACTIVISTS

Identificación de temas prioritarios	Identifying priority issues
Voluntario(a): Tengo interés en sus prioridades. Por favor, me podría decir, si Ud. pudiera cambiar dos o tres cosas sobre el país, ¿qué cambiaría?	*Volunteer:* I'm interested in your priorities. Please tell me, if you could change two or three things about the country, what would you change?
Votante: • Viviendas a precios accesibles • Trabajos y la economía • Proteger Obamacare y el Seguro Social • La inmigración / la separación de familias en la frontera • La educación	*Voter:* • Affordable housing • Jobs and the economy • Protect Obamacare and Social Security • Immigration / the separation of families at the border • Education
Voluntario(a): La senadora Jacky Rosen votó: • para defender y expandir Obamacare. También luchó para limitar los precios de los medicamentos, incluyendo la insulina. Rudy Salas está luchando para: • crear más viviendas a precios accesibles. • crear trabajos buenos que paguen más que el salario mínimo • proteger Obamacare y el Seguro Social • invertir en la educación pública • proteger a los inmigrantes y crear un sendero hasta la ciudadanía para los Dreamers y los campesinos. • *(Si el votante tiene preguntas y Ud. no sabe la respuesta):* Es una excelente pregunta. ¿Podría enviarle el sitio web con más información? Y si yo encontrara la respuesta, ¿podría enviársela a este número? *Ahora regrese a la parte ☺ de arriba para identificar el nivel de apoyo de este votante.*	*Volunteer:* Senator Jacky Rosen voted: • to defend and expand Obamacare. She also fought to limit the prices of prescription medications, including insulin. Rudy Salas is fighting to: • create more affordable housing. • create good jobs that pay more than the minimum wage. • protect Obamacare and Social Security. • invest in public education. • protect immigrants and create a path to citizenship for the Dreamers and farmworkers. • *(If the voter has questions and you don't have the answer):* That's a great question. May I send you the website with more information? And if I find the answer, could I send (text) it to this number? *Now return to the ☺ part above to identify the voter's level of support.*

Votación: hacer un plan: votar por correo	Voting: making a plan: vote by mail
Voluntario(a): ¿Cómo va a votar: en persona o por correo?	*Volunteer:* How will you vote: in person or by mail?
Votante: Por correo.	*Voter:* By mail.
Voluntario(a): ¡Excelente! ¿Ya recibió su boleta por correo?	*Volunteer:* Excellent! Have you received your ballot in the mail yet?
Votante (respuestas posibles): • Sí, ya la recibí. • Sí, ya la envié. • No, todavía no.	*Voter (possible responses):* • Yes, I've already received it. • Yes, I've already sent it. • No, not yet.
Voluntario(a): • (*Sí, ya la recibí*) Yo le recomiendo que llene su boleta y la envíe lo más pronto posible. También puede llevarla al centro de votación temprana (o en un buzón electoral*), o en el Día de las Elecciones. Por favor, asegúrese de firmar y ponerle la fecha al sobre, y también de que su firma sea la misma que la de su ID (su licencia de manejar). **depende del estado / condado: chequen con su capitán del phone bank* • (*Sí, ya la envié*) ¡Perfecto! • (*No, todavía no*) [Preguntarle al capitán del phone bank como responder.] (*Ahora vaya a la parte de "Triplicar el voto" abajo.*)	*Volunteer:* • (*Yes, I've already received it*) I recommend that you fill out your ballot and mail it as soon as possible. You can also bring it in person to an early voting center (or a ballot drop box*), or on Election Day. Please make sure to sign and date the envelope, and make sure your signature is the same as it is on your ID (driver's license). **depending on the state / county: check with your phone bank captain* • (*I've already sent it*) Perfect! • (*No, not yet*) [Ask your phone bank captain how to respond.] (*Now go to "Vote tripling" below.*)

APPENDIX D: SPANISH FOR ACTIVISTS

Votación: hacer un plan: votar en persona	Voting: making a plan: vote in person
Voluntario(a): ¿Cómo va a votar: en persona o por correo?	*Volunteer:* How will you vote: in person or by mail?
Votante: En persona.	*Voter:* In person.
Voluntario(a): • Está bien. Le recomiendo que vote antes del Día de las Elecciones en un centro de votación temprana si fuera posible. • [Si Ud. se registra para votar por correo, tiene la opción de enviar su boleta o llevarla al lugar de votación. Puede registrarse por internet para votar por correo. Puedo enviarle un enlace del sitio web.*] *depende del estado y condado: chequen con su capitán del phone bank	*Volunteer:* • OK. I recommend that you vote before Election Day at an early voting center if you can. • [If you register to vote by mail, you have the option to mail your ballot or bring it into your polling place. You can register online to vote by mail. I can send you a link to the website.*] *depending on the state and county: check with your phone bank captain
Triplicar el voto y "cerrar el trato"	**Vote tripling and "close the deal"**
Voluntario(a): • Los resultados para las elecciones casi podrían ser un empate. • ¡Es posible que un solo voto decida las elecciones! • ¡Cada voto cuenta! • Por favor, no olvide votar lo más pronto posible, y corra la voz con sus familiares, amigos y vecinos. • ¿Contamos con su apoyo para que hable con tres conocidos y se asegure de que voten? *(Si "Sí"):* ¿Podría nombrarme a esas tres personas?	*Volunteer:* • The results of these elections could almost be a tie. • It's possible that a single vote could decide the elections! • Every vote counts! • Please don't forget to vote as soon as possible, and spread the word to your family, friends and neighbors. • Can we count on you to talk with three people you know and make sure they vote? *(If "Yes"):* Could you tell me their first names?

Las despedidas	Goodbyes
Voluntario(a): • Fue un placer hablar con usted. • Muchas gracias por su tiempo y por ser un(a) votante. • Le agradezco su apoyo. Cuídese mucho. • Qué tenga un buen día / una buena tarde / una buena noche.	*Volunteer:* • It was a pleasure talking with you. • Thank you very much for your time and for being a voter. • I appreciate your support. Take very good care. • Have a good day / evening / night.

Appendix E:
'Election Spanish' for Absolute Beginners: Phrase List

*Developed by Elizabeth Chur and
Mayela Amayrani Galindo Vásquez*

(gray = voter; white = volunteer)

Votante (por teléfono): • Sí, bueno. • ¿Dígame?	Voter (on the telephone): • Hello? • Hello?
Votante (en persona): • Buenos días / Buenas tardes.* • ¿Qué se lo ofrece? * Buenos días = before noon; Buenas tardes = noon to sundown	Voter (in person): • Good morning / Good afternoon. • What can I do for you?
Voluntario / voluntaria: • Buenos días / Buenas tardes. • ¿Habla usted inglés?	Volunteer: • Good morning / Good afternoon. • Do you speak English?

Votante: • Sí. • No.	*Voter:* • Yes. *(Continue conversation in English.)* • No.
You may also hear these phrases: • ¿De parte de quién? • ¿Quién es?	*You may also hear these phrases:* • Who's calling? / Who are you with? • Who is it?
Voluntario / voluntaria (frases opcionales): • *Disculpe, pero no comprendo.* • *¿Podría hablar más despacio, por favor?*	*Volunteer (optional phrases):* • *Excuse me, but I don't understand.* • *Could you speak more slowly, please?*

Voluntario / voluntaria:
• Lo siento. Mi español no es bueno, pero me llamo _____.
• Soy voluntario (voluntaria) con el Partido Demócrata y
  ♦ el senador (la senadora) _____.
  ♦ el congresista (la congresista) _____.
  ♦ el candidato (la candidata) _____.
¿Hay alguien que hable inglés?
	Volunteer:
	• I'm sorry. My Spanish is not good, but my name is _____.
	• I'm a volunteer with the Democratic Party and
	  ♦ Senator _____.
	  ♦ Congressman / Congresswoman ___.
	  ♦ candidate _____.
	Is there someone who speaks English?

Votante: • Sí. • No.** *(Skip to next section below)*	*Voter:* • Yes. • No.** *(Skip to next section below)*
Voluntario / voluntaria: • ¿Podría hablar con él o ella, por favor?	*Volunteer:* • May I speak with him or her, please?
Votante: • Sí. Un momento, por favor.	*Volunteer:* • May I speak with him or her, please?
Voluntario / voluntaria: • Muchas gracias.	*Volunteer:* • Thank you very much.

APPENDIX E: 'ELECTION SPANISH' FOR ABSOLUTE BEGINNERS

Votante:	*Voter:*
• No / No está disponible / No está aquí.** *(Go to next section below.)*	• No / They're not available / They're not here.** *(Go to next section below)*

**No English-speakers available*

Voluntario / voluntaria:	*Volunteer*
• Muy bien. Otro día mi compañera va a contactarle. Ella habla español. *(brief pause; listen if voter responds)* • Muchas gracias. ¡Qué tenga un buen día!	• Very good. Another day my colleague will contact you. She speaks Spanish. *(brief pause; listen if voter responds)* • Thank you. Have a good day!
Votante: • ¡Igualmente! • ¡A usted!	*Voter:* • Likewise! • And you as well!

Bonus Phrases

Voluntario / voluntaria:	*Volunteer*
• ¿Ha escuchado de _____? • ¿Contamos con su voto por _____ y los demócratas? • Muchas gracias. ¡Qué tenga un buen día!	• Have you heard of _____? • Can we count on your vote for _____ and the Democrats? • Thank you. Have a good day!
Votante: • ¡Igualmente! • ¡A usted!	*Voter:* • Likewise! • And you as well!

Endnotes

1. "*Congressional District 22, CA,*" *Census Reporter,* U.S. Census Bureau, 2022. Accessed May 7, 2024. *https://censusreporter.org/profiles/50000US0622-congressional-district-22-ca/*
2. John Donegan, "Bakersfield, Kern County top list for worst air pollution in the nation," Bakersfield.com, April 27, 2024. Accessed April 29, 2024. *https://www.bakersfield.com/news/bakersfield-kern-county-top-list-for-worst-air-pollution-in-the-nation/article_f2d855a2-041f-11ef-84b8-0fde88198831.html*:
3. Shawn Hubler, Thomas Fuller, Anjali Singhvi and Juliette Love. "Many Latinos Couldn't Stay Home. Now Virus Cases Are Soaring in Their Communities," *New York Times*, June 26, 2020. Accessed May 7, 2024. *https://www.nytimes.com/2020/06/26/us/corona-virus-latinos.html.*
4. "Jurisdictions previously covered by Section 5." U.S. Department of Justice Civil Rights Division website. Accessed April 14, 2024. *https://www.justice.gov/crt/jurisdictions-previously-covered-section-5*:
5. John Schwartz, "Shelby County v. Holder: Between the Lines of the Voting Rights Act Opinion," *New York Times*. Accessed April 14, 2024. *https://archive.nytimes.com/www.nytimes.com/interactive/2013/06/25/us/annotated-supreme-court-decision-on-voting-rights-act.html.*

6   Jon Sabin, "Motivational Interviewing," Citizens' Climate Lobby webinar. June 9, 2022. Accessed January 21, 2024. https://community.citizensclimate.org/resources/item/19/123.

7   "Field Research Overview," Sister District Action Network. Updated January 27, 2020. Accessed January 21, 2024. https://sisterdistrict.com/wp-content/uploads/2020/01/Field-Research-Overview.pdf

8   Donald P. Green and Alan S. Gerber, *Get out the vote: How to increase voter turnout*. 3rd ed. Washington, DC: Brookings Institution Press; 2015.

9   James M. Lindsay, "The 2020 Election by the Numbers," Council on Foreign Relations. December 15, 2020 blog post. Accessed January 24, 2024. https://www.cfr.org/blog/2020-election-numbers

10 Aaron Blake, "Republicans came within 90,000 votes of controlling all of Washington," *Washington Post,* February 9, 2021. Accessed January 24, 2024. https://www.washingtonpost.com/politics/2021/02/09/republicans-came-within-90000-votes-controlling-all-washington/.

11 David W. Nickerson, "Quality is job one: Professional and volunteer voter mobilization calls," *American Journal of Political Science*, 51(2), 269-282, 2007.

12 "Historical Database of Sundown Towns," History and Social Justice website. Accessed April 11, 2024. https://justice.tougaloo.edu/sundown-towns/using-the-sundown-towns-database/state-map/.

13 Tina Rosenberg, "It Takes a Friend to Get a Friend to Vote," *New York Times,* March 19, 2019. Accessed April 11, 2024. https://www.nytimes.com/2019/03/19/opinion/it-takes-a-friend-to-get-a-friend-to-vote.html.

14 David W. Nickerson and Todd Rogers. "Do you have a voting plan? Implementation intentions, voter turnout, and organic plan making." Psychol Sci. 2010 Feb;21(2):194-9.

doi: 10.1177/0956797609359326. Epub 2010 Jan 8. PMID: 20424044. Accessed April 11, 2024.

15 "Presidential Election Results: Biden Wins," *New York Times*. Accessed May 4, 2024. https://www.nytimes.com/interactive/2020/11/03/us/elections/results-president.html.

16 "2020 Presidential Election Voting and Registration Tables Now Available," U.S. Census Bureau. Accessed May 4, 2024. https://www.census.gov/newsroom/press-releases/2021/2020-presidential-election-voting-and-registration-tables-now-available.html.

17 Donnie Fowler, with data analysis by Mike Podhorzer, "The 2020 Elections: Trends, Observations, & Where We're Headed," Swing Left San Francisco/Democracy Action San Francisco webinar, March 2, 2021.

18 "Presidential election, 2020," Ballotpedia.com. Accessed May 4, 2024. https://ballotpedia.org/Presidential_election,_2020.

19 Hannah Hartig, Andrew Daniller, Scott Keeter and Ted Van Green, "Voter turnout, 2018-2022," Pew Research Center, July 12, 2023. Accessed May 4, 2024. https://www.pewresearch.org/politics/2023/07/12/voter-turnout-2018-2022/.

20 William R. Miller, "The evolution of motivational interviewing," *Behavioural and cognitive psychotherapy*, 51(6), 616–632, 2023. https://doi.org/10.1017/S1352465822000431

21 William R. Miller and Stephen Rollnick, *Motivational Interviewing: Helping People Change and Grow*. United States: Guilford Publications; 2023.

22 "Motivational Interviewing – Victoria and Steve's phone call," Swing Blue Alliance video, posted February 22, 2022. https://www.youtube.com/watch?v=O3KH_C02XKE.

23 "The Romero Prayer," The Archbishop Romero Trust website. Accessed May 18, 2024. http://www.romerotrust.org.uk/romero-prayer

About the Author

Author photo © Tom Shaw

Elizabeth Chur is a Swing Left San Francisco volunteer and freelance medical writer. She has trained more than 2,500 volunteers nationally through three acclaimed workshops – Phone Bank and Canvassing Training for Introverts (& Friends), Spanish for Activists, and You and the 34%: How to Have Meaningful Conversations with High-Potential Voters.

A former journalist and documentary radio producer, she studied development of free press in Eastern Europe as a Thomas J. Watson Fellow, and was part of a UC Berkeley team which won a George Polk Award for their radio documentary, "Reports from a Warming Planet." She has also worked in homeless services and arts administration. She is a graduate of Oberlin College and the Salt Institute for Documentary Studies.

www.elizabethchur.com

www.ingramcontent.com/pod-product-compliance
Lightning Source LLC
Chambersburg PA
CBHW020532030426

42337CB00013B/822